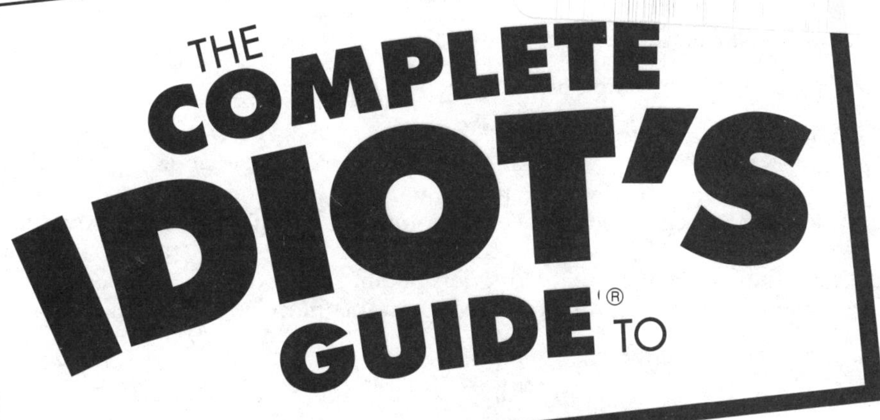

the Internet,

Special Edition

by Peter Kent

201 W. 103rd Street, Indianapolis, IN 46290

The Complete Idiot's Guide to the Internet, Special Edition

International Standard Book Number: 0-7897-1984-3

Library of Congress Catalog Card Number: 98-84855

Printed in the United States of America

First Printing: September 1998

00 99 98 4 3 2 1

Trademarks

Executive Editor
Karen Reinisch

Acquisitions Editor
Don Essig

Development Editor
Melanie Palaisa

Managing Editor
Thomas F. Hayes

Project Editor
Karen A. Walsh

Copy Editor
Heather Stith

Indexer
Craig Small
Chris Wilcox

Technical Editor
Bill Bruns

Production
Terri Edwards
Cyndi Davis-Hubler
Donna Martin
Eric S. Miller
Elise Walter

Book Designer
Glenn Larsen

Cover Designer
Mike Freeland

Cartoonist
Judd Winick

This one's dedicated to fellow limey Tim Berners-Lee, who invented the World Wide Web and then watched the rest of the world get rich on it.

Contents at a Glance

Contents

About the Author

Peter Kent is the author of around 34 computer and business books, including *Poor Richard's Web Site: Geek-Free, Commonsense Advice on Building a Low-Cost Web Site*. His work has appeared in numerous publications, from the *Manchester Guardian* to *Internet World*, the *Dallas Times Herald* to *Computerworld*.

Acknowledgments

Thanks to the huge team at Que (see the list of people at the front of the book) who helped me put this together. There's a lot more to writing a book than just, well, writing. I'm very grateful to have people willing and able to do all the stuff that comes once the words are on the computer screen.

Tell Us What You Think!

As the reader of this book, *you* are our most important critic and commentator. We value your opinion and want to know what we're doing right, what we could do better, what areas you'd like to see us publish in, and any other words of wisdom you're willing to pass our way.

As the Executive Editor for the General Desktop Applications team at Macmillan Computer Publishing, I welcome your comments. You can fax, email, or write me directly to let me know what you did or didn't like about this book—as well as what we can do to make our books stronger.

Please note that I cannot help you with technical problems related to the topic of this book, and that due to the high volume of mail I receive, I might not be able to reply to every message.

When you write, please be sure to include this book's title and author as well as your name and phone or fax number. I will carefully review your comments and share them with the author and editors who worked on the book.

Fax: 317-817-7448

Email: `internet@mcp.com`

Mail: Executive Editor
General Desktop Applications
Macmillan Computer Publishing
201 West 103rd Street
Indianapolis, IN 46290 USA

Introduction

Welcome to *The Complete Idiot's Guide to the Internet, Fifth Edition*. That's five editions in less than five years. The Internet just keeps rolling on, growing and changing...although not quite as fast as it did in its first years. The Internet is reaching another phase in its life, a more "mature" phase. Between 1993 and 1996 the Internet changed tremendously; the Internet you'll use while working your way through this book is almost nothing like the Internet of 1993. It's easier to use, far bigger, and much, much busier.

If you're just now learning about the Internet, in one way you're lucky. In 1993, most Internet users were computer geeks, and that was okay because you needed a high degree of geekhood to get anything done on the Internet. For the average business or home computer user, getting an Internet account was like stepping into a time warp. One moment you were in your whiz-bang multimedia mouse-clicking graphical user interface—Windows, OS/2, or the Mac—and the next minute you were back in the 1970s, working on a dumb UNIX terminal (dumb being the operative word), typing obscure and arcane—not to mention funky and strange—UNIX commands. You probably found yourself wondering, "What's this `ftp ftp.microsoft.com` thing I have to type?" or "What's *grep* all about and why do I care?" or "Why can't UNIX programmers actually *name* their programs instead of giving them two- or three-letter acronyms?" (Acronyms are so important in the UNIX world that there's even an acronym to describe acronyms: TLA, Three Letter Acronym.)

Most Internet users today don't need to know the answers to these ancient questions. These days the majority of new users are back in the 1990s, working in the graphical user interfaces they love (or love to hate, but that's another issue). Since 1993, thousands of fancy new Internet access programs have been written. Today, it's easier to get on the Internet, and it's easier to get around after you are there.

So, Why Do You Need This Book?

Even if you've never stumbled along the information superhighway (or "infotainment superhighway," as satirist Al Franken calls it), you've almost certainly heard of it. A recent survey found that although only 2.3 percent of American high school students could tell you the name of the U.S. President., 93.7 percent knew how to get to the Penthouse Online Web site—and a whopping 112 percent knew how to download bootleg copies of Hootie and the Blowfish songs.

Chances are, though, that if you've picked up this book, you are not an experienced international traveler along the highways and byways of this amazing system called the Internet. You probably need a little help. Well, you've come to the right place.

Yes, the Internet is far easier to get around now than it was in 1993, but there's still a lot to learn. The journey will be more comfortable than it was then, and you can travel much farther.

Now, I know you're not an idiot. What you do, you do well. But right now, you don't do the Internet, and you need a quick way to get up and running. You want to know what the fuss is about, or maybe you already know what the fuss is about and you want to find out how to get in on it. Well, I'm not going to teach you how to become an Internet guru, but I will tell you the things you really *need* to know, such as

- How to get up and running on the Internet
- How to send and receive email messages
- How to move around on the World Wide Web (and what is the Web, anyway?)
- How to find what you are looking for on the Internet
- What "push" is all about, how to push what you want pushed, and where to push it
- Protecting life and limb on the information superhighway fast lane
- How to participate in Internet discussion groups (this could take over your life and threaten your relationships if you're not careful)
- How to talk to Aunt Edna in Walla Walla for a few cents an hour
- How to make your fortune in cyberspace

I am, however, making a few assumptions. I'm assuming that you know how to use your computer, so don't expect me to give basic lessons on using your mouse, switching between windows, working with directories and files, and all that stuff. There's enough to cover in this book without all that. If you want really basic beginner's information, check out *The Complete Idiot's Guide to PCs* (also from Que), a great book by Joe Kraynak.

How Do You Use This Book?

I've used a few conventions in this book to make it easier for you to follow. For example, things you type, press, click, and select will appear in bold like this:

type **this**

If I don't know exactly what you'll have to type (because you have to supply some of the information), I'll put the unknown information in italic. For example, you might see the following instructions. In this case, I don't know the filename, so I made it italic to indicate that you have to supply it.

type **this *filename***

Also, I've used the term "Enter" throughout the book, even though your keyboard may have a "Return" key instead.

Finally, Internet addresses are in a monospace type font. They'll look something like this:

`http://www.microsoft.com`

In case you want a greater understanding of the subject you are learning, you'll find some background information in boxes. You can quickly skip over this information if you want to avoid all the gory details. On the other hand, you may find something that will keep you from getting into trouble. Here are the special icons and boxes used in this book.

Check This Out

These boxes contain notes, tips, warnings, and asides that provide you with interesting and useful (at least theoretically) tidbits of Internet information.

Techno Talk

The Techno Talk icon calls your attention to technical information you might spout off to impress your friends, but that you'll likely never need to know to save your life.

Part 1
Start at the Beginning

You want to start, and you want to start quickly. No problem. In Part 1, you're going to do just that. First, I'll give you a quick overview of the Internet, and then I'll have you jump right in and use the two most important Internet services: email and the World Wide Web. (The Web is so important these days that many people think the Internet is the Web. I'll explain the difference in Chapter 1, "The Internet: What's It All About?") By the time you finish this part of the book, you'll be surfing around the Web like a true cybergeek—and you'll be ready to move on and learn the other Internet services.

Chapter 1

The Internet: What's It All About?

In This Chapter

- The obligatory "What is the Internet?" question answered
- A quick history of the Internet
- What sort of information flies across the Internet
- Internet services, from Archie to the World Wide Web
- Getting a connection to the Internet
- Four types of Internet connections
- The difference between the Internet and the online services

Yes, this is the obligatory "What is the Internet?" chapter. But before you skip ahead, let me tell you that I'll be covering some other subjects, too, and that I promise not to go into too much detail about Internet history. Quite frankly, most people are tired of hearing about the history of the Internet; they just want to get on the Net and get something done. However, for those of you who may have been holed up in an FBI or ATF siege for the past few years, or stuck on the Mir space station, or perhaps chatting with Kenneth Starr's grand jury, here's my abbreviated history of the Internet:

1. The Internet was created by the U.S. military-industrial complex in the late 1960s as a way of enabling government researchers who were working on military projects to share computer files.

2. The Internet *wasn't* set up to figure out how computer networks could be made to survive nuclear war. Or maybe it *was*. I still haven't figured out this one. Although the nuclear war story is "common knowledge," some people involved in the early days of the Internet say it's untrue. I'll admit that I've repeated the nuclear war story in earlier books, as have a gazillion other Internet authors, but then I read an article by one of the founders of the Internet claiming that nuclear survivability wasn't the initial purpose of the Internet. Since then I've seen it said, by authoritative sources, that it was. Either way, at some stage in the Internet's early life, testing survivability became an important purpose.
3. Everyone and his dog in academia jumped on the bandwagon. The Internet became a sort of secret academic communication link, connecting hundreds of academic institutions, while America went on watching *Starsky and Hutch*, not realizing what was going on.
4. Eventually, the people in the press figured out what was happening. Granted, it took them almost a quarter of a century, but during that time they were busy being spoon-fed by our political institutions, and the Internet didn't have a public relations company.
5. In 1993, the press started talking about the Internet. In 1994 and 1995, it was about all they could talk about.
6. Ordinary Americans—and then ordinary Brits, Aussies, Frenchies, and others all around the world—began to wake up and realize that the Internet might be worth looking into. And look into it they did—by the millions.
7. The World Wide Web appeared on the scene at the same time that thousands of software companies started producing Internet programs that could be used by people who don't regard Jolt Cola as the equivalent of a fine wine—in other words, by the average non-geek. The Internet was transformed, if not exactly overnight, certainly within a year.
8. The Internet today has become a haven for all the people the U.S. military-industrial complex loathes: pinkos, body piercers, eco-anarchists, people who wear clothing more suited to the opposite sex, and Democrats. Along with, of course, all sorts of "ordinary" people, businesses, schools, churches, and the like.

That's my quick history of the Internet. If you want more, you'll have to look elsewhere. I want to move on to what today's Internet is.

Okay Then, What Is the Internet?

Let's start with the basics. What's a computer network? It's a system in which computers are connected so they can share "information." (I'll explain what I mean by that word in a moment.) There's nothing particularly unusual about this in today's world. There are millions of networks around the world. True, they are mostly in the industrialized world, but there isn't a nation in the world that doesn't have at least a few. (I don't know that for sure, but I can't think of one.)

The Internet is something special, though, for two reasons. First, it's the world's largest computer network. Second, it's pretty much open to anyone with the entrance fee, and the entrance fee is constantly dropping. Many users have free accounts, and many more are paying as little as $10 to $20 a month, sometimes for "unlimited" usage. ("Unlimited," in Internetspeak, is a euphemism meaning "if your computer can manage to connect to the service, and if the service's computers let you stay connected, you can use it as much as you want.") Consequently, millions of people all over the world are getting online.

Just how big is the Internet? Many of the numbers thrown about in the past few years are complete nonsense. In 1993, people were saying 25 million. Considering that the majority of Internet users at the time were in the United States, and that 25 million is 10 percent of the U.S. population, and that most people in this great nation thought that the Internet was some kind of hair piece sold through late-night infomercials, it's highly unlikely that anywhere near 25 million people were on the Internet. In fact, they weren't.

These days, estimates vary all over the place, ranging from 10 or 20 million to 50 or 80 million or so. Just recently I've seen advertisements claiming 80 million, probably based on the reasoning that "it was 40 million a few months ago, so it must be over 80 million by now." The truth is that nobody knows how many people are using the Internet. I believe, however, that many of the claims are gross exaggerations. Also, remember that many users are only infrequent visitors to cyberspace, visiting just now and again, maybe once a week or so. That little bit of information may not be important to the average user, but it *is* worth bearing in mind if you plan to set up shop on the Internet.

Cyberspace

The term *cyberspace* means the "area" in which you can move around online. When you are on the Internet, on an online service, or even connected to a computer BBS (bulletin board system), you are in cyberspace.

One way or another, though, there are a whole lot of people out there; the numbers are definitely in the tens of millions.

What Exactly Is "Information"?

What, then, do I mean by "information"? I mean anything you can send over lines of electronic communication, and that includes quite a lot these days (and seems to include more every day). I mean letters, which are called *email* on the Internet. I mean reports, magazine articles, and books, which are called *document files* on the Internet. I mean music, which is called *music* on the Internet.

You can send your voice across the Internet; but for now let me just say that you'll find it much cheaper than talking long-distance on the phone (although most certainly not as easy), as long as you can find someone to talk to. You can also grab computer files of many kinds (programs, word processing files, clip art, sounds, and anything else that can be electronically encoded) from huge libraries that collectively contain literally millions of files.

A Word About Numbers

When I first started writing about the Internet, I tried to be specific; I might have said "2.5 million files." However, I've given up that practice for two reasons. First, many of the numbers were made up, not by me, but by Internet gurus who were trying to be specific and made "educated" guesses. Second, even if the numbers were correct when I wrote them, they were too low by the time the book got to the editor, *much* too low by the time the book got to the printer, and *ridiculously* low by the time the book got to the readers. But you can be pretty sure that there are at least 2,536,321 files available for you to copy.

"Information" could also be a type of conversation. You want to talk about Palestinian/ Israeli conflict? There's a discussion group waiting for you. Do you want to meet like-minded souls with a passion for daytime soap operas? They're talking right now. Feel the need to know more about Bill Clinton's latest liaison? Plenty of people are willing to fill you in with the details.

Anything that can be sent electronically is carried on the Internet, and much that can't be sent now probably will be sent in a few months. "Such as?," you ask. How about a three-dimensional image of your face? In the next year or so, special face scanners will appear on the scene. You'll be able to scan your face, and then send a three-dimensional image of your face to someone, or use the image for your chat *avatar*. You'll learn about avatars in Chapter 9, "Yak, Yak, Yak: Chatting in Cyberspace."

The Internet Services

The following list provides a quick look at the Internet services available to you. This list is not exhaustive. Other services are available, but these are the most important ones:

- *Email.* This is the most used Internet service. Hundreds of millions of messages—some estimates go over a billion (another of those completely unconfirmable figures)—wing their way around the world each day, between families, friends, and businesses. The electronic world's postal system is very much like the real world's postal system, except that you can't send fruit, bombs, or this month's selection from the Cheese of the Month club. (You *can*, however, send letters, spreadsheets, pictures, sounds, programs, and more.) It's much quicker and cheaper, too. And the mailman isn't armed. Come to think of it, it's not much like the real world's postal system, but in principle it's very similar: helping people communicate with others all over the world. See Chapter 2, "The Premier Internet Tool: Email," for more information about this essential service.
- *Chat.* Chat's a bit of a misnomer. Not much chatting goes on, but there is an awful lot of typing. You type a message, and it's instantly transmitted to another person, or to many other people, who can type their responses right away. If you enjoy slow and confusing conversations in which it's tough to tell who's talking to whom, in which the level of literacy and humor is somewhere around fourth grade, and in which many of the chat-room members claiming to be handsome and successful businessmen are actually spotty teenage boys...you'll *love* chat! (Okay, maybe I'm being a little harsh; some people enjoy chat. On the other hand, some people enjoy eating monkey brains and going bungee-jumping too.) You'll learn more about this service in Chapter 9.
- *Internet "Phones."* Install a sound card and microphone, get the Internet phone software, and then talk to people across the Internet. This service is not very popular today, and to be quite honest, despite all the hype, it probably won't be popular anytime soon, either. But just think: You can, in some cases, make international phone calls for *nothing*.
- *FTP.* The whole purpose of the Internet was to transfer files from one place to another, and for years, FTP was how it was done. FTP provides a giant electronic library of computer files.
- *Gopher.* Poor old Gopher. If not crippled, he's at least been hobbled. Just a couple of years ago this service was supposed to revolutionize the Internet by converting a

command-line computer system to a menu system. You wouldn't have to remember and use arcane commands anymore; you could just use the arrow keys or type a number corresponding to a menu option. Then along came the World Wide Web.

- *World Wide Web.* The Web is driving the growth of the Internet because it's *cool*! (Are you sick of that word yet?) Containing pictures, sounds, and animation, the Web is a giant *hypertext* system in which documents around the world are linked to one another. Click a word in a document in, say, Sydney, Australia, and another document (which may be from Salzburg, Austria) appears. You'll begin learning about this amazing system in Chapter 3, "The World of the World Wide Web."
- *Telnet.* Very few people use Telnet, but it can be quite useful. Telnet provides a way for you to log on to a computer that's connected somewhere out there on the Internet—across the city or across the world. Once logged on, you'll probably be using arcane commands or a text-based menu system. You may be playing one of the many role-playing *MUD* games (that stands for Multiple User Dungeons or Multiple User Dimensions), or perhaps a *MUCK* game (which I won't define, but perhaps you can guess what it's about based on the sound of the word), or even perusing a library catalog.
- *Newsgroups.* Newsgroups are discussion groups. Want to learn all about what Kathleen Willey *really* did with Bill? (Or, at least, what the members of the discussion group say she did?) Want to learn an unusual kite-flying technique? Want to learn about...well, anything really. There are approximately 40,000 internationally distributed newsgroups, and you'll find out how to work with them in Chapter 7, "Newsgroups: the Source of All Wisdom," and Chapter 8, "Your Daily News Delivery." (I broke my "no specific numbers rule" there, but 40,000 is fairly close, at least for the moment; the number has grown by around 10,000 in the past year or so, though.)
- *Mailing lists.* If 40,000 discussion groups are not enough for you, here are 150,000 more. (This number's more of a guess. One large directory lists 90,000 mailing lists, although its list contained only 72,000 last year. There are certainly many, many more, along with thousands of Web forums.) Mailing lists are another form of discussion group that works in a slightly different manner—you send and receive messages using your email program. Web forums are discussion groups located at Web sites. In these forums, you read and submit messages using your Web browser.
- *Push programs.* These systems are so named because information from the Internet is "pushed" to your computer. Rather than you going out onto the Internet to find information, information is periodically sent to your computer without your direct

intervention (all you need to do is state what information you want to retrieve and how often). "Push" is another Internet misnomer (I don't get to pick these names!); this system is really a scheduled pull system.

These services are all tools, not reasons to be on the Internet. As a wise man once said, "Nobody wants a 1/4-inch drill bit, they want a 1/4-inch hole." Nobody wants a car, either; they want comfortable, affordable transportation. Nobody wants the Web, FTP, or Telnet; they want...well, what do they want? As you read this book, you'll get ideas for how you can use the Internet tools for profit and pleasure (along with a good measure of incidental frustration, unfortunately). Chapter 14, "Ideas," gives loads of examples of how real people use the Internet.

Getting on the Net

So you think the Net sounds great. How do you get to it, though? You might get Internet access in a number of ways:

- Your college provides you with an Internet account.
- Your company has an Internet connection from its internal network.
- You've signed up with an online service such as America Online (AOL), CompuServe, The Microsoft Network (MSN), or Prodigy.
- You've signed up with a small, local Internet service provider.
- You've signed up with a large, national Internet service provider such as PSINet, Earthlink, or SpryNet.
- You've signed up with one of the phone companies, such as AT&T, Sprint, or MCI.
- You've signed up with a Free-Net or other form of free community computer network.

The Internet is not owned by any one company. It's more like the world's telephone system: Each portion is owned by someone, and the overall system hangs together because of a variety of agreements between those organizations. So there is no single *Internet, Inc.* where you can go to get access to the Internet. No, you have to go to one of the tens of thousands of organizations that already have access to the Internet and get a connection through it.

At this stage, I'm going to assume that you already have some kind of Internet connection. But if you don't, or if you're considering finding another Internet account or a replacement, you can learn more about finding a connection (and about those Free-Nets) in Appendix A, "Finding Internet Access and the Right Equipment."

The Difference Between the Internet and Online Services

I often hear the questions, "What's the difference between the Internet and AOL, or CompuServe, or whatever?" and "If I have an AOL account, do I have an Internet account?" Services such as AOL (America Online), CompuServe, Prodigy, GEnie, MSN (The Microsoft Network) and so on are not the same as the Internet. They are known as *online services*. Although they are similar to the Internet in some ways (yes, they are large computer networks), they are different in the sense that they are private clubs.

For instance, what happens when you dial into, say, CompuServe? Your computer connects across the phone lines with CompuServe's computers, which are all sitting in a big room somewhere. All those computers belong to CompuServe (well, now they belong to America Online, which recently bought CompuServe). Contrast this with the Internet. When you connect to the Internet, you connect to a communications system that's linked to millions of computers, which are owned by tens of thousands of companies, schools, government departments, and individuals. If the Internet is like a giant public highway system, the online services are like small private railroads.

However, at the risk of stretching an analogy too far (I'm already mixing metaphors, so why not?), I should mention that these private railroads let you get off the tracks and onto the public highway. In other words, although AOL, CompuServe, and the others are private clubs, they do provide a way for you to connect to the Internet. So, although the barbarians on the Internet are held at the gates to the private club, the private club members can get onto the Internet.

The online services view themselves as both private clubs and gateways to the Internet. As Russ Siegelman of The Microsoft Network stated, Microsoft wants MSN to be "the biggest and best content club and community on the Internet." So it's intended to be part of the Internet—but a private part. In fact, although I (and many others) call these services "online services," Microsoft now refers to MSN as an "Internet Online Service."

To summarize:

- The Internet is a public highway system overrun with barbarians.
- Online services are private railroads or exclusive clubs…or something like that.
- Even if you use the Internet, you can't get into the online services unless you're a member.
- If you are a member of the online services, you *can* get onto the Internet.

The answer to the second question I posed earlier, then, is "yes." If you have an online-service account (at least with the services mentioned here), you also have an Internet account. Interestingly, these services are now being merged into the Internet. In particular, MSN is making great efforts to appear as an integral part of the Internet. Parts of MSN are already open to the public. People on the Internet can now access the private areas in

MSN if they sign up for the service. They don't have to dial into a phone number provided by Microsoft; they can get onto the Internet any way they like and then use their World Wide Web browser to get into MSN.

What Do You Need?

What does it take to get onto the infotainment superhypeway? Many of you already have Internet accounts; our high-priced research shows that most readers buy this book after they have access to the Internet (presumably because they got access and then got lost). However, I want to talk about the types of accounts (or connections) that are available because they all work in slightly different ways. This discussion will help ensure that we are all on the same wavelength before we get going.

There are basically four types of Internet connections:

- Permanent connections
- Dial-in direct connections (PPP, SLIP, and CSLIP)
- Dial-in terminal connections (shell accounts)
- Mail connections

Generally, if you ask an online service or service provider for an account these days, you'll be given a dial-in direct connection, even though you won't hear it called that. Different service providers use slightly different terms, and the terminology can become blurred. The following sections define each one, which should clarify things a little.

Service Provider

A service provider is a company that sells access to the Internet. You dial into its computer, which connects you to the Internet. The online services are an anomaly. Strictly speaking, they are Internet service providers because they provide Internet access. However, they aren't normally called service providers; they're simply known as online services. The companies known as service providers generally provide access to the Internet and little, if anything, more. The online services, on the other hand, have all sorts of file libraries, chat services, news services, and so on within the private areas of the services themselves.

Note, by the way, that the online services sometimes provide two types of access telephone numbers. One provides you with a dial-in direct connection to the Internet and access to the online service. The other provides access to the online service only, not to the Internet. For instance, if you use Microsoft Network you have two connection choices: The Internet and Microsoft Network and The Microsoft Network. You must pick the former if you want to use the Internet (in the Sign In dialog box, click **Settings**, **Access Numbers**, and then select **The Internet and Microsoft Network** from the **Service Type** drop-down list box). If you're working with an online service, make sure you've set up the correct connection. (This distinction is disappearing, though, as the major online services are merging lines, making all their lines handle both types of connection.)

Permanent Connections

If you have a permanent connection, your computer connects directly to a TCP/IP (Transmission Control Protocol/Internet Protocol) network that is part of the Internet. To be a little more specific, what is most likely is that your organization has a large computer connected to the network, and you have a terminal or computer connected to that computer. This sort of connection is often known as a *dedicated connection* or sometimes as a *permanent direct connection.*

What's a Protocol? A protocol defines how computers should talk to each other. It's like a language: If a group of people agrees to speak French (or English or Spanish), they can all understand each other. Communication protocols provide a similar set of rules that define how modems, computers, and programs can communicate.

Permanent connections are often used by large organizations, such as universities and corporations. The organization has to set up special equipment to connect its network to the Internet, and it has to lease a special telephone line that can transfer data very quickly. Because that organization has a leased line, it is always connected to the Internet, which means there's no need to make a telephone call and use a modem to reach the service provider's computer. Instead, the user simply logs on to the Internet from his terminal.

Dial-in Direct Connections

Dial-in direct connections are often referred to as PPP (Point-to-Point Protocol), SLIP (Serial Line Internet Protocol), or CSLIP (Compressed SLIP) connections (PPP is the most common form these days). Like the permanent connection, this is also a TCP/IP connection, but it's designed for use over telephone lines instead of a dedicated network. This type of service is the next best thing to the permanent connection. Although a permanent connection is out of the price range of most individuals and small companies, a dial-in direct connection is quite cheap, often available for $20–$25 a month for unlimited use (I've seen them as low as $12 a month). Once you've connected across your dial-in direct connection, though, you'll use it in the same way you would use a permanent connection. (You may have a permanent connection at work, and a dial-in direct connection at home, but you'll use the same skills and techniques in both places.)

A dial-in direct connection is a *dial-in* service. That is, you must have a modem, and you have to dial a telephone number given to you by the service provider or online service. The following figure shows an example of one type of software you can run while working with a dial-in direct or permanent connection. The figure shows Microsoft's FTP site, a large file library that's open to the public, displayed within Netscape Navigator 4. The main reason I'm showing you this right now is so that you can compare it to the horrible-looking dial-in terminal connection I'll talk about next. With a dial-in direct connection you can use all the nice GUI (Graphical User Interface) software that the computer industry has spent billions of dollars on over the last few years. With a dial-in terminal account, you're back in the 1970s.

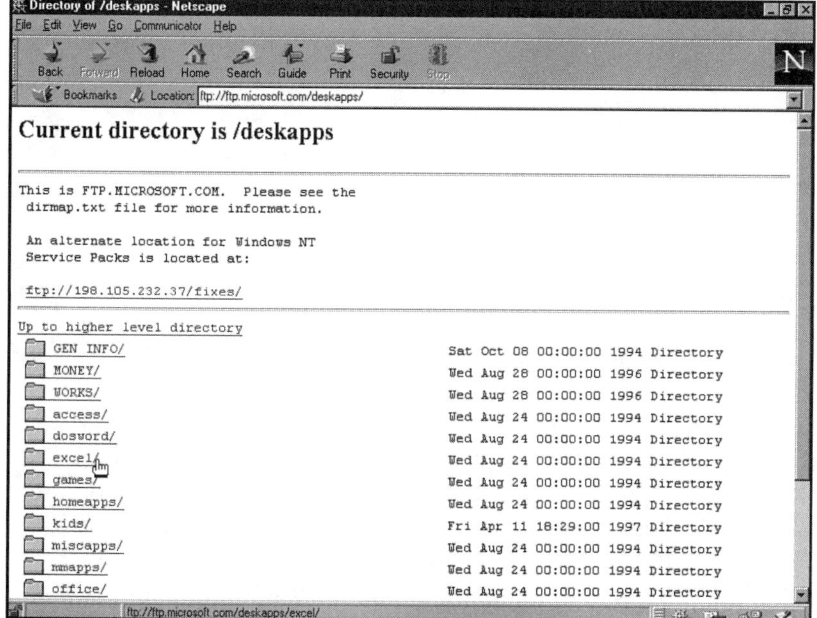

Microsoft's FTP site as viewed from a program running in a dial-in direct connection (SLIP, CSLIP, or PPP) or a permanent connection. To change directories or transfer a file, just click with the mouse.

Dial-in Terminal Connections

With a dial-in terminal connection, you also have to dial into the service provider's computer. When the connection is made, your computer becomes a terminal of the service provider's computer. All the programs you use are running on the service provider's computer. That means that you can transfer files across the Internet to and from your service provider's computer, but not to and from yours. You have to use a separate procedure to move files between your computer and the service provider's.

If you want to see just how ugly this sort of connection is, take a look at the next figure. This figure shows Microsoft's FTP site, the same service you saw in the first figure, in a simple serial communications program (specifically Windows's Hyperterminal). If you're working with a dial-in terminal connection, you have to remember all the commands you need to use to get around, or you'll soon be lost. There's no pointing and clicking here; you'll have to type arcane commands such as `ls -l "|more"`.

Back at Microsoft's FTP site, this time with a dial-in terminal account. Now, what was the command to change the directory?

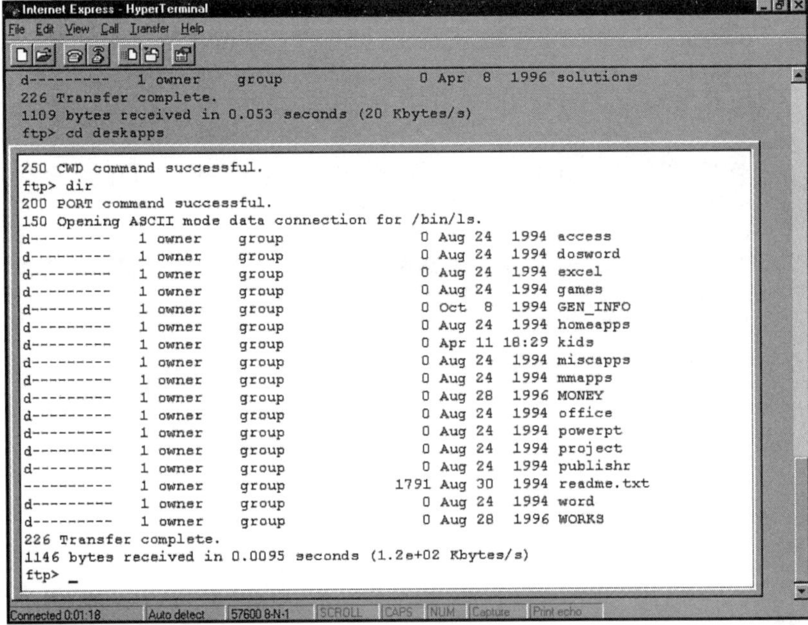

Who uses this sort of connection? Up until 1993, and well into 1994, most Internet users did. It wasn't until the middle of 1994 that people began using dial-in direct accounts and the more convenient GUI software. Today, few users in the industrialized world use dial-in terminal connections, unless perhaps they're using a free Internet account or studying at Podunk University. In the third world, this type of account may be more common, so many users in poorer countries are still using dial-in terminal connections.

Techno Talk

Clearing Up the Confusion

A dial-in terminal connection is often called a *dial-up connection*. That term can be confusing because you have to dial a call before connecting to a PPP or SLIP account as well. To differentiate between the two, some service providers call a dial-in terminal connection an interactive service, which seems only slightly less ambiguous, or a shell account. Wherever I mention this sort of account (which isn't often), I call it a dial-in terminal connection because you dial the call to your service provider, and once it's connected, your computer acts as a terminal of the other computer.

Mail Connections

A mail connection lets you send and receive Internet email and, perhaps, read the Internet newsgroups. But you can do nothing more. This is hardly a real Internet account, so I've ignored it in this book. I'll assume you have one of the first three types of accounts.

What Do You Have?

So what kind of connection do you have, and why do you care? We're interested only in the permanent, dial-in direct, and dial-in terminal connections. The first two connections are the most important for the following reasons:

- They are easier to use.
- You use both in pretty much the same way.
- You probably have one of these connections.

If you have an Internet account provided by your employer at work and you access it across your network connection, you have a permanent connection. How do you connect? Ask your system administrator. You might have to log on in some way, or you may find that you are permanently logged on. If your company has set up the network so that you can connect using your graphical user interface—Windows, the Mac, a UNIX graphical user interface, or OS/2—you can use all the fancy Internet software that's available for your particular operating system.

If you have an account through one of the major online service providers, you have a dial-in direct account: PPP, SLIP, or CSLIP (almost certainly PPP, but it makes little difference). You must use the software the online service provider gives you to dial in and connect, but once you're connected properly, you can use whatever Internet software you want. (You'll learn about various programs as you go through the book.) With any of these accounts, you'll be using GUI software with windows, dialog boxes, and so on. In fact, you can use the same sort of software as the permanent connection users.

The dial-in terminal connection is the nasty "I'll use it if I absolutely have to" connection. If you are completely broke and have to use the very cheapest service you can find (perhaps a free service, one of the Free-Nets I talk about in Appendix A) or if, perhaps, you are at a college that hasn't yet upgraded its Internet access, you might have to work with a dial-in terminal (shell) account. If so, you'll find yourself working at the command line, where you have to know a bunch of geeky little UNIX commands to get around.

When I wrote the first edition of this book in 1993, it was based on this sort of account, because it was pretty much the only type of account available. These days most users are working with a graphical interface instead of the command line, so this book is based on the newest software. However, if you are still working with a command-line account (if you have a dial-in terminal account, or if your company or college has given you a dumb terminal connected to a UNIX computer connected to the Internet), you can still get help.

Almost the entire first edition of *The Complete Idiot's Guide to the Internet* is available to you using an email responder, a special program that automatically sends you information when you send it an email message. The first edition has all the old command-line information that's required if you're using a dial-in terminal connection. When you get to a subject in which you need more information about the UNIX command line, I'll tell you where to send an email message and what to put in the body of that message. You'll automatically receive a response that includes the relevant chapter from the book.

I Have AOL (CompuServe, MSN, or Such), But Where's the Internet?

I've told you that the online services provide access to the Internet, but when you first install their software and connect to the service, the Internet connection might not be enabled. You might see a message telling you that if you want to connect to the Internet, you'll have to download some more software. Follow the instructions to do so. Just in case, though, here's how to find out more about setting up an Internet connection on the three most popular online services:

- *America Online.* Log on, and then click the **Internet** bar in the Welcome window, or click the **Internet Connection** bar in the Channels window, or use the keyword **INTERNET**.
- *CompuServe.* Log on, and then click the **Internet** button in the main menu, or use the GO word **INTERNET**.
- *The Microsoft Network.* Log on, then select **Communicate**, **Internet Center**.

You Want Help Setting Up?

Unfortunately, I can't help you with the initial setup of your software. There are too many systems to cover. So here's my (very general) advice: If your service provider or online service can't help you set up, find another one!

Don't let me frighten you. In many cases, the initial software installation is quite easy. You simply run some kind of setup program and follow any instructions, and in a few minutes, you'll be up and running. (If you're just now learning about the Internet, you're lucky. Installing this fancy GUI Internet software back in the early days was a real nightmare.)

Some providers—in particular, many of the small service providers—are not terribly helpful. However, things are certainly better than they were a few years ago, when many service providers had the attitude "we give you the account to connect to, it's up to you to figure out how to do it!" These days, most providers are making more of an effort. But if you run into a service provider that isn't willing to explain, absolutely clearly, what you need to do to connect, you should move on. This is a very competitive business, and there are many good companies that are willing to help you.

That's All, Folks!

I don't need to talk any more about getting an Internet account. Most of you already have an account, so it's time to move on and get down to the meat of the subject: how to work with the account you have. If, on the other hand, you *don't* have an account yet, flip to Appendix A, in which I explain how to find one and tell you what computer equipment you need. Even if you do have an account, you may want to look at this appendix because you may eventually want to swap to a cheaper or more reliable service. Moving along, I'll assume that you have an Internet account you are completely happy with and that you know how to log on to that account. (Check with your system administrator or look in your service documentation if you need information about logging on to the Internet.)

The Least You Need to Know

- The Internet is the world's largest computer network, a huge public information highway.
- The Internet's motto might be "Designed by the military-industrial complex, used by the people they hate!"
- You can do many things on the Internet: send email, join discussion groups, grab files from electronic libraries, cruise the World Wide Web, and much more.
- There are four types of Internet connections: mail connections, which aren't much good; dial-in terminal connections, which are better, but you're working with the command line or text menus; and permanent connections and dial-in direct (SLIP and PPP) connections, both of which are much better.
- The Internet is a public system. The online services, such as America Online, CompuServe, and The Microsoft Network, are private services with gateways to the Internet.
- A member of an online service can use the Internet, but an Internet user cannot use an online service unless he joins that service.
- You can get Internet access through your company or school, a small local Internet service provider, a giant Internet service provider (such as AT&T or PSINet), or an online service.

Chapter 2

The Premier Internet Tool: Email

In This Chapter

- Which email program are you using?
- All about email addresses
- Setting up your email program
- Sending a message
- Retrieving your messages—then what?
- Sending files across the Internet
- Avoiding fights

Some of you may think the title of this chapter is a joke. It's not. Although email may not be exciting, cool, or compelling, it is the most popular and, in many ways, the most useful Internet service. More people use email on any given day than use any other Internet service. Tens of millions of messages fly across the wires each day—five million from America Online alone (at least it was five million the last time I checked, but it's probably several times that by now). According to *Wired* magazine, publishing via email—newsletters, bulletins, even small books—is growing very quickly, perhaps more quickly than publishing on the World Wide Web.

Despite all the glitz of the Web (you'll learn about that glitz in Chapter 3, "The World of the World Wide Web," Chapter 4, "More About the Web," Chapter 5, "Forms, Applets, and Other Web Weirdness," and Chapter 6, "Web Multimedia"), the potential of Internet Phone systems, and the excitement—for some—of the many chat systems (Chapter 9, "Yak, Yak, Yak: Chatting in Cyberspace"), email is probably the most productive tool there is. It's a sort of Internet workhorse, getting the work done without any great fanfare.

After spending huge sums of money polling Internet users, we've come to the conclusion that the very first thing Internet users want to do is send email messages. It's not too threatening, and it's an understandable concept: You're sending a letter. The only differences are that you don't take it to the post office and that it's much faster. So that's what I'm going to start with: how to send an email message.

Dial-in Terminal (Shell) Accounts

If you are working with a dial-in terminal account (also known as a shell account), this information on email—beyond the basic principles—won't help you much. To learn more about working with email with your type of account, you can use the autoresponder to get the mail chapters from *The Complete Idiot's Guide to the Internet.* Of course, to use the autoresponder, you need to be able to send an email message! So, if necessary, ask your service provider how to send the first message. When you've got that figured out, send email to `ciginternet@mcp.com` with **allmail** in the Subject line to receive the email chapters.

What Email System?

Which email system do you use? If you are a member of an online service, you have a built-in mail system. But if you are not a member of one of the major online services, who the heck knows what you are using for email! I don't. For that matter, even with an online service, there are different options; CompuServe, for instance, offers a number of different programs you can use.

Basically, it all depends on what your service provider set you up with. You might be using Netscape, a World Wide Web browser (discussed in Chapter 3) that has a built-in email program. Or perhaps you're using Microsoft Exchange, which comes with Windows 95 and NT4, or if you are working with a very recent version of Windows 95 (yes, there are different versions of Windows 95, but we won't get into that) or Windows 98, you might be using Outlook Express. You could be using Eudora, which is one of the most popular email programs on the Internet, or perhaps Pegasus. Or you might be using something else entirely. Luckily, the email concepts are all the same, regardless of the type of program you are using—even if the buttons you click are different.

Start with What You Were Given

I suggest you start off using the email program that you were given when you set up your account. You may be able to use something else later. If you'd like to try Eudora later, go to `http://www.qualcomm.com/`. (You'll see how to use a URL, one of these Web addresses, in Chapter 3.) A free version called Eudora Light is available for the Macintosh and Windows. My current favorite is AK-Mail, a shareware email program (`http://akmail.com/`). You can find Pegasus at `http://www.pegasus.usa.com/`.

To POP or Not to POP

POP (Post Office Protocol) is a very common system used for handling Internet email. A POP server receives email that's been sent to you and holds it until you use your mail program to retrieve it. However, POP's not ubiquitous; some online services and many companies do not use POP.

Why do you care what system is used to hold your mail? After all, all you really care about is the program you use to collect and read the mail, not what arcane system your company or service provider uses. However, the POP issue becomes important if you want to change mail programs. In general, the best and most advanced email programs are designed to be used with POP servers. So if you need some specific email features and have decided you want to switch to another mail program, you may find you can't do so.

Suppose that you have an America Online or CompuServe account. The mail programs provided by these systems are quite basic. They lack many features that programs such as AK-Mail and Eudora have, such as advanced filtering. (Filtering allows you to automatically carry out actions on incoming email depending on the characteristics of that mail. For instance, you could set up the program to automatically delete all the email messages received from your boss. That way you won't be lying when you tell him you didn't receive his message.) But you may be stuck with what you've got. At the time of this writing, you could not use a POP program with an America Online account, so you couldn't install Eudora or AK-Mail or any other POP program. On the other hand, CompuServe now *does* provide POP mail, but you have to sign up for this optional service (it's free; use **GO POPMAIL** to find more information).

Another common mail system, IMAP (Internet Message Access Protocol), is generally used by corporate networks, not Internet service providers. If you're using a corporate network, you probably won't have much choice about which mail program you can use.

You Have a New Address!

I recently discovered how you can tell an absolute beginner on the Internet: He often talks about his email number, equating email with telephones. They are both electronic, after all. However, you have an email *address*. That address has three parts:

- Your account name
- The "at" sign (@)
- Your domain name

What's your account name? It's almost always the name you use to log on to your Internet account. For instance, when I log on to my CompuServe account, I have to type `71601,1266`. That's my account name. When I log on to MSN, I use `CIGInternet`, and on AOL, I use `PeKent`. (Note that the CompuServe account name is a special case; when using this account in an email address, I have to replace the comma with a period, like this: `71601.1266@compuserve.com`.)

After your account name, you use the @ sign. Why? How else would the Internet mail system know where the account name ends and the domain name starts?

Finally, you use the domain name, which is the address of your company, your service provider, or your online service. Think of it as the street part of an address: one street (the domain name) can be used for thousands of account names.

Techno Talk

Account Names: They're All the Same

CompuServe calls the account name a *User ID*, MSN calls it a *Member Name*, and AOL calls it a *Screen Name*. In addition, you might hear the account name called a *username* or *logon ID*. All these names mean the same thing: the name by which you are identified when you log on to your account. However, I discovered that some large service providers (mainly the phone companies, for some reason, who "don't quite get it") do something a little odd. You get some strange number as the account name, and you get *another* name to use when accessing your email. Someone at AT&T's WorldNet gave me a flip answer as to *why* they do this, using a sort of "well, of course, we *have* to do this, but you probably wouldn't understand" tone of voice; I wasn't convinced.

Where do you get the domain name? If you haven't been told already, ask the system administrator or tech support people. (Later in this chapter you'll learn the domain names of the larger online services.)

A Word About Setup

You might need to set up your email system before it will work. In many cases, this setup will already be done for you. If you are with one of the online services, you don't need to worry—it's done for you. Some of the Internet service providers also do all this configuring stuff for you. Others, however, expect you to get into your program and enter some information. It doesn't have to be difficult. The following figure shows some of the options you can configure in Netscape Messenger, the new email program that comes, along with Navigator, as part of the Netscape Communicator package, but the options will be similar in other programs.

Pronouncing Your Email Address Here's the "correct" way to say an email address out loud. You say "dot" for the periods and "at" for the @ sign. Thus, `pkent@topfloor.com` is "p kent at topfloor dot com."

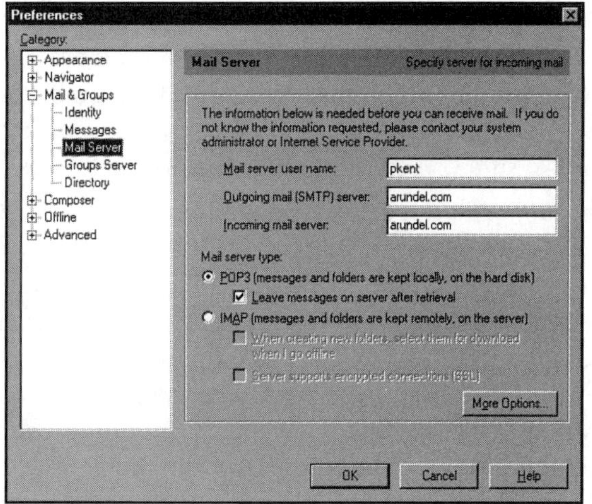

One of several mail-related panels in Netscape Messenger's Preferences dialog box, in which you can configure the mail program before you use it.

Whatever program you have, you may have to enter the following information:

- *Incoming Mail Server*. This is usually a POP account, although if you're on a corporate network it may be an IMAP (Internet Message Access protocol) account. When you connect to your service provider, your email program needs to check with the mail server (a program running on your service provider's system) to see if any mail has arrived. This mail server holds the messages that arrive for you until your mail program asks for them. Your account name is usually the same as the account name that you use to log on to your service. You might need to enter the full account name and the server hostname (for instance, in Netscape Messenger, I enter **pkent**, my account name, in the Mail Server User Name box, and then enter the server name—**topfloor.com**—in the Incoming Mail Server text box, and click the **POP** option button). On some systems, such as Eudora, you may have to enter the account name and server name all together in one box.

- *SMTP (Simple Mail Transfer Protocol) Server.* This mail program is used to *send* mail. While the POP account holds your incoming mail, the SMTP server transmits your messages onto the Internet. This time you'll enter a hostname (`mail.usa.net`, for instance) or maybe a number (something like `192.156.196.1`) that your service provider has given to you.
- *Password.* You'll need to enter your password so the email program can check the POP for mail. This password is generally the same one you use to log onto the system. Some programs, however, don't request your password until the first time you log on to retrieve your mail.
- *Real Name.* This is, yes, your actual name. Most mail programs will send your name along with the email address when you send email in the From line of the message.
- *Return or Reply To Address.* You can make the email program place a different Reply To address on your messages. For instance, if you send mail from work but want to receive responses to those messages at home, you'd use a different Reply To address. If you do this, make sure you enter the full address (such as `pkent@topfloor.com`).
- *All Sorts of Other Stuff.* You can get a good mail program to do all sorts of things. You can tell it how often to check the POP to see if new mail has arrived, choose the font you want the message displayed in, and get the program to automatically include the original message when you reply to a message. You can even tell it to leave messages at the POP server after you retrieve them. This might be handy if you like to check your mail from work; if you configure the program to leave the messages at the POP, you can retrieve them again when you get home, using the program on your home machine. You can also define how the program will handle attachments, but that is a complicated subject that I'll get to in the later section "Sending Files Is Getting Easier."

What Else Can I Do with My Mail Program?

You might be able to do lots of things. Check your documentation or Help files, or browse through the configuration dialog boxes to see what you can do. Note, however, that the online services' email programs generally have a limited number of choices. Email programs such as Eudora, Pegasus, AK-Mail, and those included with Netscape Communicator and Internet Explorer have many more choices.

There are so many email programs around, I can't help you configure them all. If you have trouble configuring your program, check the documentation or call the service's technical support. As I've said before, if your service doesn't want to help, find another service!

Sending a Message

Now that you understand addresses and have configured the mail program, you can send a message. So who can you mail a message to? You may already have friends and colleagues whom you can bother with your flippant "Hey, I've finally made it onto the Internet" message. Or mail me at `testmail@topfloor.com`, and I'll send a response back to you. (To do that, I'll use something called an *autoresponder*, a program that automatically replies to messages that it receives.)

So start your email program, and then open the window in which you are going to write the message. You may have to double-click an icon or choose a menu option that opens the mail's Compose window. For instance, in Eudora, once the program is open, you click the **New Message** button on the toolbar or choose **Message**, **New Message**.

Online Services

If you are working in one of the CompuServe programs, choose **Mail, Create New Mail.** In AOL, choose **Mail, Compose Mail.** In MSN, you'll open the **Communicate** menu and select **Send or Read Email.** (If you're still working with the old version of the MSN software, click the big **Email** bar in MSN Central.) If you are using Netscape's email program, there are all sorts of ways to begin: select **File**, **New**, **Message**, for instance.

In all the email programs, the Compose window has certain common elements. Some programs have a few extras. Here's what you might find:

- *To.* This line is for the address of the person you are mailing to. If you are using an online service and you are sending a message to another member of that service, all you need to use is the person's account name. For instance, if you are an AOL member and you're mailing to another AOL member with the screen name of PeKent, that's all you need to enter. To mail to that member from a service other than AOL, however, you enter the full address: `pekent@aol.com`. (I'll explain more about mailing to online services in the section "We Are All One: Sending Email to Online Services," later in this chapter.)
- *From.* Not all mail programs show this line, but it shows your email address, which is included in the message header (the clutter at the top of an Internet message). It lets the recipient know who to reply to.
- *Reply To.* You may have both a From address (to show which account the message came from) and a Reply To address (to get the recipient to reply to a different address).

- *Subject.* This line is a sort of message title—a few words summarizing the contents. The recipient can scan through a list of subjects to see what each message is about. (Some mail programs won't let you send a message unless you fill in the Subject line; others, perhaps most, don't mind if you leave it blank.)

Don't Cc to a list! If you want to mail a message to a large list of people, don't put all the addresses into the Cc line. Addresses in the Cc line will be visible to all recipients, and most people don't like the idea of their email address being given away to strangers. Instead, put the list into the Bcc line. Addresses in the Bcc line will not be displayed anywhere in the email message.

- *Cc.* You can enter an address here to send a copy to someone other than the person whose address you placed in the To line.
- *Bcc.* This means "blind copy." As with the Cc line, a copy of the message will be sent to the address (or addresses) you place in the Bc (or Bcc) line; however, the recipient of the original message won't be able to tell that the Bcc address received a copy. (If you use Cc, the recipient of the original message sees a Cc line in the header.)
- *Attachments.* This option is for sending computer files along with the message. (Again, I'll get to that later in this chapter, in the section "Sending Files Is Getting Easier.")
- *A big blank area.* This area is where you type your message.

Email programs vary greatly, and not all programs have all these features. Again, the online service mail programs tend to be a bit limited. The following figures show the Compose window in two very different mail programs.

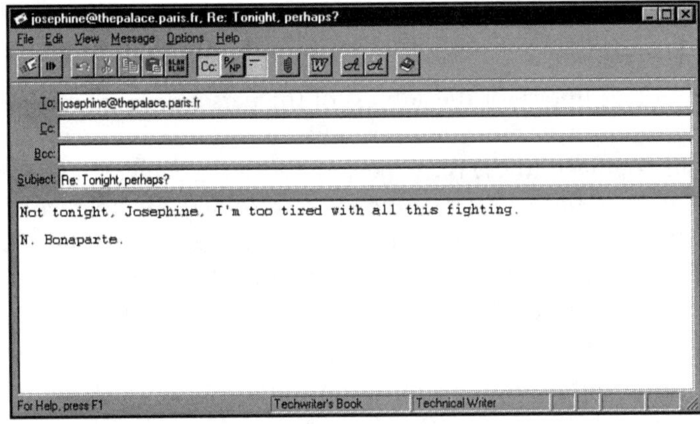

This is AK-Mail, my current favorite.

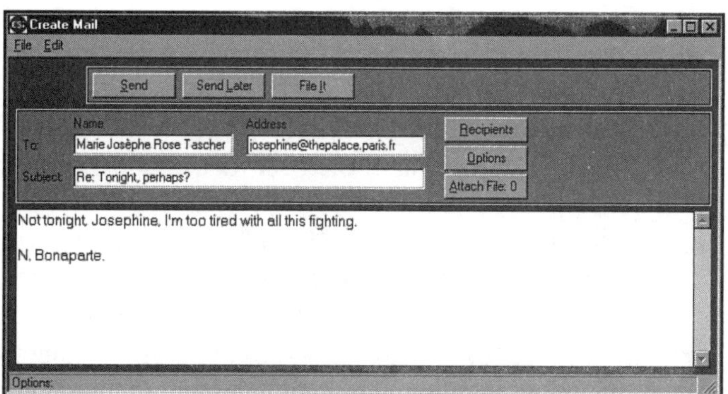

This is CompuServe's mail composition window.

Go ahead and type a To address. Email `testmail@topfloor.com`, and you'll get a response. Or email to your own address. If you use an online service, you might as well use the entire Internet address (for instance, on AOL type *`name`*`@aol.com`). The message will probably go out onto the Internet and then turn around and come back to you. I'll explain those online service addresses in the next section.

We Are All One: Sending Email to Online Services

One of the especially nice things about the Internet, from an email point of view, is that because all the online services are now connected to the Internet, you can send email between online services. (Not so long ago the online services were completely separate; you could only email someone on a service if you had an account with that service.) Perhaps you have an America Online account because AOL sent you a disk in the mail. Perhaps your brother has a CompuServe account because he's a geek, and that's where the geeks have been hanging out for years. (Before you email me to complain, I've had a CompuServe account for almost 15 years.) You can send email to each other, using the Internet as a sort of bridge. How? You just have to know the other person's account name on that service and that service's domain name.

For instance, CompuServe has this Internet domain name: `compuserve.com`. Say you want to send an email message to someone at CompuServe who has the account name (or User ID as it's called on CompuServe) of `71601,1266`. You add the two together with the @ in the middle. Then you have `71601,1266@compuserve.com`. However, you can't have a comma in an Internet address. So you replace it with a period, and you end up with `71601.1266@compuserve.com`. (Some CompuServe users have "proper" email addresses, names instead of numbers. If you use CompuServe and want one of these real addresses, use **GO REGISTER**.) The following table lists a few services and tells you how to send email to them.

Sending email to other services

Service	Method of Addressing
America Online	Add `@aol.com` to the end of an America Online address.
CompuServe	Replace the comma in the User ID with a period, and then add `@compuserve.com` to the end.
GEnie	Add `@genie.geis.com` to the end of a GEnie address.
MCImail	Add `@mcimail.com` to the end of an MCImail address.
Microsoft Network	Add `@msn.com` to the end of the MSN Member name.
Prodigy	Add `@prodigy.com` to the end of the user's Prodigy address.

These addresses are quite easy. Of course, there are more complicated Internet addresses, but you'll rarely run into them. If you have trouble emailing someone, though, call and ask *exactly* what you must type as his email address. (There's no rule that says you can't use the telephone anymore.)

Write the Message

Now that you have the address onscreen, write your message—whatever you want to say. Then send the message. How's that done? There's usually a big **Send** button, or maybe a menu option that says **Send** or **Mail**. What happens when you click the button? That depends on the program and whether you are logged on at the moment. Generally, if you are logged on, the mail is sent immediately. Not always, though. Some programs will put the message in a queue and won't send the message until told to do so. Others will send the message immediately, and if you are not logged on, they will try to log on first. Watch closely, and you'll usually see what's happening. A message will let you know if the message is being sent. If it hasn't been sent, look for some kind of **Send Immediately** menu option or perhaps **Send Queued Messages**. Whether the message should be sent immediately or put in a queue is often one of the configuration options available to you.

Where'd It Go? Incoming Email

You've sent yourself an email message, but where did it go? It went out into the electronic wilderness to wander around for a few seconds or maybe a few minutes. Sometimes email messages can take a few hours to reach their destinations. Very occasionally, it even takes a few days. (Generally, the message comes back in a few minutes, especially if you're sending yourself a message, unless you mistyped the address, in which case you'll get a special message telling you that it's a bad address.)

Now it's time to check for incoming email. If you are using an online service, as soon as you log on you'll see a message saying that email has arrived. If you are *already* online, you may see a message telling you that mail has arrived, or you may need to check periodically; you may find a Get New Mail menu option. If you are working with an Internet service provider, you generally won't be informed of incoming mail; rather your email program has to go and check. Either you can do that manually (for instance, in Eudora, there's a **File, Check Mail** command), or you can configure the program to check automatically every so often.

Fancy Fonts

Some of the online services allow you to use fancy text formatting features. For example, MSN and AOL let you use colors, indents, different fonts, bold, italic, and so on. But in general these features only work in messages sent *within* the online services. Internet email is plain text—nothing fancy. Don't bother getting fancy in your Internet email because the online service's email system will strip out all that attractive stuff when the message is sent out onto the Internet. However, there is a system you can use to send formatted email, if both you and the recipient have the right type of mail program—HTML Mail.

What Now?

What can you do with your incoming email? All sorts of things. I think I'm pretty safe in saying that *every* email program allows you to read incoming messages. Most programs also let you print and save messages (if your program doesn't, you need another). You can also delete them, forward them to someone else, and reply directly to the sender. These commands should be easy to find. Generally you'll have toolbar buttons for the most important commands, and more options will be available if you dig around a little in the menus, too.

A Word About Quoting

It's a good idea to quote when you respond to a message. This means that you include part or all of the original message. Some programs automatically quote the original message. Different programs mark quoted messages in different ways; usually, you'll see a "greater than" symbol (>) at the beginning of each line. The following figure shows a reply message that contains a quote from the original message.

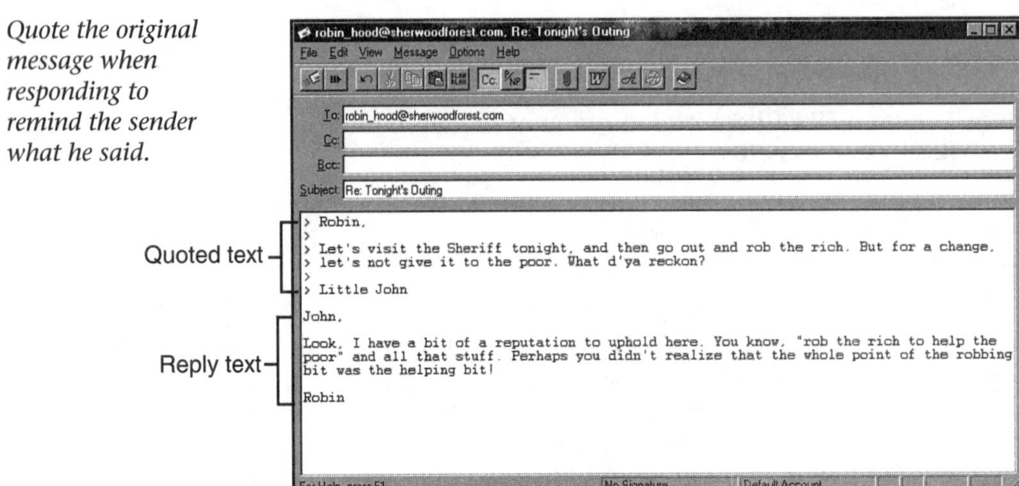

Quote the original message when responding to remind the sender what he said.

You aren't required to quote. But if you don't, the recipient might not know what you are talking about. I receive scores of messages a day, and I know people who get hundreds. (Of course, the radiation emitted from their computer screens is probably frying their brains.) If you respond to a message without reminding the recipient exactly which of the 200 messages he sent out last week (or which of the five he sent to you) you are responding to, he might be slightly confused. Quoting is especially important when sending messages to mailing lists and newsgroups (discussed in Chapter 7, "Newsgroups: The Source of All Wisdom"), where your message might be read by people who didn't read the message to which you are responding.

Sending Files Is Getting Easier

I used to hate sending files. Not because it's so difficult to send files across the Internet (although it is—or at least used to be until very recently), but because it was sort of embarrassing to admit how difficult it was. Now before you misunderstand, let me say that I *did* know how to send files across the Internet. However, very few other people seemed to understand, and even when they did understand, they didn't seem to have software that worked properly. Unless both parties involved (the sender and the recipient) understand the process and have the correct software, things sometimes won't work.

I recall, for instance, the incredible problems I had transferring computer files to a magazine early in 1995. It didn't matter what transmission format I used (I'll discuss that in a moment), nor what program I was working with; the staff at the magazine couldn't seem to open those files—never mind that this magazine just happened to be a major *Internet* magazine. Today the situation is much improved, and the problems inherent in file transfers are, for many users, a thing of the past. Still, the situation isn't perfect, and problems can still occur.

Files are commonly sent across cyberspace in one of four ways:

- *MIME.* Multimedia Internet Mail Extensions is a system designed to make sending files across the Internet easier. It converts the file to text, sends it with the message, and converts it back at the other end. (You can send only text files in the Internet's email system, hence the need to convert files to text.) What's the difference between uuencode and MIME? Whereas uuencode, the following method, is a sort of quick fix, MIME was intended to be a nicely integrated system that works transparently so that all you have to do is select the file you want to send, and MIME does the rest. MIME also has a method for identifying the type of file that is being transferred. (MIME is now used on the World Wide Web to identify multimedia files linked to Web pages.) MIME is the most common method used for sending files across the Internet these days. Most users now have email programs that handle the file transfer, but a few have to use utilities to convert a MIMEd file back to its original format.
- *uuencode.* In this system, a computer file is converted to plain ASCII text. It may start out as a sound file or a word processing file, but when it's converted it looks like gibberish text. This process is called *uuencoding*. An encoded file can be placed into an email message and sent. The person at the other end must then either receive the message with a mail program that can convert uuencoded files back to their original format or save the message as a text file and *uudecode* it—convert it back to its original format—using a special utility. This system is falling out of favor because most email programs now handle MIME.
- *BinHex.* This system is used on the Macintosh, and it's very similar to uuencode. Files are converted into text and then converted back at the other end. It seems to be dying out, though (relatively speaking; please don't email me to tell me it's alive and well, and how the Macintosh is a better machine, and how Bill Gates should be crucified for stealing Macintosh design features…). Even many Macintosh mail programs use MIME and uuencode.
- *Online Service Systems.* Each of the online services has a file-transfer system. In AOL and CompuServe, you can attach a file to a message and then send that message to another member of the same online service. In MSN, you can insert all sorts of things directly into messages—pictures, formatted text, or computer files—and then send them to other MSN members.

Now, here's the problem. If you want to send a message to another person on the Internet, you may have to know which system to use. The following guidelines can help you make a good decision:

1. The first time you have to send a file to someone, just go ahead and use whatever system your mail program works with. A couple of years ago you'd have a fifty-fifty

chance of the file getting through, but these days it will probably work. If it doesn't, though, move on to the next step.

2. Check to see if the other person has an account on the same online service you do. Even if you've been given an Internet email address that is obviously not an online service, ask just in case. It's more reliable to send a file between CompuServe accounts, between AOL accounts, or between MSN accounts, for instance, than to use MIME, BinHex, or uuencode. (You'll find that many people—especially geeks—have accounts on two or more services.) I used to tell people that it's *far* more reliable to use the online service rather than the other systems, but the gap is closing.
3. If you have to use the Internet email system, check to see which system the recipient can work with (MIME, uuencode, or BinHex). In the past I've advised that you *shouldn't* simply pick one and send the file because if the recipient didn't have the right software, he wouldn't be able to use the file. However, these days MIME is in fairly wide use, so if you're not able to check with the recipient first, you could try MIME, and it will probably work. (However, see the following discussion of the online services.) The most popular POP mail programs all work with MIME: Eudora, Netscape Communicator's mail program (Messenger), Pegasus, Microsoft Internet Mail, Outlook Express, and so on.
4. Consider which file-transfer systems are built into your email program. If you are lucky, the system that's built into your email program is the same system the recipient uses—but if that was the case, you wouldn't have had a problem in the first place. However, the program may have two or more systems built in, so that you can choose one or the other. For example, Eudora Light can send files using MIME or BinHex—but it can't send files using uuencode. (At least, Eudora can't do so directly. However, you'll see in a moment how to send uuencoded messages even if it's not built into your email program.) Netscape Navigator has both MIME and uuencode, so you can use either. Many mail programs only work with MIME, though.

What if you don't have a match? Or what if the recipient has an online service account? Or if *you* have an online service account? Some of the online services may not work with either MIME or uuencode. The major online services have recently been upgrading their mail services so you can use MIME—perhaps. You can send files to and from CompuServe using MIME, although to receive them you may have to upgrade your mail system (use the **GO NEWMAIL** command). AOL also allows file transfers to and from the Internet. Surprisingly, MSN didn't allow incoming and outgoing file attachments until recently; version 2.5 of the MSN software, which uses Outlook Express as the mail program, *does* work with attachments, so if you have an earlier version, you might want to upgrade.

Note, however, that even if an online service's mail system uses MIME, it may not do so *properly*. For instance, I found that when I sent a file from CompuServe to an Internet account the file was transferred correctly, but without a filename. CompuServe had trouble accepting incoming files that had MIME attachments, too. AOL, on the other hand, may strip out the file extension on *incoming* files, yet transfer outgoing files correctly, although the new version 4.0 seems to work well. (By the way, the online services' mail systems are very slow; I think they employ people to retype all the incoming messages. I'm not sure what they do with attachments, but attachments slow down incoming mail even further.) If you are working with a service that won't work with MIME or uuencode, you'll have to use a utility to convert the incoming file for you, which I'll discuss next.

Conversion Utilities

There are things you can do to get around incompatibilities between your mail system and the recipient's, but they may be a hassle. Say you want to send someone a file using uuencode because that's the only thing he can work with. But you have a CompuServe account, which means your email program won't automatically uudecode files. You can go to a software archive and download a uuencode program. (For instance, if you use Windows, you can use a program called Wincode.) Then you use that program to convert the file to a text file, you copy the text from the file and paste it into the message, and you send the message. (And then you cross your fingers.)

How about MIME? Say someone just sent you a MIME-encoded file, but you have a mail program that won't decode MIME attachments. What can you do? Go to the software libraries and search for MIME. For instance, I use little DOS programs called Mpack and Munpack. You can save the message you received as a text file (virtually all email programs let you do this, generally with the **File**, **Save As** command), and then use Munpack to convert that text file to the original file format. (Mpack and Munpack are also available for the Macintosh and for UNIX systems.)

How about BinHex? I sometimes receive files from Macintosh users; I use a Windows program called StuffIt Expander to extract the file from BinHex. (StuffIt Expander was originally a Macintosh program, so Mac versions are available, too, of course; it also works with uuencoded files and archive files such as .SIT and .ZIP files—see Chapter 10, "What on Earth Are All Those File Types?," for more information. You can find these programs at `http://www.aladdinsys.com/`.)

If you are lucky, though, your email program has MIME and uuencode built in, as well as some kind of command that lets you insert or attach a file. For instance, in Eudora Light, choose **Message**, **Attach File** and use the small drop-down list at the top of the Compose window to choose between **BinHex** and **MIME**. In AOL, click the **Attach** button; in CompuServe (see the next figure), use the **Mail**, **Send File** command in the main window, or click the **Attach File** button in the Create Mail window.

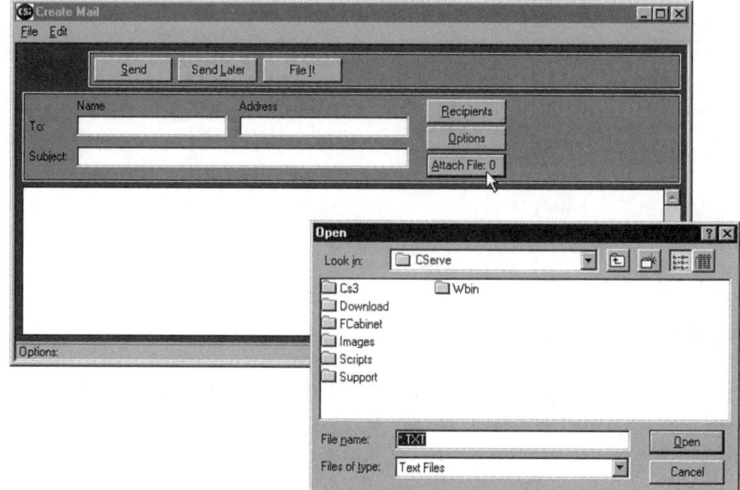

Sending a file with your email is usually as simple as clicking a button and selecting the file.

Cool Things You Can Do with Email

Once you understand your email system and realize that it won't bite, you might begin to enjoy using it. The following list contains suggestions of some things you might want to do with your email program:

- *Create a mailing list.* You can create a special mailing list that contains the email addresses of many people. For instance, if you want to send a message to everyone in your department (or family, or club) at the same time, you can create a mailing list. Put all the addresses in the list, and then send the message to the list. Everyone on the list receives the message, and you save time and hassle. Some programs will have a mailing list dialog box of some sort; others let you create a nickname or alias for the mailing list and then associate the addresses with it.
- *Create an address book.* Virtually all email systems have address books, and they're usually quite easy to use. You can store a person's complicated email address and then retrieve it quickly using the person's real name.
- *Use aliases.* An alias, sometimes known as a *nickname*, is a simple identifier you give to someone in your address book. Instead of typing **peter kent** or **pkent@topfloor.com**, for instance, you could just type a simple alias such as **pk** to address a message to that person.
- *Work with mail while you're offline.* Most programs these days let you read and write email offline. The program quickly logs on to send and retrieve messages, and then logs off again automatically. This feature is of particular importance with services that charge you for the amount of time you are online.
- *Forward your mail.* After being on the Internet for a while, there's a risk of attaining real geekhood by getting multiple Internet accounts, such as one with your favorite online service, one at work, one with a cheap service provider, and so on. (Right

now, I have about eight, I think.) That's a lot of trouble logging on to check for email. However, some services let you forward your email to another account so that if a message arrives at, say, the account you use at home, you can have it automatically sent on to you at work. Ask your service provider how to do this; you may need to log on to your shell account to set this up (discussed in Chapter 13, "21 Questions: The Complete Internet FAQ"). Although most Internet service providers let you do this, the online services generally *don't*.

- *Create a vacation message.* When you go on vacation, your email doesn't stop. That's why so many cybergeeks never go on vacation, or take a laptop if they do: They can't bear the thought of missing all those messages. Still, if you manage to break away, you may be able to set a special vacation message, an automatic response to any incoming mail that says basically, "I'm away, be back soon." (You get to write the response message.) Again, ask your service provider. The online services generally *don't* have this service.
- *Filter your files.* Sophisticated email programs have file-filtering capabilities. You can tell the program to look at incoming mail and carry out certain actions according to what it finds. You can place email from your newsgroups into special inboxes, grab only the message subject if the message is very long, delete mail from certain people or organizations, and so on.

Caution: Email Can Be Dangerous!

The more I use email, the more I believe that it can be a dangerous tool. There are three main problems: 1) people often don't realize the implications of what they are saying, 2) people often misinterpret what others are saying, and 3) people are comfortable typing things into a computer that they would never say to a person face-to-face. Consequently, online fights are common both in private (between email correspondents) and in public (in the newsgroups and mailing lists).

The real problem is that when you send an email message, the recipient can't see your face or hear your tone of voice. Of course, when you write a letter, you have the same problem, but email is replacing conversations as well as letters. The U.S. Post Office is as busy as ever, so I figure email is *mainly* replacing conversations. That contributes to the problem because people are writing messages in a chatty conversational style, forgetting that email lacks all the visual and auditory "cues" that go along with a conversation.

In the interests of world peace, I give you these email guidelines to follow:

- *Don't write something you will regret later.* Lawsuits have been based on the contents of electronic messages, so consider what you are writing and whether you would want it to be read by someone other than the recipient. A message can always be forwarded, read over the recipient's shoulder, printed out and passed around, backed up onto the company's archives, and so on. You don't *have* to use email—there's always the telephone. (Oliver North has already learned *his* lesson!)

- *Consider the tone of your message.* It's easy to try to be flippant and come out as arrogant or to try to be funny and come out as sarcastic. When you write, think about how your words will appear to the recipient.
- *Give the sender the benefit of the doubt.* If a person's message sounds arrogant or sarcastic, consider that he might be trying to be flippant or funny! If you are not sure what the person is saying, ask him to explain.
- *Read before you send.* It will give you a chance to fix embarrassing spelling and grammatical errors and to reconsider what you've just said. (Some mail programs have spell checkers.)
- *Wait a day…or three.* If you typed something in anger, wait a few days and read the message again. Give yourself a chance to reconsider.
- *Be nice.* There's no need for vulgarity or rudeness (except in certain newsgroups, where it seems to be a requirement for entrance).
- *Attack the argument, not the person.* I've seen fights start when someone disagrees with another person's views and sends a message making a personal attack upon that person. (This point is more related to mailing lists and newsgroups than email proper, but we are on the subject of avoiding fights.) Instead of saying, "Anyone who thinks *Days of Our Lives* is not worth the electrons it's transmitted on must be a half-witted moron with all the common sense of the average pineapple," consider saying "You may think it's not very good, but clearly many other people find great enjoyment in this show."
- *Use smileys.* One way to add some of those missing visual and auditory cues is to add smileys—keep reading.

You're Being Baited Some people send rude or vicious messages because they *enjoy* getting into a fight like this—where they can fight from the safety of their computer terminals.

Smile and Be Understood!

Over the past few years, email users have developed a number of ways to clarify the meaning of messages. You might see <g> at the end of the line, for example. This means grin and is shorthand for saying, "You know, of course, that what I just said was a joke, right?" You may also see :-) in the message. Turn this book sideways, so that the left column of this page is up and the right column is down, and you'll see that this symbol is a small smiley face. It means the same as <g>, "Of course, that *was* a joke, okay?"

Emoticons Galore

Little pictures are commonly known as *smileys*. But the smiley face, although by far the most common, is just one of many available symbols. You might see some of the emoticons in the following table, and you may want to use them. Perhaps you can create a few of your own.

Share the Smiles

Many people call these character faces "smiley faces." But if you'd like to impress your friends with a bit of technobabble, you can call them *emoticons*. If you really want to impress your colleagues, get hold of *The Smiley Dictionary* by Seth Godin. It contains hundreds of these things.

Commonly used emoticons

<table>
<tr><th>Emoticon</th><th>Meaning</th></tr>
<tr><td>:-(</td><td>Sadness, disappointment</td></tr>
<tr><td>8-)</td><td>Kinda goofy-looking smile, or wearing glasses</td></tr>
<tr><td>:-></td><td>A big smile</td></tr>
<tr><td>;-)</td><td>A wink</td></tr>
<tr><td>*<|:-)</td><td>Santa Claus</td></tr>
<tr><td>:-&</td><td>Tongue-tied</td></tr>
<tr><td>:-o</td><td>A look of shock</td></tr>
<tr><td>:-p</td><td>Tongue stuck out</td></tr>
<tr><td>,:-) or 7:^]</td><td>Ronald Reagan</td></tr>
</table>

Personally, I don't like smileys much. They strike me as being just a *tiiiny* bit too cutesy. However, I do use them now and again to make *absolutely* sure that I'm not misunderstood!

Message Shorthand

There are a couple of other ways people try to liven up their messages. One is to use obscure acronyms like the ones in this table.

Online shorthand

Acronym	Meaning
BTW	By the way
FWIW	For what it's worth
FYI	For your information
IMO	In my opinion

continues

continued

Acronym	Meaning
IMHO	In my humble opinion
LOL	Laughing out loud (used as an aside to show your disbelief)
OTFL	On the floor, laughing (used as an aside)
PMFBI	Pardon me for butting in
PMFJI	Pardon me for jumping in
RTFM	Read the &*^%# manual
ROTFL or ROFL	Rolling on the floor laughing (used as an aside)
ROTFLMAO	Same as above, except with "laughing my a** off" added on the end. (You didn't expect me to say it, did you? This is a family book, and anyway, the editors won't let me.)
TIA	Thanks in advance
YMMV	Your mileage may vary

The real benefit of using these is that they confuse the average neophyte. I suggest that you learn them quickly, so you can pass for a long-term cybergeek.

You'll also see different ways of stressing particular words. (You can't use bold and italic in most Internet email, remember?) You might see words marked with an underscore on either side (_now!_) or, perhaps frequently, with an asterisk (*now!*).

The Least You Need to Know

- There are many different email systems, but the basic procedures all work similarly.
- Even if your online service lets you use fancy text (colors, different fonts, different styles) within the service, that text won't work in Internet messages.
- Sending files across the Internet is much easier now than it was just a year or so ago, but problems still arise; sending files *within* the online services is always easy.
- On the Internet, the most common file-transfer method is MIME; uuencode is also used now and then. These are often built into mail programs, or you can use external utilities to convert the files.
- Don't send a file until you know which system the recipient is using. Or if you do, use MIME.
- Get to know all the neat little things your email program can do for you, such as create mailing lists and filter files.
- Be careful with email; misunderstandings (and fights) are common.

Chapter 3

The World of the World Wide Web

In This Chapter

- What is the Web?
- Which browser should you use?
- The home page
- Moving around the Web
- The history list and bookmarks
- Using URLs

The World Wide Web is also known as *The Web*, *WWW*, and sometimes (among really geeky company) *W3*. In really confused company, it's called *the Internet*. The World Wide Web is *not* the Internet. It's simply one software system running on the Internet. Still, it's one of the most interesting and exciting systems, so it has received a lot of press, to the extent that many people believe that the terms Web and Internet are synonymous. However, the Web seems to be taking over roles previously carried out by other Internet services; at the same time, Web programs, called *browsers*, are including utilities to help people work with non-Web services. For instance, you can send and receive email with some Web browsers, and you also can read Internet newsgroups with some browsers.

What's the Web?

Imagine that you are reading this page in electronic form, on your computer screen. Then imagine that some of the words are underlined and colored. Use your mouse to point at one of these underlined words on your screen and press the mouse button. What happens? Another document opens, a document that's related in some way to the word you clicked.

That's a simple explanation of *hypertext.* If you've ever used Apple's Hypercard or a Windows Help file, you've used hypertext. Documents are linked to each other in some way, generally by clickable words and pictures. Hypertext has been around for years, but until recently most hypertext systems were limited in both size and geographic space. Click a link, and you might see another document held by the same electronic file. Or maybe you'll see a document in another file, but one that's on the same computer's hard disk, probably the same directory.

The World Wide Web is a hypertext system without boundaries. Click a link, and you might be shown a document in the next city, on the other side of the country, or even on another continent. Links from one document to another can be created without the permission of the owner of that second document, and nobody has complete control over those links. When you put a link in your document connecting to someone else's, you are sending your readers on a journey that you can't predict. They will land at that other document, from which they can take another link somewhere else—to another country, another subject, or another culture from which they can follow yet another link, and on and on.

The Web has no capacity limit, either. Web pages are being added every minute of the day, all over the world; the Web is pushing the growth of the Internet. Creating and posting a Web page is so easy that thousands of people are doing it, and more are joining them each day.

If you haven't seen the Web, this description may sound a little mundane. Okay, so one document leads to another that leads to another; what's the big deal? I try to avoid the Internet hype we've been inundated with over the past couple of years, but the Web really is a publishing revolution. Publishing to an international audience is now quick and simple. I don't mean to imply (as some Internet proponents seem to) that every Web page is a jewel that is widely read and appreciated (much of it is closer to a sow's ear than to silk), but it's a medium with which people can make their words available so that they can be widely read if they have some value.

Check This Out...

Dial-In Terminal (Shell) Accounts

Using the Web with a dial-in direct account is very different from using it with a dial-in terminal (shell) account. If you are working with a dial-in terminal account, much of the information in this chapter won't help at all. To learn more about working with the Web with your type of account, you can use the autoresponder to get the Web chapters from the first edition of *The Complete Idiot's Guide to the Internet.* Send email to `ciginternet@mcp.com`, with `web` in the Subject line to receive the email chapters.

Let's Start

If you want to listen to a CD, you need a CD player. If you want to watch a video, you need a video player. If you want to view a Web page, you need a Web player: a *Web browser.*

The Web equation has two parts. First, a *Web server* is a special program running on a host computer (that is, a computer connected directly to the Internet). This server administers a Web site, which is a collection of World Wide Web documents. The second part is the *browser,* which is a program on your PC that asks the server for the documents and then displays the documents so that you can read them.

> Check This Out...
>
> **Servers and Clients** If you hang around on the Internet long enough, you'll hear the terms server and client used over and over. A *server* is a program that provides information that a *client* program can use in some way.

There are two big contenders in the Web browser war (yes, there's a war going on). One is Netscape Navigator. Right now, somewhere around 50% of all Web users are working with Netscape, although in the past Netscape owned 80%–90% of the market. Netscape is available in versions for Windows 3.1, Windows 95 and Windows NT, the Macintosh, and various flavors of UNIX. Netscape Navigator is now part of the Netscape Communicator suite of programs. The following figure shows the Netscape Navigator Web browser.

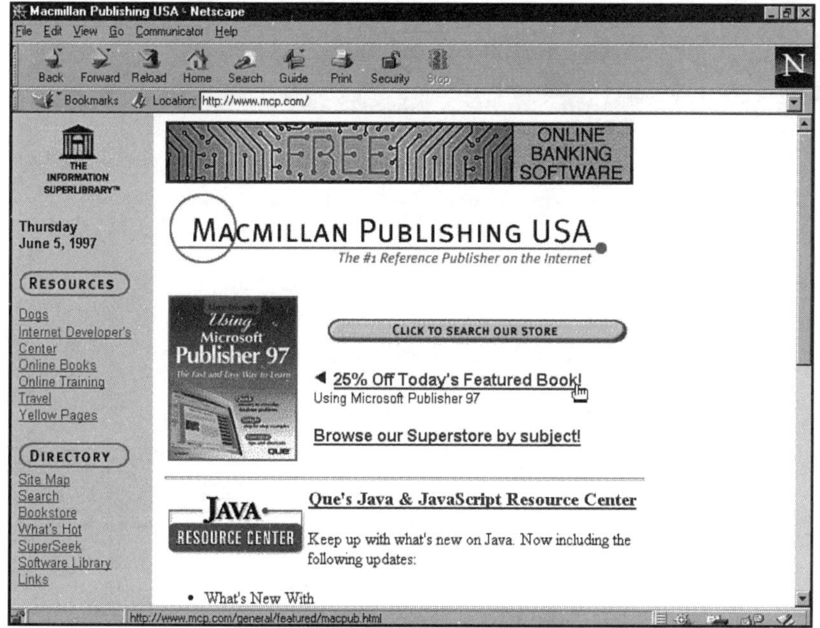

Netscape Navigator, part of the Netscape Communicator suite of programs, is the most popular browser on the Web, for the moment.

Netscape Navigator

Netscape Communications manufactures Netscape Navigator. You might think that it would be known as Navigator for short, but it's not. It's known as Netscape, mainly for "historical" reasons. The Netscape programmers came from NCSA (National Center for Supercomputing Applications). They originally created the first graphical Web browser, called Mosaic. Netscape was originally known as Netscape Mosaic, and the company was Mosaic Communications. Thus, the browser was known as Netscape to differentiate it from Mosaic.

The second most popular browser is Internet Explorer from Microsoft (shown in the following figure). Originally this browser ran only on Windows 95 and Windows NT, but now it's available for the Mac and Windows 3.1. This browser has almost all the rest of the browser market share, perhaps around 40%. Its share of the market is growing (if you can call it a market; few people buy their Web browser). Chances are you are using either Netscape Navigator or Internet Explorer.

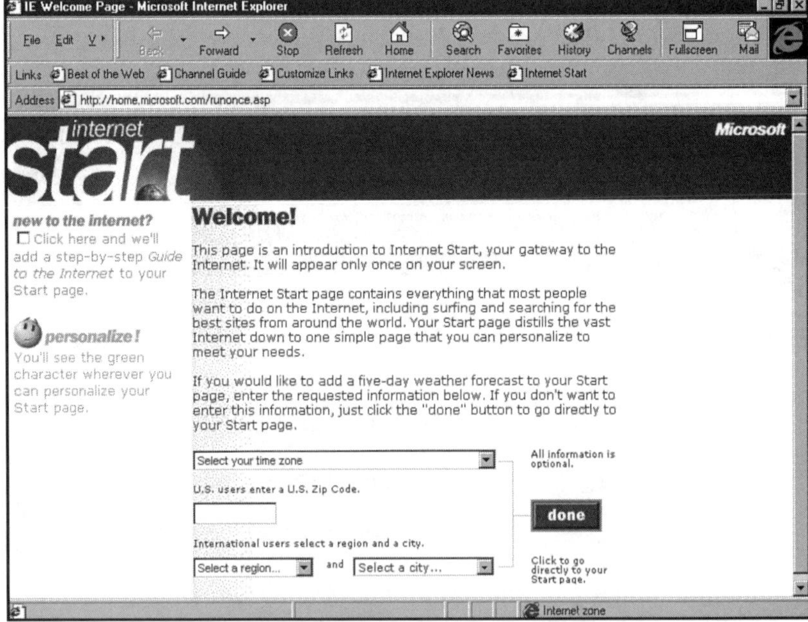

MS Internet Explorer 4, Microsoft's latest weapon in the Web war with Netscape.

I'm going to keep my head down because what I'm about to say may incite an assault by Web purists. Netscape is not the "be all and end all" of Web browsers. It is undoubtedly a good browser, but you shouldn't feel that if you don't have Netscape you're missing out on something. Dozens of other browsers are available, ranging from pretty awful to very good. Probably the best two are Netscape and Internet Explorer. At the moment, I prefer Netscape Navigator, although in the past I've preferred Internet Explorer. They seem to leapfrog each other. For a few months, Netscape Navigator is better, and then a new version of Explorer comes out, and it seems better. Then, a few weeks later, Navigator is modified again, and it has a few nice features and bug fixes that make it better than Explorer, and so on.

Getting a Browser

Which browser should you use? If your service provider has given you one, I suggest you start with that. You'll probably be given either Netscape or Explorer—most likely Internet Explorer these days because CompuServe, AOL, and (of course!) Microsoft Network provide that browser to their members.

If you have to pick a browser, try Explorer first (if you are using Windows NT or Windows 95); then try Netscape later and see if you like it. If you are using a Mac or Windows 3.1, you might want to do it the other way around: start with Netscape (even though the new Explorer for the Mac is getting good reviews). There's a new version of Internet Explorer that runs on UNIX, too.

For now, I'm going to assume that you have a Web browser installed, and that you have opened it and are ready to start. One nice thing about Web browsers is that they all work similarly, and they look very similar, too. So whatever browser you use, you should be able to follow along with this chapter.

Browsing Begins at Home

When you open your browser, whatever page you see is, by definition, your *home page*. (I like that kind of definition; it's easy to understand.) Ideally, the home page is a page that has lots of useful links, which take you to places on the Web that you will want to go to frequently. You can create your own home page by using something called HTML, the Web document language or even using one of the fancy new customizing systems you'll find on the Web. (Both Netscape and Microsoft have systems that automatically create customized pages for you, if you have their browsers. Go to `http://www.netscape.com/custom/index.html` for the Netscape system or `http://home.microsoft.com/` for the Microsoft system (Internet Explorer 4 has an Internet Start button you can click to get to this page). I'll explain how to use these "addresses" later in this chapter, in the section "A Direct Link: Using the URLs."

Home Page, Start Page

Microsoft's programmers can't seem to decide whether to use the term *home page* or *start page*. The term home page originally meant the page that appeared when you opened your browser or when you used the Home button. Then all of a sudden, everybody was using the term to mean a person or company's main Web page (the page you see when you go to that Web site) such as NEC's home page, Netscape's home page, and so on. So Microsoft's programmers evidently thought it made more sense to rename the home page to "start page." Unfortunately, they're using *both* terms, so Internet Explorer 3 and 4 have a Home button on the toolbar; Explorer 3 has a Go, Start Page menu option; some versions of Explorer 4 have a Go, Home Page menu option and a Home button, but mention start page in the options dialog box. More recent versions of Explorer 4 have completely replaced the term start page with home page.

Moving Around on the Web

Whatever browser you are using, you'll almost certainly find links on the home page. Links are the colored and underlined words. You may also find pictures that contain links, perhaps several different links on a picture (a different link on each part of the picture). Use your mouse to point at a piece of text or a picture; if the mouse pointer changes shape—probably into a pointing hand—you are pointing at a link. (Just to confuse the issue, some pictures contain links even though the pointer doesn't change shape.)

Click whatever link looks interesting. If you are online (I'm assuming you are!), your browser sends a message to a Web server somewhere, asking for a page. If the Web server is running (it may not be) and if it's not too busy (it may be), it transmits the document back to your browser, and your browser displays it on your screen.

You've just learned the primary form of Web "navigation." When you see a link you want to follow, you click it. Simple, eh? But what about going somewhere useful, somewhere interesting? Most browsers these days either have toolbar buttons that take you to a useful Web page or come with a default home page with useful links. For example, in Netscape Navigator 4, you can click the Guide button to open the Guide page, or click the Guide button and hold it down to display these options:

- *The Internet.* This option also takes you to the Guide page, the page that appears if you simply single-click the Guide button.
- *People.* This option provides links to sites that can help you track down other Internet users.

- *Yellow Pages.* This option displays a page from which you can select a regional Yellow Pages system and search for a business.
- *What's New?* This option provides links to a selection of new and interesting Web sites from the people at Netscape.
- *What's Cool?* This option provides links to Web sites chosen for their usefulness or CQ—coolness quotient. (Personally, I'm getting tired of the word *cool*. But hey, that's my job: Internet Curmudgeon.)

Techno Talk

How Does the Browser Know Where to Go?

How does your browser know which server to request the document from? What you see on your computer screen is not quite the same document that your browser sees. Open the source document (which you can probably do using the **View**, **Page Source** menu option), and you'll see what the Web document *really* looks like. The source document is just basic ASCII text that contains all sorts of instructions. One of the instructions says, in effect, "if this guy clicks this link, here's which document I want you to get." You don't normally see all these funky commands because the browser *renders* the page, removing the instructions and displaying only the relevant text.

Internet Explorer 3 has a special QuickLinks toolbar (click **QuickLinks** in the Address toolbar to open the QuickLinks toolbar). In Explorer 4, this toolbar is simply named the Links bar and can be opened or closed by selecting **View**, **Toolbars**, **Links**. On this toolbar, you'll find a variety of buttons designed to take you to useful starting points. (The button names vary between versions.)

Whatever browser you are using, take a little time to explore. Go as far as you want. Then come back here, and I'll explain how to find your way back to where you came from.

Check This Out...

Link Colors

Some links change color after you click them. You won't see it right away, but if you return to the same page later, you'll find that the link is a different color. The color change indicates that the particular link points to a document that you've already seen. The "used-link" color does expire after a while, and the link changes back to its original color. How long it takes for this to happen is something that you can generally control with an option in your browser's Preferences or Options area.

The Hansel and Gretel Dilemma: Where Are You?

Hypertext is a fantastic tool, but it has one huge drawback: it's easy to get lost. If you are reading a book and you flip forward a few pages, you know how to get back. You flip back, right? But with hypertext, after a few moves through the electronic library, you can become horribly lost. How do you get back to where you came from? And where did you come from, anyway?

Over the years, a number of systems have been developed to help people find their way around this rather strange freeform medium. This table explains some tools you can use in most Web browsers to move through the pages and sites you've seen.

Web page navigation tools

Button	Description
Back	Click the **Back** button or choose **Back** from a menu (probably the **Go** menu) to return to the previous Web page.
Forward	Click the **Forward** button or choose the **Forward** menu option to return to a page you've just come back from.
Home	Click the **Home** button (or the **Start** button on some versions of Internet Explorer) to go all the way back to your home page or start page.
Bookmarks or Favorites	You can set bookmarks on pages you think you'll want to come back to (they're known as Favorites in Internet Explorer); bookmarks can be very helpful because you don't have to struggle to find your way back to the page the next time.
History	This is a list of pages you've seen previously. The **Back** and **Forward** commands take you back and forward through this list. You can also go directly to a page in the history list by selecting it from the **Go** menu. (In Explorer 2, you select from the **File** menu. In Explorer 4, click the small triangle on the **Back** button.)

Bookmarks

The bookmark system (known as Favorites in Internet Explorer) is an essential tool for finding your way around. Get to know it right away.

In most browsers, you can just click a button or select a menu option to place a bookmark. Each system works a little differently, of course. In Netscape, choose **Bookmarks, Add Bookmark** (Navigator 3), or click the **Bookmarks** button and choose **Add Bookmark** (Navigator 4). The bookmark is added to the bottom of the Bookmark menu (you can move it to a folder or submenu later). In Navigator 4, you can even select which folder you want to put the bookmark in by clicking the **Bookmarks** button and then choosing **File Bookmark**.

In Internet Explorer, choose **Favorites**, **Add to Favorites**, and then click the **Create In** button and select the folder into which you want to place the bookmark.

Both systems have Bookmarks windows and an associated Bookmarks menu. (In Explorer, they're called the Favorites window and menu.) Creating a folder in the window automatically creates a submenu in the menu.

To open Netscape's Bookmarks window choose **Bookmarks, Go to Bookmarks** (Navigator 3) or **Bookmarks, Edit Bookmarks** (Navigator 4). In the latest version of Explorer, you can click the **Favorites** button in the toolbar to open a Favorites panel in the browser window.

You can even search Bookmarks or Favorites. For instance, you can search Internet Explorer's Favorites using the Windows 95 or 98 **Find** tool on the **Start** menu. In Explorer 4, right-click a folder in the Favorites list and choose **Find** to search the folder.

Click here to open the Favorites panel

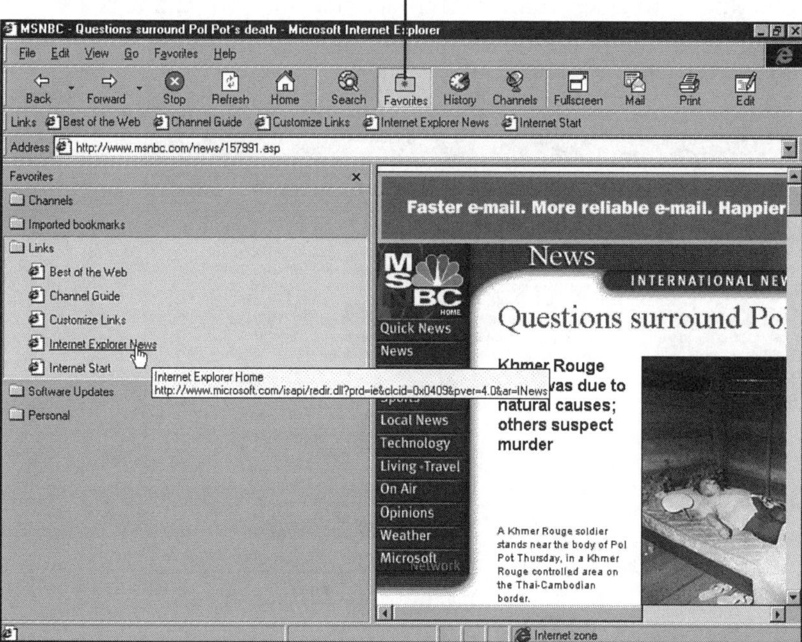

Internet Explorer 4's new "in-browser" Favorites panel.

A Little History

The history list varies tremendously. Netscape 3's history list is not very helpful. It lists some, but not all, of the pages you've visited in the current session. Other browsers,

In or Out? In Internet Explorer 2, the History window is separate from the browser window; in versions 3 and 4, the history list is shown within the browser window. Click on Internet Explorer 4's **Favorites** button, and a panel opens on the left side of the browser window to display the Favorites list. But select **Favorites, Organize Favorites** to open a separate Favorites window.

including Netscape Navigator 4, show much more, often listing pages from previous sessions. Explorer, for instance, keeps a record of up to 3,000 pages (including all the pages from the current session and earlier sessions). You can view the list in a window (see the following figure) sorted by date or by name. Double-click an entry in the history list to open that Web page.

Whatever system you have, though, using the history list is simple. In Netscape Navigator, you can select an entry from the **Go** menu. To keep us on our toes, Microsoft's programmers keep moving the history list. In Internet Explorer 2, you'll find the history entries on the **File** menu; in Explorer 3 and some versions of 4, the history list is on the **Go** menu.

You can also open the history window to see more history entries, perhaps thousands. In version 4 of Internet Explorer, click the **History** button in the toolbar; in version 3, choose **Go**, **Open History Folder**, and in version 2, choose **File**, **More History** (sometimes I wonder what drugs these Microsoft programmers are on). In Netscape, choose **Window**, **History** (or **Communicator**, **History** in some 4 versions, depending on the operating system).

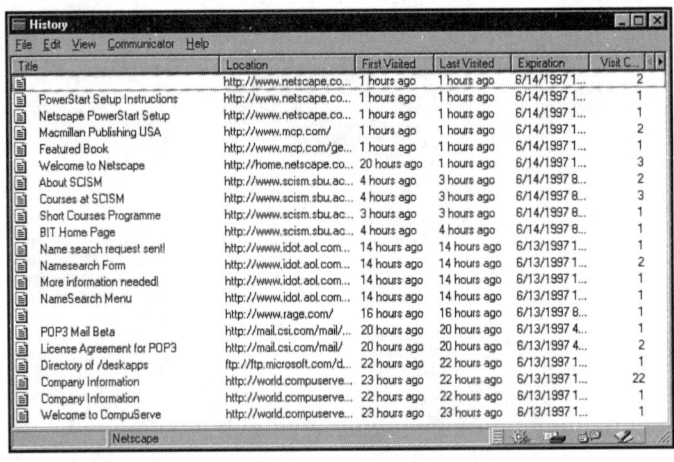

Title	Location	First Visited	Last Visited	Expiration	Visit C...
	http://www.netscape.co...	1 hours ago	1 hours ago	6/14/1997 1...	2
PowerStart Setup Instructions	http://www.netscape.co...	1 hours ago	1 hours ago	6/14/1997 1...	1
Netscape PowerStart Setup	http://www.netscape.co...	1 hours ago	1 hours ago	6/14/1997 1...	1
Macmillan Publishing USA	http://www.mcp.com/	1 hours ago	1 hours ago	6/14/1997 1...	2
Featured Book	http://www.mcp.com/ge...	1 hours ago	1 hours ago	6/14/1997 1...	1
Welcome to Netscape	http://home.netscape.co...	20 hours ago	1 hours ago	6/14/1997 1...	3
About SCISM	http://www.scism.sbu.ac...	4 hours ago	3 hours ago	6/14/1997 8...	2
Courses at SCISM	http://www.scism.sbu.ac...	4 hours ago	3 hours ago	6/14/1997 8...	3
Short Courses Programme	http://www.scism.sbu.ac...	3 hours ago	3 hours ago	6/14/1997 8...	1
BIT Home Page	http://www.scism.sbu.ac...	4 hours ago	4 hours ago	6/14/1997 8...	1
Name search request sent!	http://www.idot.aol.com...	14 hours ago	14 hours ago	6/13/1997 1...	1
Namesearch Form	http://www.idot.aol.com...	14 hours ago	14 hours ago	6/13/1997 1...	2
More information needed!	http://www.idot.aol.com...	14 hours ago	14 hours ago	6/13/1997 1...	1
NameSearch Menu	http://www.idot.aol.com...	14 hours ago	14 hours ago	6/13/1997 1...	1
	http://www.rage.com/	16 hours ago	16 hours ago	6/13/1997 8...	1
POP3 Mail Beta	http://mail.csi.com/mail/...	20 hours ago	20 hours ago	6/13/1997 4...	1
License Agreement for POP3	http://mail.csi.com/mail/	20 hours ago	20 hours ago	6/13/1997 4...	2
Directory of /deskapps	ftp://ftp.microsoft.com/d...	22 hours ago	22 hours ago	6/13/1997 1...	1
Company Information	http://world.compuserve...	23 hours ago	22 hours ago	6/13/1997 1...	22
Company Information	http://world.compuserve...	22 hours ago	22 hours ago	6/13/1997 1...	1
Welcome to CompuServe	http://world.compuserve...	23 hours ago	23 hours ago	6/13/1997 1...	1

With Netscape Navigator 4's history list, you can go back days or even weeks in your Web travels. The list even indicates how long it's been since you visited the page and how often you've been there.

A Direct Link: Using the URLs

Earlier in this chapter I mentioned a couple of URLs. *URLs* are Web addresses, such as `http://www.msn.com/` or `http://www.netscape.com/`. These addresses provide a direct link to a particular Web page. Instead of clicking links to try to find your way to a page, you can tell your browser the URL and say "go get this page."

Most browsers have a bar near the top in which you can type the URL of the page you want to go to. The bar's almost certainly already displayed; it's a long text box. If it's not there, someone must have removed it; in Netscape, use the **Options**, **Show Location** or **View**, **Show Location Toolbar** menu command to display the bar (depending on the version you're working with); in Internet Explorer, choose **View**, **Toolbar**, or **View**, **Toolbars**, **Address Bar**.

If you don't want the bar there all the time (after all, it takes up room that is sometimes better given to the Web pages), you can leave it turned off. If you keep it turned off, you can generally use a shortcut key to display a dialog box in which you can type a URL. In Netscape, press **Ctrl+L** to open the box (or try **Ctrl+O** if that doesn't work; the shortcut key varies between versions); in Internet Explorer, choose **File**, **Open** or press **Ctrl+O**. In either case, you type the URL in the box that appears. If you prefer to use the Address or Location box at the top of the browser window, click in the box, type the address, and press **Enter**.

Check This Out...

New History List Trick

Starting with version 4, the Internet Explorer and Netscape Navigator browsers have a handy new feature that enables you to see the history list from the **Back** and **Forward** buttons. In Navigator, click the button and hold down the mouse button; in Explorer, right-click the button, or click the little downward pointing arrow on the button. In both cases, you'll see a list of pages that you've visited.

Check This Out...

URL This acronym stands for Uniform Resource Locator, which is a fancy name for Web address.

Maximizing the Web Page

Browsers have so many controls and tools that sometimes there's not enough room for the Web page. Internet Explorer 4 has a "new" feature. Click the **Fullscreen** button to remove almost all the controls (except a small toolbar at the top of the window), giving the Web page the maximum room. You can even remove the small toolbar using an Autohide feature similar to that used by the Windows 98 toolbar (right-click the toolbar and select **Autohide**). Actually this feature isn't new; it's from the ancient history of the graphical Web browser (way back in 1994). It used to be called a Kiosk feature, but it disappeared for a while.

The URL Explained

A URL consists of certain distinct parts. For example, here's a long URL:

```
http://www.poorrichard.com/newsltr/instruct/subsplain.htm
```

Each part of this URL has a specific meaning:

`http://`	This part tells the browser that the address is for a Web page. The `http://` stands for *Hypertext Transfer Protocol*, the system used on the Internet to transfer Web pages. In addition to `http://`, you might see similar prefixes for an FTP site or a Gopher menu (see the following table).
`www.poorrichard.com`	This part is the hostname, the name of the computer holding the Web server that is administering the Web site you want to visit.
`/newsltr/instruct/`	This part is the directory in which the Web server has to look to find the file you want. In many cases, multiple directories will be listed, so the Web server looks down the directory tree in subdirectories. In this example, the Web server has to look in the instruct directory, which is a subdirectory of the newsltr directory.
`subsplain.htm`	This part is the name of the file you want, the Web page. These files are generally .HTM or .HTML files (that extension stands for Hypertext Markup Language, the "coding" used to create Web pages). Sometimes the URL has no filename at the end; in that case, the Web server generally sends a default document for the specified directory.

The URL is not complicated; it's just an address so your browser knows where to look for a file. The different types of URLs are identified by a different *protocol* portion of the address. The Web page URLs all begin with `http://`. This table lists some other protocols you'll see on the Internet.

Other Internet protocols

Protocol Prefix	Description
`ftp://`	The address of an FTP file library.
`gopher://`	The address of a Gopher site.
`news:`	The address of a newsgroup, discussed in Chapter 7, "Newsgroups: The Source of All Wisdom." Note that this prefix doesn't have the // after the name; neither does `mailto:` (below).
`mailto:`	When you use this prefix, the browser's email program opens so you can send mail. Web authors often create links using the `mailto:` URL so that when someone clicks the link, he can quickly send a message to the author.

Protocol Prefix	Description
`telnet://`	The address of a Telnet site.
`tn3270://`	The address of a tn3270 site. This protocol is similar to Telnet.
`wais://`	The address of a WAIS site; WAIS is a little-used database-search tool, and you probably won't run into many WAIS links. In any case, most browsers don't recognize the `wais://` protocol.

Forget http://

In most browsers these days (including Netscape and Internet Explorer), you don't need to type the full URL. You can omit the `http://` piece, and the browser will assume that the `http://` piece should be added. If you type something beginning with `gopher` (as in `gopher.usa.net`, for instance) or `ftp` (as in `ftp.microsoft.com`), you can omit the `gopher://` or `ftp://` part, too. Also, in some browsers, you can even drop the `www.` and `.com` bits. For instance, in Netscape Navigator and Internet Explorer, you can type **mcp** and press **Enter** to get to the `http://www.mcp.com/` Web site (this only works if the domain ends with `.com`). The newest browsers, Navigator and Explorer 4, have an auto-fill-in feature, something you may have seen in personal-finance programs. Start typing a URL, and if the browser recognizes that you've entered it before, it will fill in the rest for you.

What Will You Find on Your Web Journey?

When you travel around the Web, you'll find a lot of text documents and much, much more. As a system administrator at a Free-Net once said to me, "The Web is for people who can't read!" It was a slight exaggeration, perhaps, but his point was that, on the Web, the nontext stuff is often more important than the words.

While traveling around the Web, you'll find these sorts of things:

- *Pictures.* You'll find pictures both inside the text documents and on their own. Sometimes when you click a link (at a museum site, for example), a picture—not a document—is transferred to your browser.
- *Forms.* These days, most browsers are forms-compatible (Navigator and Explorer have always been forms-compatible). In other words, you can use forms to interact with the Web site to send information about yourself (to subscribe to a service, for instance), to search for information, or to play a game, for example.

- *Sounds.* Most browsers can play sounds, such as voices and music. Many Web sites contain sounds. For instance, IUMA (the Internet Underground Music Archive at `http://www.iuma.com/`) has song clips from many new bands.
- *Files.* Many Web sites have files you can download, such as shareware, demos of new programs, and documents of many kinds. When you click a link, your browser begins the file transfer (see Chapter 4, "More About the Web").
- *Multimedia of other kinds.* All sorts of strange things are on the Web: 3D images, animations, Adobe Acrobat .PDF hypertext files, videos, slide shows, 2D and 3D chemical images, and plenty more. Click a link, and the file starts transferring. If you have the right software installed, it automatically displays or plays the file. For instance, in the following figure, you can see a Bubbleviewer image. (See `http://www.omniview.com/` for information about the Bubbleviewer, and Chapter 5, "Forms, Applets, and Other Web Weirdness" and Chapter 6, "Web Multimedia" to learn more about multimedia.)

Where Do I Find What I Want on the Web?

You can follow any interesting links you find, as discussed earlier in this chapter. You can also search for particular subjects and Web pages by using a Web search site, as discussed in Chapter 11, "Finding Stuff."

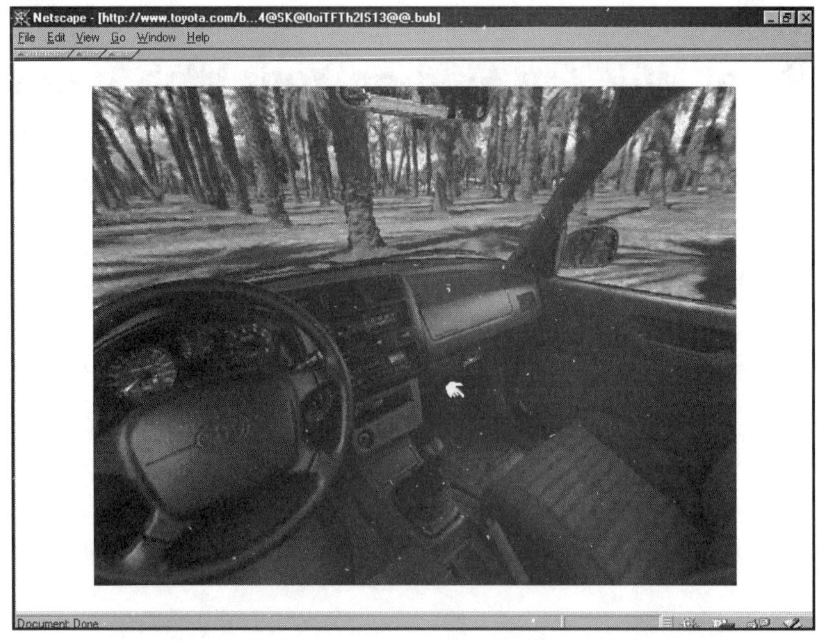

A BubbleViewer image in Netscape. You can move around inside the car, viewing up, down, and all around.

Speeding Up Your Journey by Limiting Graphics

The Web used to be a very fast place to move around. The first Web browsers could display nothing but text, and text transfers across the Internet very quickly. These days, though, thanks to something commonly known as "progress," things move more slowly. The things I just mentioned—pictures, video, sounds, and so on— slow down the process. Although video is the slowest thing on the Web (moving at an almost glacial pace in most cases), pictures are more of a nuisance; very few sites use video, but most use static pictures.

Most browsers provide a way for you to turn off the display of pictures. In Netscape Navigator, for instance, choose **Options**, **Auto Load Images**, and remove the check mark from the menu option to turn off images. In Netscape Navigator 4, choose **Edit**, **Preferences**, and then click the **Advanced** category and clear **Automatically Load Images**. In Internet Explorer, you can turn off images in the Options dialog box, and you can turn off sounds and video, too. Choose **View**, **Options** and click the **General** tab to see the options that are available. (In Explorer 4, you'll have to click the **Advanced** tab, and then clear the **Show Pictures** check box in the list box below **Multimedia**.) Because the images are no longer transmitted to your browser, you see the pages much more quickly.

Of course, you often need or want to see those images. Many images have links built into them, and although some Web pages have both graphic links and corresponding text links (for people using a browser that can't display pictures), other Web pages are unusable unless you can see the pictures. However, you can usually grab the picture you need quickly. Where there *should* be a picture, you'll see a little icon that functions as a sort of placeholder.

In Netscape, you can right-click the placeholder and choose **Load Image** (**Show Image** in some versions) from the shortcut menu that appears. Or you can click the **Images** button in the toolbar to see all of them. To view an image when you have images turned off in Internet Explorer, right-click the placeholder and choose **Show Picture** from the shortcut menu.

There's Plenty More!

There's a lot more to say about the Web than I've said in this chapter. In fact, one could write a book about it (I already have: *Using Netscape Communicator 4*). In the next few chapters, you'll learn a few advanced Web travel tips and all about Web multimedia.

The Least You Need to Know

- The World Wide Web is a giant hypertext system running on the Internet.
- The two best browsers available are Netscape Navigator and MS Internet Explorer.
- The home page (sometimes called the start page in Internet Explorer) is the page that appears when you open your browser.

- Click a link in a document to see another document. To find your way back, use the **Back** or **Home** button.
- The history list shows where you've been. In Netscape Navigator 3, it includes just some of the pages you've seen in the current session; in some other browsers, including Netscape Navigator 4 and Internet Explorer, the history list includes all the pages from the current session and many pages from previous sessions.
- A URL is a Web address. You can use the URL to go directly to a particular Web page.

Chapter 4

More About the Web

In This Chapter

- Running multiple Web sessions
- Opening files from your hard disk
- All about the cache and reloading
- Searching documents and using the pop-up menu
- Copying things you find to the Clipboard
- Saving images, documents, and files

You've seen the basic moves; now you are ready to learn more techniques to help you find your way around the Web. In the last chapter, you learned how to move around on the Web using a Web browser such as Netscape Navigator or Internet Explorer. In this chapter, you'll find out how to run multiple Web sessions at the same time, how to deal with the cache, how to save what you find, and so on. You need to know these advanced moves to work efficiently on the Web.

Multiple Windows: Ambidextrous Browsing

These days, most browsers enable you to run more than one Web session at the same time. Why would you want to do that? There could be many reasons. While you wait for an image to load in one window, you can read something in another window. Or maybe you need to find information at another Web site but don't want to "lose your place" at the current one. (Yes, you have bookmarks and the history list, but sometimes it's just easier to open another window.) You can open one or more new browser windows, as shown in the following figure, so that you can run multiple Web sessions. In this example you can see two Internet Explorer 4 windows. To make the one at the back take up the entire screen, I clicked the **Fullscreen** button and turned on the **Autohide** feature (see Chapter 3, "The World of the World Wide Web").

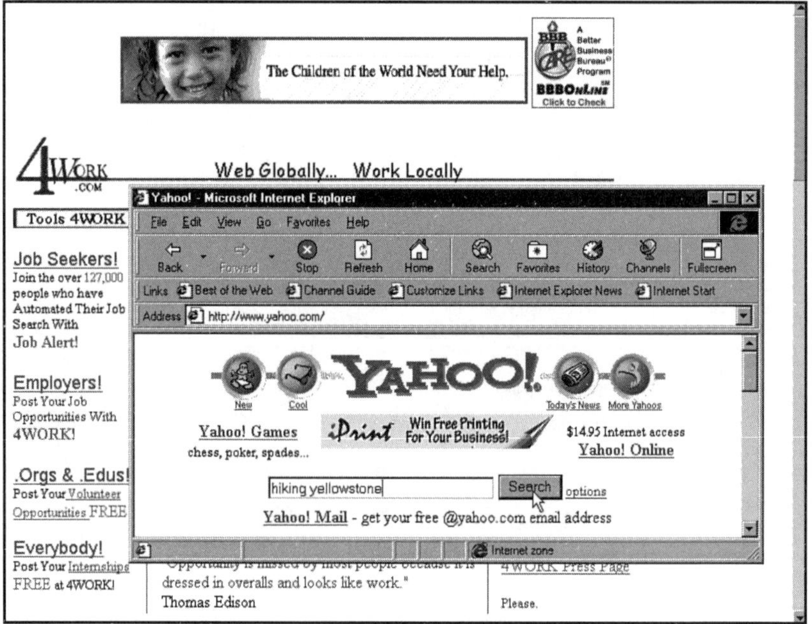

Opening multiple windows is a good way to keep from getting lost or to do more than one thing at a time.

Exactly how you open a new window varies among browsers; however, most are similar. In Netscape Navigator, try these procedures:

- Right-click the link that you want to follow in a new window, and then choose **Open in New Window**. A new Netscape window opens, and the referenced document opens in that window.
- Choose **File**, **New Web Browser**, or **File**, **New**, **Navigator Window**, or press **Ctrl+N** to open a new window displaying the home page.

Internet Explorer gives you several options:

- Right-click the link you want to follow, and then choose **Open in New Window**. A new window opens, displaying the referenced document.
- Press **Tab** until the link becomes highlighted, and then press **Shift+Enter**.
- Choose **File**, **New Window** (or, in some versions, **File**, **New**, **Window**) or press **Ctrl+N** to open a new window that displays the same document as the one you've just viewed.
- Type a URL into the **Address** text box, and then press **Shift+Enter** to display that document in a new window.

You may encounter some problems when running multiple Web sessions. Web browsers are turning into real memory hogs, so you may find that you don't have enough memory to run multiple sessions or to run more than one additional session. In addition, your modem can do only so much work. If you have several Web windows open and each is transferring things at the same time, every transfer will be slower than if it were the only thing the modem had to do.

Automatic Multiple Sessions

Now and then, windows will open automatically. If you suddenly notice that the browser's Back button is disabled, it may be that when you clicked a link, a secondary window opened and you didn't notice. Web authors can create codes in their Web pages that force browsers to open secondary or targeted windows.

Your Hard Disk as Web Server?

If you enjoy working on the Web and spend most of your waking hours there, eventually, you'll end up with .HTM or .HTML files on your hard disk. You'll have them in your cache (discussed next), or you may save documents using the **File**, **Save As** command. Your browser provides a way to open these HTML files—generally a **File**, **Open** command or something similar. You'll see a typical Open box from which you can select the file you want to open.

Here's a geek trick for you. If you know the exact path to the file you want to open, and if you can type quickly, click in the **Address** or **Location** text box. Then type the entire path and filename, such as **`C:/Program Files/Netscape/Navigator/ownweb.htm`**. This trick should work in both Netscape and Internet Explorer. In some browsers, however, you may need to use the more formal (and older) method by entering the file path in this format: **`file:///C¦/Program Files/Netscape/Navigator/ownweb.htm`**. Notice that in the second format, you precede the path with **`file:///`** and replace the colon after the disk letter (in this case **C**) with a pipe symbol (|).

Forward Slash or Backslash

UNIX computers use a forward slash (/) between directory names. DOS computers use a backslash(\). Because the Web was developed on UNIX computers, URLs use forward slashes. Thus `C:/Program Files/Netscape/Navigator/ownweb.htm` is correct, even though in normal DOS notation this would appear as `C:\Program Files\Netscape\Navigator\ownweb.htm`. However, you can type it whichever way you please when you're opening a file on your hard disk or a page on the Web; both Internet Explorer and Netscape will figure it out.

HTM or HTML?

Depending to some degree on the operating system you use, the file extension of the HTML Web files might be .HTM or .HTML. Originally, the Web was developed using UNIX computers, and Web files had the extension .HTML. Later, when Windows 3.1 machines started appearing on the Web, the .HTM extension came into use because Windows 3.1 could work only with three-character file extensions, and many people were creating Web pages in Windows. Today, you'll see both extensions. Even though Windows 95 and 98 can accept four-letter extensions, not all Windows HTML-editing programs can, so people are still creating files with three-letter extensions. Also, many people still use Windows 3.1 machines to create Web pages.

Turbo Charging with the Cache

Have you noticed that when you return to a Web document that you've previously viewed, it appears much more quickly than when you first accessed it? That's because your browser isn't taking it from the Internet; instead, the browser is getting it from the *cache*, an area on your hard disk or in your computer's RAM (memory) in which it saves pages. The cache is handy because it greatly speeds up the process of working on the Web. After all, why bother to reload a file from the Internet when it's already sitting on your hard drive? (Okay, you may think of some reasons to do so, but I'll come back to those when I talk about the Reload command.)

When the browser loads a Web page, it places it in the cache. You can generally control the size of the cache. Not all browsers let you do so, but Netscape, Internet Explorer, and many others do. When the cache fills up, the oldest files are removed to make room for newer ones. Each time the browser tries to load a page, it might look in the cache first to see if it has the page stored. (Whether it does depends on how you set up the cache.) If it finds that the page is available, it can retrieve the page from the cache very quickly.

Putting the Cache to Work

To take full advantage of the cache's benefits, you need to do some configuring. To configure the cache in Netscape Navigator 2 or 3, choose **Options**, **Network Preferences**, and then click the **Cache** tab. In Navigator 4, select **Edit**, **Preferences**, and then open the **Advanced** category and click the **Cache** subcategory. The following figure shows Netscape's cache information.

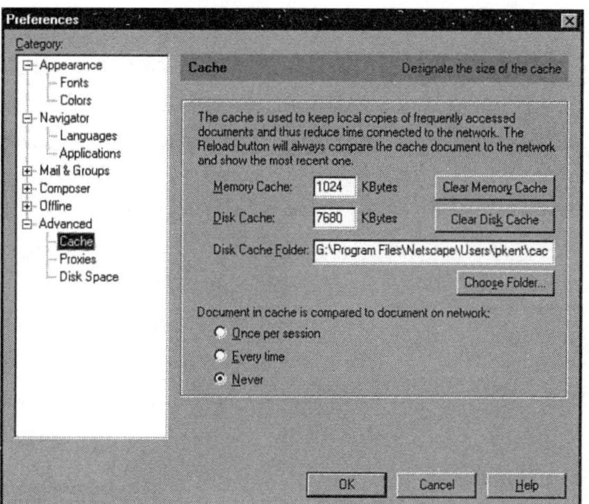

You have several options when setting up Netscape's cache.

Configure any of the available settings to meet your needs:

- *Memory Cache.* You can tell Netscape how much of your computer's memory you want to assign to the cache. Netscape stores a few documents in the memory so that it can retrieve them extremely quickly. The button to the right of this option enables you to remove all the pages from the memory cache.
- *Disk Cache.* You can also tell Netscape how large the disk cache should be—that is, how much of your disk space you want to give to Netscape. How much should you give? That all depends on how much disk space you have free. (I always say that you can never have too much hard disk space, money, or beer; I've been proven wrong once or twice, though.) The button to the right of this option enables you to clear out the disk cache, which is handy when you finally run out of disk space.
- *Disk Cache Folder.* You can tell Netscape where to place the disk cache. If you have several hard disks, put the cache on the fastest disk or the one with the most room.
- *Document in cache is compared to document on network.* Now for the complicated one. This setting tells Netscape when to verify documents. When you request a document (by clicking a link or entering a URL), Netscape can send a message to the Web server asking (basically), "Has this document changed since the last time I grabbed it?" If it has changed, Netscape downloads a new copy. If it hasn't changed, Netscape grabs the page from the cache. You can configure Netscape to ask the Web server to verify documents Once per Session (in which case, Netscape checks the first time you try to retrieve a document, but it doesn't bother after that); Every Time (so that Netscape checks every time you try to get a document, regardless of how many times you view that document in a session); or Never (in which case, Netscape doesn't even bother to check to see whether the document has been updated, unless you use the Reload command).

The Hard Disk Cache Note that you are not reserving an area of your hard disk for the cache. For instance, if you have a 30,000KB (almost 30MB) disk cache, your browser doesn't create a 30,000KB file that prevents other programs from using that disk space. You're just telling the browser that it can use up to that much disk space for the cache if it's available—if other programs don't use up the space first. When you fill up the available cache space, the browser starts clearing out older files to make way for newer ones.

- *Allow Persistent Caching of Pages Retrieved Through SSL.* This feature is in older versions of Netscape (it's not in the latest version), and it's related to Internet security. SSL stands for secure sockets level (which probably means no more to you than SSL, so I'm not sure why I told you that). An SSL Web browser can use secure transmission of information; the information is encrypted before being transmitted. (See Chapter 12, "Staying Safe on the Internet," for a discussion of encryption.) This feature tells the browser to cache pages that were sent in a secure manner.

Internet Explorer uses a similar system. Choose **View**, **Options** (or **Internet Options**), and click the **General** tab (or the **Advanced** tab, depending on which version of Explorer you're using). Then click the **Settings** button under the **Temporary Internet Files** area. Although Explorer's programmers (ever the innovators) have taken to referring to the cache as Temporary Internet Files, it's the same thing. The following figure shows Explorer 4.0's settings.

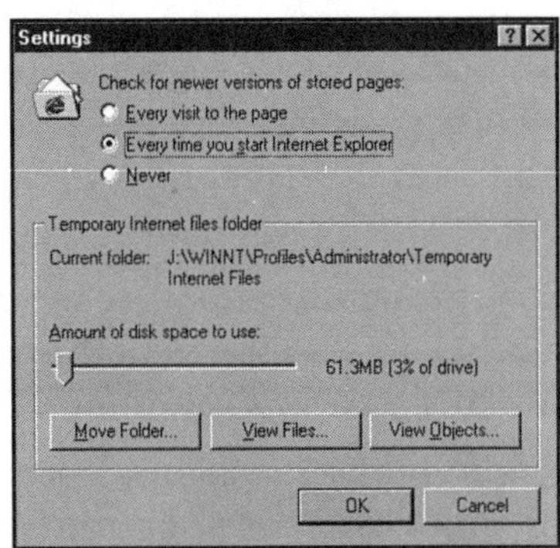

Internet Explorer enables you to modify the cache and view its contents directly.

Near the top of the box, you can tell the browser when to check to see whether there's a newer version of the file. You can tell it to check Once per Session in Explorer 3; this option is ambiguously labelled Every Time You Start Internet Explorer in Explorer 4, but it's the same thing. Or you can turn it off altogether (select Never). In Explorer 4, you also have the option to check Every Visit to the Page.

You also can modify the size of the cache by dragging a slider to set the percentage of the drive you want to use (instead of by entering an MB value). You can select the cache directory using the **Move Folder** button, but notice that Explorer offers something extra: a View Files button. Click the **View Files** button to display a list of the files stored in the cache; you can double-click a file to open it in the browser. The most recent versions of Explorer 4 also have a View Objects button, which opens a window containing ActiveX controls downloaded to your computer (see Chapter 5, "Forms, Applets, and Other Web Weirdness"). You can also clear the cache; you may find an Empty Folder button in this dialog box or perhaps a Delete Files button back in the Internet Options dialog box.

Decisions, Decisions

Which of the cache options should you use? I prefer Never because it makes my Web sessions *much* quicker. Whenever I tell a browser to go to a Web page that's already in the cache, it loads the page from the hard disk right away, without sending a verification message to the server first. Even if the browser doesn't have to retrieve the page again because the page hasn't changed, checking with the Web server can slow you down noticeably.

On the other hand, I have to remember to keep using the Reload command to make sure I'm viewing the latest version of the Web page. Some people may prefer to use the Once Per Session option to ensure that recent page.

What Is Reload?

Sometimes you want to get a file from the Web again. Reload is a "cure" for the cache. If you get a page from the cache, you are not getting the latest document. Sometimes getting the most recent document doesn't matter, but in a few cases, it does.

For instance, say you want to return to a site you visited several weeks ago. If you have a very large cache, that document may still be available. If you have the Never option button selected in the Preferences dialog box, your browser displays the old document, without checking to see whether the corresponding document stored on the Web has changed. Or perhaps you are viewing a Web document that changes rapidly, such as a stock quote page. Even if you viewed the page only a few minutes ago, it could already be out of date.

The cure for replacing those old, stale Web pages is to reload them. Click the **Reload** button or choose **View, Reload**. Internet Explorer's programmers, in their attempt to rename everything they can, use the term Refresh instead of Reload. (The fact that Reload is a term the Web's been using for several years and that Refresh has a different meaning—Netscape has a Refresh command that simply "repaints" the display using the contents of the memory cache—doesn't seem to matter to Microsoft's programmers.) Anyway, the Reload command (Refresh in Explorer) tells the browser, "Throw away the copy held in the cache and get the latest version."

You'll sometimes see a Reload Frame command, which reloads just one frame in a framed document. (Chapter 5 covers frames.) Netscape Navigator has a "super reload" command that few people know about. Holding down the Shift key and then selecting the Reload command says to Netscape Navigator "make absolutely sure you really do reload the page!" Navigator's Reload command has had a bug living in it for a couple years and in some cases doesn't reload the page. (This problem seems to be related to forms and scripts not being reloaded correctly.) Holding down the Shift key ensures that the page really is reloaded.

Long Documents: Finding What You Need

Some Web pages are large. Some are positively huge—thousands of lines long with links at the top of the document that take the user to sections lower on the same page. Many Web authors prefer to create one large page than to create lots of small linked ones, the advantage being that once the page has been transferred to your browser you can use links to move to different parts of the page very quickly.

Don't Forget Find The Find command can come in very handy for searching long Gopher menus and FTP file listings, as well as large Web documents.

Virtually all browsers have some kind of Find command; it's generally Edit, Find or a Find button on the toolbar. Internet Explorer's programmers (as you might guess) have a command called Edit, Find (on this page), which I must admit is a good idea. This command tells the browser to search the current page instead of the Web; I'm sure some new users get confused about that issue. (On the other hand, Explorer's Search toolbar button is not the same as the Find command; it's for searching the Web. You'll learn how to search the Web in Chapter 11, "Finding Stuff.")

The Find command works in a way that's very similar to what you've probably used in other programs (in particular, in word processors). Click the **Find** button, or choose **Edit, Find**, and the Find dialog box opens. Type the word or words you are looking for, choose **Match Case** (if necessary), and then click **Find Next**. The browser moves the document so that the first line containing the word or words you are searching for is at the top of the window.

Remember to Right-click

Remember to use the shortcut menus that appear when you right-click on items. Both Netscape and Internet Explorer use them, as do other browsers. The shortcut menu is a new toy in the programmer's toy box—and a very nice one at that. (The Macintosh mouse has only one button; on Macintosh browsers, you may be able to access a pop-up menu by pressing the button and holding it down.) Experiment by right-clicking links, pictures, and the background, and you'll find all sorts of useful commands, such as those listed here:

- *Copy Shortcut or Copy Link Location.* This command copies the URL from the link to the Clipboard.
- *Open.* This command opens the related document, just as if you clicked the link.
- *Open in New Window.* This command opens a new window and loads the document referenced by the link you clicked.
- *Save Target As or Save Link As.* This command transfers the referenced document and saves it on your hard disk without bothering to display it in the browser first.
- *Add Bookmark or Add to Favorites.* This command places an entry for the document referenced by the link in the Bookmark or Favorites system.

Look to see what other commands are available. You'll find commands for moving back through framed documents, saving image files, saving background images as your desktop wallpaper, adding wallpaper, sending the Web page in an email message, and so on. Which reminds me, maybe you should learn how to save such things from the Web, eh?

Is It Worth Saving?

A lot of it is. Yes, I know that multimedia consultant and author William Horton has called the Web a GITSO (Garbage In, Toxic Sludge Out) system. Although there *is* a lot of sludge out there, it's not *all* sludge. Much of it is worth saving. And now and then that's just what you'll want to do: Save some of it to your hard disk. Let's look at two aspects of saving in particular: how to save and what you can save.

You can save many things from the Web. Most browsers work in much the same way, although one or two have a few nice little extra "save" features. Here's what you can save:

- *Save the document text.* You can copy text from a browser to the Clipboard and then paste the text into another application. Or you can use the **File**, **Save As** command, which enables you to choose to save the document as plain text (that is, without all the little codes used to create a Web document.
- *Save the HTML source document.* The source document is the HTML (Hypertext Markup Language) document used to create the document that you see in your browser. Once you begin creating your own Web pages (You are planning to do that, aren't you? Everyone else and his dog is), you may want to save source documents so you can "borrow" bits of them. Use **File**, **Save As** and choose to save as HTML.

> Check This Out...
>
> **It's Not Yours**
>
> Remember that much of what you come across on the Web is copyrighted material. Unless you are sure that what you are viewing is not copyrighted, you should assume that it is.

- *Save the text or HTML source for documents you haven't even viewed.* You don't have to view a page before you save it (although to be honest, I haven't yet figured out why you would want to save it if you haven't seen it). Right-click the link and choose **Save Target As** or **Save Link As** from the shortcut menu.
- *Save inline images in graphics files.* You can copy images you see in Web pages directly to your hard drive. Right-click an image and choose **Save Image As** or **Save Picture As**.
- *Save the document background.* Internet Explorer even lets you save the small image that is used to put the background color or pattern in many documents. Right-click the background and choose **Save Background As**.
- *Create Windows wallpaper.* Internet Explorer also lets you quickly take an image or background from a document and use it as your Windows wallpaper image. Right-click the picture or the background and choose **Set as Wallpaper**.
- *Copy images to the Clipboard.* With this neat Explorer feature, you can copy images and background images directly to the Clipboard. Right-click the image, and then choose **Copy** or **Copy Background** from the shortcut menu.
- *Print the document.* Most browsers have a File, Print command and maybe even a Print button. Likewise, you'll often find a Page Setup command that lets you set margins and create headers and footers.
- *Save URLs to the Clipboard.* You can save URLs to the Clipboard so that you can copy them into another program. Copy the URL directly from the Address or Location text box, or right-click a link and choose **Copy Shortcut** or **Copy Link Location**. Some versions of Netscape also allow you to drag a link onto a document in another program; the link's URL will then appear in the document.
- *Grab files directly from the cache.* Remember that the cache is dynamic; the browser is constantly adding files to and removing files from it. If you have something you want to save, you can copy it directly from the cache. Internet Explorer makes this process easy; simply click the **View Files** button in the Options dialog box. With Netscape, you can view the directory holding the files. However, Netscape renames files, making them hard to identify. (Explorer names each file with its URL.) You can also find special programs that will help you view and manage files in your cache.
- *Save computer files referenced by links.* Many links do not point to other Web documents; they point to files of other formats, which opens a whole can of worms that we'll explore right now.

Grabbing Files from the Web

I like to group nondocument files into the following two types:

- *Files that you want to transfer to your hard disk.* A link might point to an .EXE or .ZIP file (a program file or a .ZIP archive file) that contains a program you want to install on your computer. Chapter 10, "What on Earth Are All Those File Types?," deals with file formats.
- *Files that you want to play or view.* Other files are not things you want to keep; instead, they are files containing items such as sounds (music and speech), video, graphics, or word processing documents that are part of the Web site you are viewing.

Both types of files are the same in one way: Whatever you want to do with them—whether you want to save them or play them—you *must* transfer them to your computer. However, the purpose of the transfer is different, and the way it's carried out is different. When you want to play or display a file, you might have to configure a special viewer, helper application, or plug-in so that when the browser transfers the file it knows how to play or display it. Chapter 6, "Web Multimedia," covers such things in detail. For now, we're only interested in the first type of file—a file that you want to transfer and save on your hard disk.

Web authors can distribute computer files directly from their Web documents. Several years ago, pretty much the only file libraries were FTP sites. Now many Web sites have links to files. Companies that want to distribute their programs (shareware, freeware, or demo programs) and authors who want to distribute non-Web documents (PostScript, Word for Windows, Adobe Acrobat, and Windows Help documents, for example) can use Web sites to provide a convenient way to transfer files.

Files Can Be in Both Categories

Files can be in both the first and second categories. What counts is not so much the type of file, but what you want to do with the file and how your browser is configured. If you want to save the file on your hard disk, perhaps for later use, it would fall into the first category: save on your hard disk. If you want to view the file right now, it would fall into the second category: view in a viewer or plug-in.

Which category a file fits into also depends on the manner in which the file was saved. In its normal format, for instance, an Adobe Acrobat file (a .PDF file) could fall into either category. In some compressed formats, it would fall into the first category only because you'd have to save it to your hard disk and decompress it before you could view it. (Compressed formats are explained in Chapter 10.)

Winsock? What's this Winsock thing? Winsock is a contraction of *Windows Sockets*, the name of the TCP/IP driver used to connect Windows programs to the Internet's TCP/IP system. Just as you need a print driver to connect a Windows program to a printer, you also need a special driver to connect a program to the Internet. The term Winsock refers to programs that can connect to a TCP/IP network.

Save It

To see how you can save a file, go to TUCOWS (The Ultimate Collection of Winsock Software) at `http://www.tucows.com/`. (Its logo is two cows.) This site contains a fantastic library of Internet software for Windows and Macintosh computers.

Suppose you find a link to a program that you want to transfer. You click it as usual, and what happens? If you're using Netscape, and if the file is an .EXE or .COM file, you'll probably see a File Save box. If so, choose the directory into which you want to save the file (download directories are discussed in Chapter 10). Or you might see the Unknown File Type dialog box (shown in the next figure). This box appears whenever Netscape tries to transfer a file that it doesn't recognize; Netscape wants you to tell it what to do. You can click the **Save File** button to get to the Save As dialog box, and then you can proceed to tell your computer where you want to save the file.

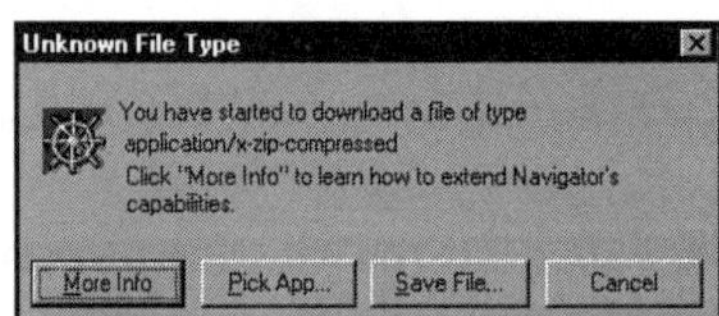

Netscape doesn't know what to do with this file type, so you have to tell it.

Explorer uses a slightly different method. First, it displays a dialog box showing that a file is being transferred. After a moment or two, you'll see another dialog box (similar to the one in the following figure).

Internet Explorer uses a slightly different method for managing file transfers.

You now have two choices:

- ➤ You can tell Explorer to open it, in which case Explorer transfers the file to your desktop and runs the file. This is a pretty lousy idea, for a couple of reasons. First, if the file is a compressed archive file, you'll be expanding all files held by the archive onto the desktop, making a huge mess and mixing them in with all the other files already there. Second, the file may be a program file that will run automatically. If it contains a virus, you could be in trouble. You should check program files with virus-check software before running them. (You'll learn more about that subject in Chapter 10.)
- ➤ You can save it to disk. This is the preferable option. Choose this option and click **OK**, and the transfer will continue. Once the file has been transferred to your hard disk, you'll see a Save As dialog box in which you can choose where to place the file.

Notice the check box titled Always Ask Before Opening This Type of File. If you clear the check box, the next time you download a file, Explorer will automatically transfer it and open it, even if you chose the **Save it to disk** option button the first time. (To recheck this check box, go to Windows Explorer, and then choose **View**, **Options**—or **View**, **Folder Options**—and click the **File Types** tab. Then click the file type in the list box, click **Edit**, click **Confirm Open After Download**, and click **OK**.)

The Least You Need to Know

- ➤ If your computer has enough memory, you can open a second Web document in a new window and keep the current window open.
- ➤ You'll probably end up saving Web documents on your hard disk; you can reopen them using the **File**, **Open** command.
- ➤ The cache stores documents you've seen on your hard disk. The browser can get those documents from the cache the next time you want to see them, which speeds up work tremendously.
- ➤ The Reload command (or Refresh in Internet Explorer) throws away the version of the page held in the cache and grabs a new one from the Web site. You can configure the cache to do this automatically once every session.
- ➤ You can copy, print, and save all sorts of things from the Web: document text, the document source file, images, background images, and more.
- ➤ If you click a link to a nondocument file, your browser may ask you what to do with it. You can save it to your hard drive if you want.

Chapter 5

Forms, Applets, and Other Web Weirdness

In This Chapter

- Unexpected things you'll run into on the Web
- Using tables and forms
- Getting into password-protected sites
- Using frames and secondary windows
- Web programming: Java, JavaScript, and ActiveX
- Pushing, pulling, and multimedia

Not so long ago the Web was filled with static documents that contained pictures and text—originally Web documents didn't even have pictures. But the Web has changed and is still changing; no longer is it just a static medium that you read. In this chapter, you're going to take a quick look at some weird and wonderful things you might find on the Web, such as tables, forms, password-protected sites, secondary or targeted windows, and frames. You'll also learn about Java, JavaScript, and ActiveX applets, as well as push and pull commands and multimedia.

Working with Tables

A *table* is...well, you know, a table. It's a set of columns and rows in which you organize text and (sometimes) pictures. Most browsers these days can display tables. So if you are using a recent one (such as Netscape or Internet Explorer), you'll have no problems. Tables are often used to display tabular data (go figure), but they can also be used as a simple page layout tool to get pictures and text to sit in the correct places. (The following figure shows a table being used in this way.) Recent improvements to the way that browsers handle tables enable Web page authors to use different background colors and different border colors in each cell.

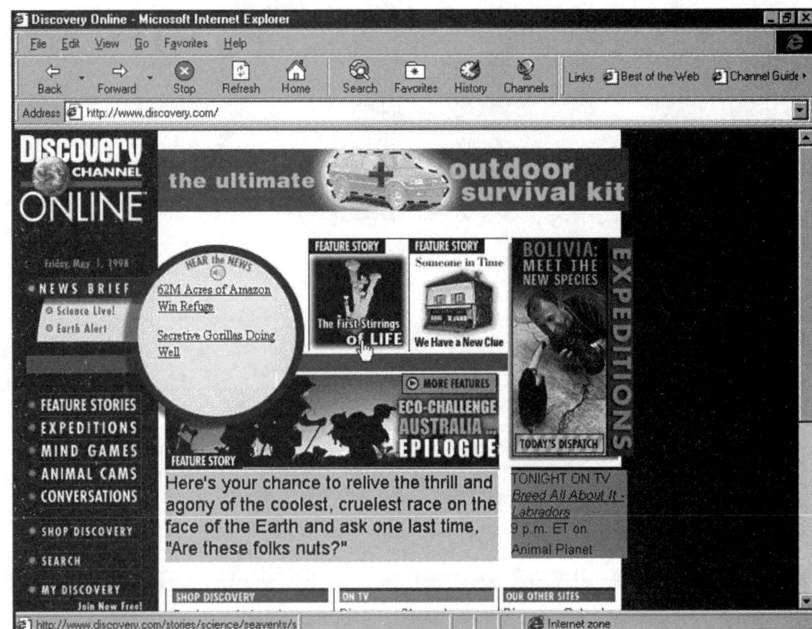

The Discovery Channel (`http://www.discovery.com/`*) page formatted using the table feature.*

Interactive Web Pages: Using Forms

A *form* is a special *interactive* Web document. It contains the sorts of components that you've become familiar with while working in today's graphical user interfaces: text boxes, option buttons (also known as radio buttons), command buttons, check boxes, list boxes, drop-down list boxes, and so on. You'll find forms at the search sites (see Chapter 11, "Finding Stuff"). You use them just like you would a Windows or Macintosh dialog box: You type a search word into a text box, select any necessary options by clicking option buttons and check boxes, and then click a command button.

Forms are also used to collect information (you might have to enter your name and address when downloading demo software, for instance) and make sales. You can choose the products you want to buy and enter your credit card information into a form. The next figure shows an order form at one of my Web sites.

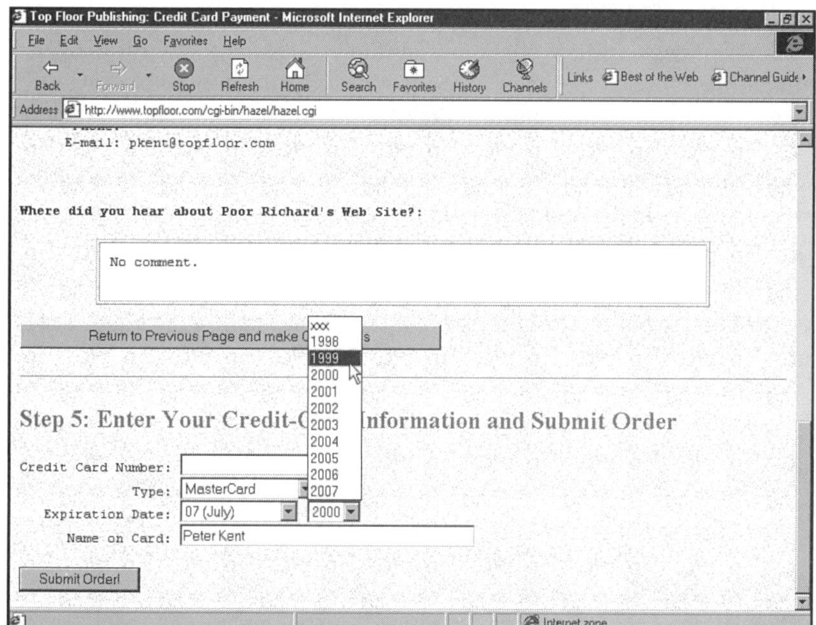

Enter all the required information, select options from the drop-down list boxes, and then click the Submit Order button.

Playing It Safe: Secure Sites

When you enter information into a form and send that information back to the Web server, there is a slight chance that it could be intercepted by someone and read. (It's not very *likely* that your information will be intercepted, but that's another story—which I'll get to in Chapter 12, "Staying Safe on the Internet".) Netscape, Internet Explorer, and some other browsers provide a way to send information *securely*. If the form you are viewing comes from a special `https://` server (a secure server), the information is *encrypted* before it's sent back from the form to the server. When the server receives the information, it decrypts the information. While the encrypted data is between your computer and the server, the information is useless; anyone who intercepted the information would end up with a load of garbled rubbish.

> Check This Out...
>
> **Just a Little Different** Forms in Web pages do function just a little differently from forms in other programs. For a start, you must click directly on an option button or check box to select it, not just on the label; in some operating systems—Windows, for instance—clicking the label will select the option or box. Although you can press **Tab** to move to the next field in a form in most browsers (or **Shift+Tab** to move to the last), this keystroke doesn't work in all browsers.

In most browsers, you know when you are at a secure site. In Internet Explorer, the little padlock icon in the lower-right corner is locked (in some versions of Explorer, no lock appears until you're displaying a secure page; in others, the lock's always there, but it's open when you're at a page that not secure). Some versions of Netscape Navigator have a key in the lower-left corner of the window; the key is whole at a secure page (it's broken on pages that are not secure). These versions of Navigator also display a blue bar just below the toolbars when the site is secure. Newer versions of Navigator (Version 4) don't have the blue bar or the key. Instead, they use a padlock icon which is closed. You'll see the padlock icon in the lower-left corner of the browser and in the toolbar; the Security button is a padlock that changes according to the type of document displayed. Other browsers use similar but slightly different methods to indicate that you are at a secure page.

One indicator of a secure site is visible in any Web browser. As you can see in the following figure, the URL of a secure Web page begins with `https://` instead of `http://`. If you send information to this site or receive information from it, you can be sure that the information will be transmitted in a secure, encrypted manner.

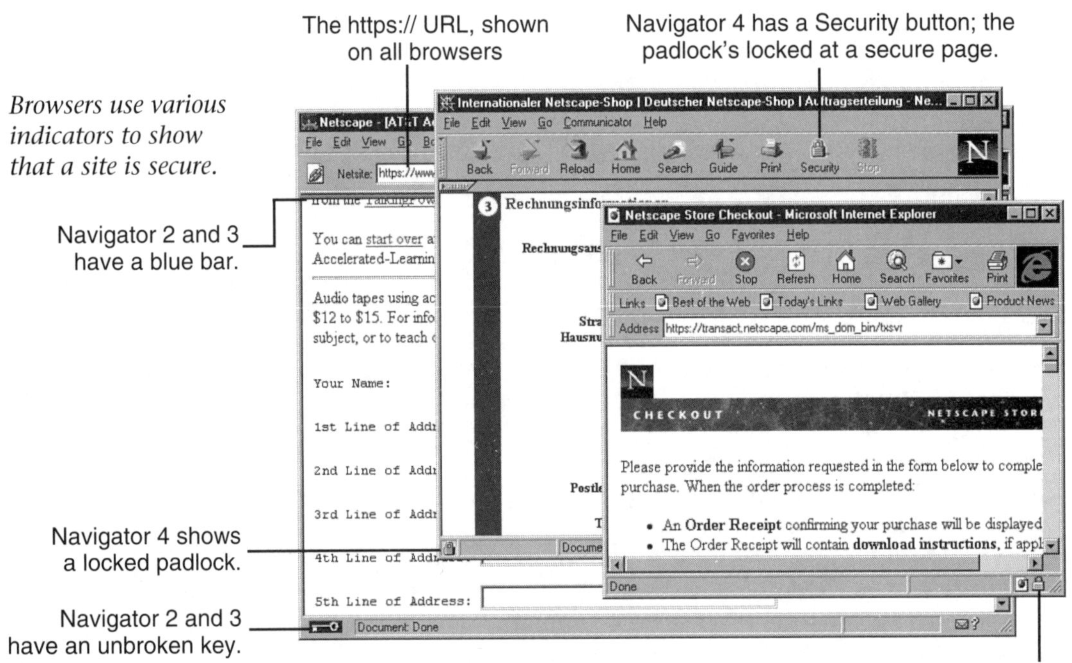

Browsers use various indicators to show that a site is secure.

For Your Eyes Only: Password-protected Sites

Many Web sites are password-protected or have an area that is password-protected. You can't enter a password-protected Web site or area unless you enter a password, which is given to you when you go through a registration process (which often, though not always, includes payment of some kind).

Why do sites use passwords? They may be selling information or some other kind of data (the single most common form of sold data, and in general the most profitable, is pornography). They may have private areas for employees of a particular company or members of a club or association. But sometimes free sites that are open to the public require that you log in. This requirement is often because these sites create an account for you and save information about you. To access that account, you have to log in (see the following figure). For instance, Expedia (`http://expedia.com/`), Microsoft's travel Web site, creates accounts for people that save information about them: their email address, zip code, the airport they generally fly from, and a subscription to an email notification of travel promotions.

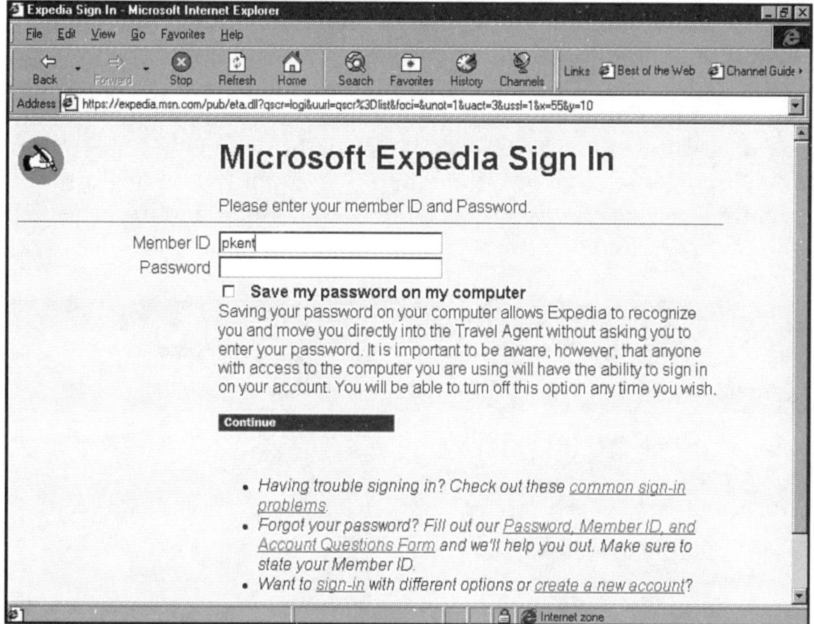

Microsoft Expedia is free, but you have to set up an account—with an account name and password—if you want to use it.

Dealing with Secondary Windows

I should know better, but once or twice I've been confused when I've suddenly discovered that Netscape Navigator's history list has disappeared. What happened? I clicked a link and then looked away for a moment. While my eyes were averted, another browser window opened automatically. I continued, unaware of what had happened.

Public Letter to Web Authors

Dear Web authors: It's bad interface design to open a secondary window full-screen. Please open your windows slightly less than full screen, so it's obvious to your users what's going on! Signed, Confused in Denver. (Unfortunately, browsers aren't very helpful. In many cases, the Web author can't determine the screen size.)

Web authors can set up a link so that when you click it, a new window opens, and the referenced document appears in that window. It's a very handy feature when used properly. These windows are called *targeted* windows. (I prefer to use an older hypertext term: *secondary* windows.)

When a targeted window opens in Netscape Navigator, the history list disappears from the previous window because the history list is linked to a particular window. In newer versions of Navigator, you *can* still use the history list from the Go menu, though the Back button won't work. That's how it works in all versions of Internet Explorer—although the Back and Forward commands stop working in that browser, you can still access the full history list and get back to a previous page.

Panes or Frames

Another new feature you may find while browsing on the Web is *frames*. (In other earlier hypertext systems, these were sometimes known as *panes*.) The following figure shows an example of frames. A framed document displays two or more documents, each within its own pane. The frames around each document may be movable (if the author set them up that way), and you may have scrollbars in each pane. Why put documents in frames? Frames can be a good way to organize a lot of information. For example, you might find a table of contents in one frame; clicking a link in the table of contents would load the specified document into the other frame.

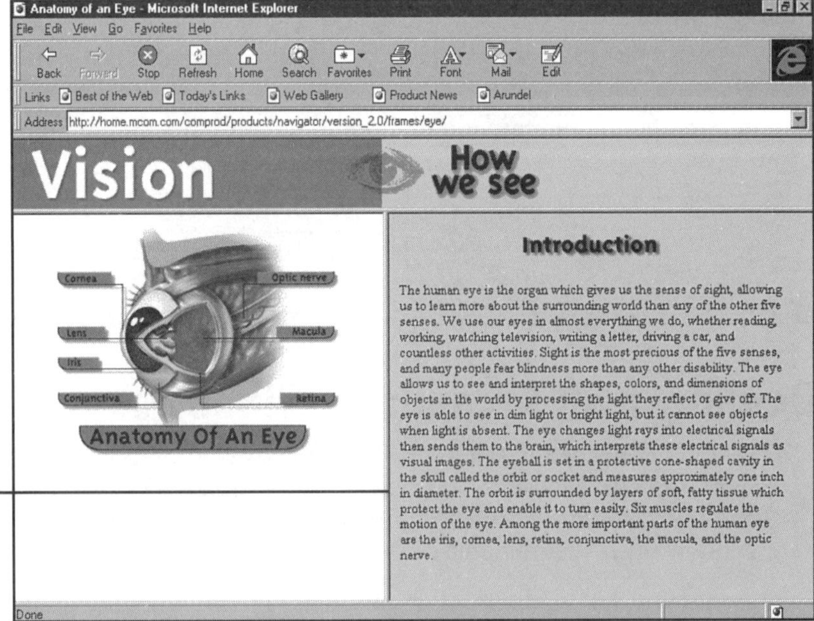

The How We See demo shows a good use of framed documents. Click parts of the eye in the left frame to see information in the right frame.

This bar divides the frames.

Some browsers have a special reload command for frames: Click inside a frame and then choose **View**, **Reload Frame** to reload the contents of that one frame. Some versions of the Netscape browser also have a **Back in Frame** command with which you can move back to the previously viewed document within the frame. Navigator Version 2 had a real problem with frames, though; using the Back command took you all the way out of the frames, perhaps many steps back, rather than showing you the previous document you viewed within the frames. Internet Explorer and the more recent versions of Navigator (Navigator Version 4) have no Back in Frame command; instead, they assume that if you're using the Back command, you want to go back step by step, not all the way out of the frames.

Frames are one of the most hated features on the Web. Although they can be very useful when designed properly, too many Web authors misuse them; they put too many frames into a window or lock frame contents so you can't scroll down the page within the frame. Such authors are often working with very high-resolution monitors on which everything works fine, but things get totally messed up on lower-resolution monitors.

Animated Icons

Animated icons are becoming popular these days. These little pictures embedded into Web documents appear to be in motion. They are relatively easy for Web authors to create, so you can expect to see many more of them appearing on the Web. They add a little motion to a page (this is known in Web jargon as "making a page more compelling") without causing a lot of extra stuff to be transmitted to your computer. Unfortunately, such animations can be extremely irritating, as user research has shown. Many authors throw in animations because they're cool, without realizing that they sometimes make the page harder to read.

If you find large and complicated things in motion, you've stumbled across some kind of video or animation file format (see Chapter 6, "Web Multimedia") or perhaps a Web program created in Java or ActiveX, which we'll look at next.

Web Programs: Java, JavaScript, and ActiveX

You may have heard of Java by now. I'm not talking about a chain of coffee bars; I'm talking about a new programming language that will (if you believe the hype) make the Web more exciting, make every appliance from toasters to dishwashers talk to you in Swahili, bring about world peace, and lead to a complete and total eradication of body odor.

Java has been hyped for a couple of years, but I think it's finally becoming useful. A number of sites now have Java applets that do something useful (in the early days Java was a toy, and the average Java applet was nothing more useful than a picture of bouncing heads). The Expedia site mentioned earlier, for instance, has Java-based maps. You can select an area to see a map showing a few hotels, and then zoom in on a particular area, or find information about one of the hotels. Java is also used to create moving banners, automatically scrolling text boxes, chat programs (see Chapter 9, "Yak, Yak, Yak: Chatting in Cyberspace"), and many other useful and not-so-useful things.

Java Interpreters

Java-compatible browsers are Java "interpreters." In effect, an interpreter is a program that can run another program, coordinating between the computer's operating system and the program. So a Java applet can run on any operating system (Windows 3.1, Windows 95, Macintosh System 7, and UNIX of various flavors) as long as there is an interpreter created for that operating system. Both Netscape Navigator and Internet Explorer are Java interpreters.

For these programs to work, you must be using a Java-compatible Web browser—and even then they may not work. Netscape 2.0 and later versions, and Internet Explorer 3.0 and later versions, are Java-compatible. The later the version, the more likely that the Java applet will function (Netscape Navigator 2, for instance, doesn't handle Java applets very well). But even if you have the very latest browser, you may still run into problems.

When you reach a Web page that has an embedded Java applet, the Java program is transmitted to your computer, and the browser then runs the program. The program may be a game of some sort, a multimedia display, a financial calculator of some kind, or just about anything else. The following figure shows one of the Java maps at Expedia.

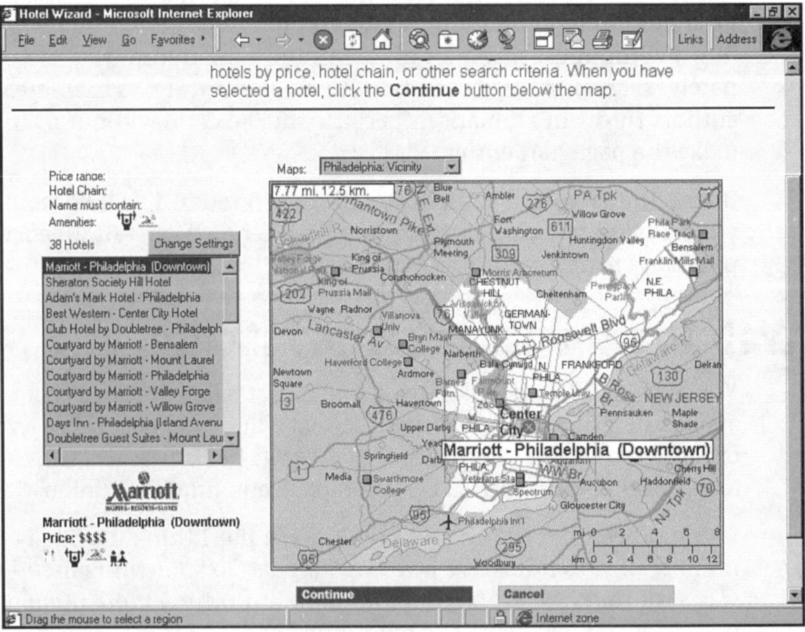

Expedia's Java maps help you find a hotel.

For all the overblown projections, many Java applets remain rarely used, unreliable, and slow. (And all too often pointless.) Searching for interesting or useful Java applets has been an experience in frustration and disappointment for some time. The situation is improving, though, with truly useful Java applets becoming more common and more reliable.

Applications Across the Net

You may have heard the theory that pretty soon, instead of buying software and installing it on your hard drive, you'll "rent" programs across the Internet, paying for the time you use. If this *ever* happens (and there are good reasons to suspect it won't), it will be a very long time from now. Internet connections are currently about as reliable and efficient as a drunk at a beer tasting, and until they are as reliable as the electricity supply, this system won't work. I've added this projection to my "yeah, right, don't hold your breath" list.

What About JavaScript and ActiveX?

JavaScript is Java's baby brother. It's a scripting language in which programs are written within the Web page. In other words, a JavaScript-compatible browser reads the Web page, extracts the JavaScript commands, and runs them. JavaScript is not as powerful a programming language as Java, but it's easier to create programs using JavaScript, so it's more common. You can find loads of JavaScript programs at Developer.com (`http://www.developer.com/directories/pages/dir.javascript.html`). The following figure shows an example of a JavaScript application, taken from a book I wrote on the subject.

A competitor to Java, ActiveX is a system from Microsoft, designed to allow Web authors to easily incorporate multimedia and programs into their Web pages. Currently, the only ActiveX browser is Internet Explorer, and you can probably expect it to stay that way for a while. With Netscape as the most popular browser, there's not much incentive for Netscape Communications to add ActiveX to Netscape and help their major competitor! (On the other hand, as Internet Explorer gains Web share—which it seems to be doing fairly steadily—that situation may change.)

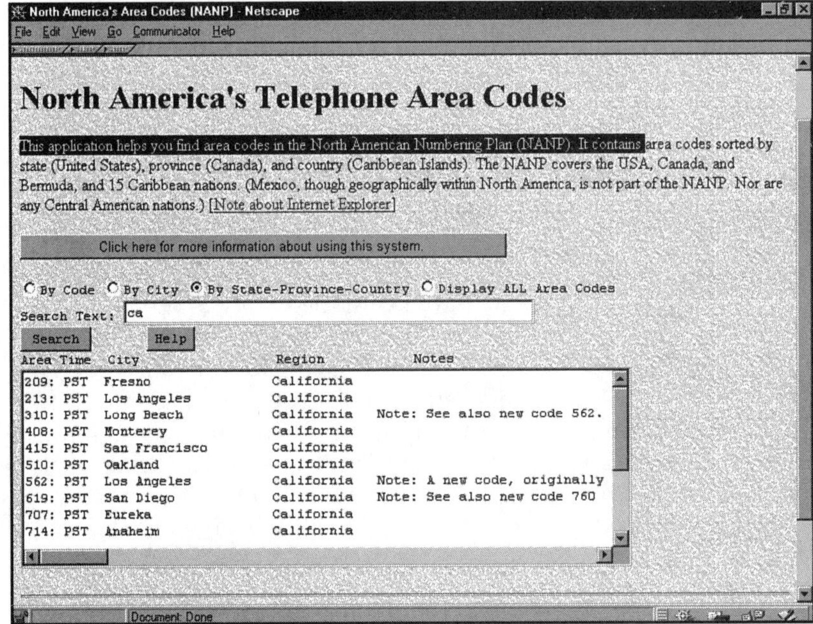

My Area Code program, written in JavaScript (`http://www.netscapepress.com/support/javascript1.2/index.htm`*).*

The Latest Programmer's Toy, Dynamic HTML

There's another way to make Web pages move, and that's with a new toy called Dynamic HTML (also called DHTML) and layers. A Web designer can now create different layers of information—pictures and text—and then shuffle these layers around on the page, making them visible and then invisible, to create an animation effect and even let people move things around on the page (see the alien head in the following illustration). People define Dynamic HTML differently; layering is a feature that's often used in conjunction with Dynamic HTML, although the purists may say it's a different thing. Microsoft and Netscape regard Dynamic HTML and layers as different things, too.

Dynamic HTML means Dynamic Hypertext Markup Language. You may remember from Chapter 3, "The World of the World Wide Web," that HTML is Hypertext Markup Language and is the coding used to create Web pages. So DHTML is sort of like HTML in motion. That's the theory, but advanced DHTML also requires programming skills, not just Web-authoring skills.

For the moment, DHTML is a programmer's toy used on few sites, although that's rapidly changing. DHTML works in both Internet Explorer 4 and Netscape Navigator 4, which means that many users don't have DHTML browsers. In any case, DHTML that works in Explorer probably won't work in Navigator and vice versa. If you'd like to see this technology at work (or not at work, depending on your browser), visit Microsoft's DHTML

Gallery (http://www.microsoft.com/gallery/files/html/) or the Netscape Communicator Demonstrations page (http://search.netscape.com/comprod/products/communicator/beta_features.html).

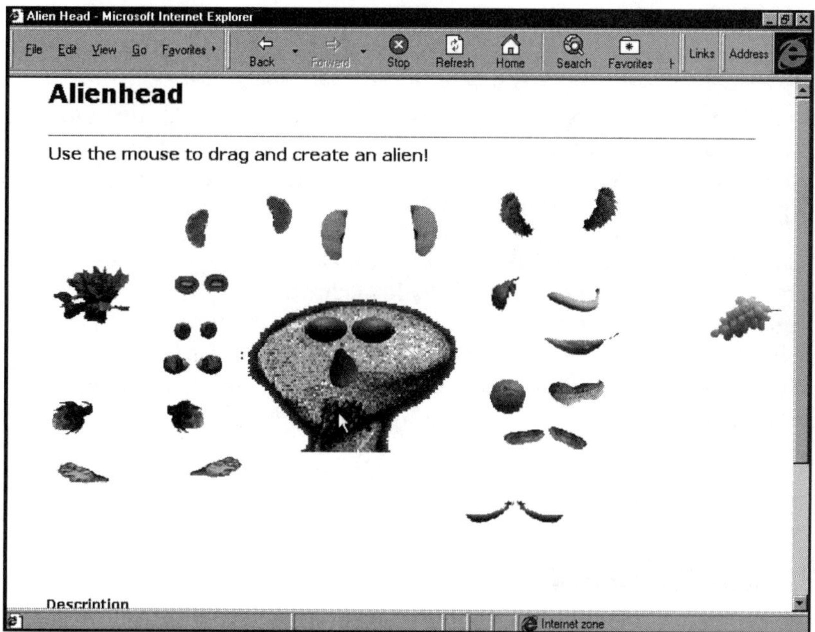

Create your own alien head through the wonders of DHTML. (You'll have to use Internet Explorer, though.)

Just a Little Shove: Pushing and Pulling

Information generally arrives at your screen because you've directly requested it by clicking a link or entering a URL. However, Web authors can set up their Web pages to use server push and client pull so you can get information without doing a thing.

The first of these, *server push*, occurs when the Web server continues sending information even though you haven't requested it. Suppose you click a link to display a Web page, and just a few minutes later, the Web page changes. Even if you don't request more information, the server sends updated information and continues to send periodic updates until you close the page.

Client pull is similar, except that the request for updates comes from the browser. For instance, you open a page. At the same time the server sends the page, it sends a special program (you don't see this; it all happens in the background). This program tells the browser when to request updates. After the defined interval, the browser sends a request to the server asking for the information. Again, these updates will continue until you leave the page.

These systems work so similarly that you usually won't know which method is being used. They are very useful when you're viewing information that changes rapidly, such as stock quotes, weather reports, news headlines, or auctions.

The Web Gets More Complicated

Creating a simple Web page is quite easy; even many of the more advanced Web-authoring techniques are not particularly complicated. Sure, there are special codes to learn, but it's all reasonably straightforward.

But the latest technologies are things that the average Web author will find much more complicated to use. Technologies such as Java, JavaScript, ActiveX, and Dynamic HTML require programming skills. As a result, it's becoming harder for Web authors to keep up with the Joneses (technologically speaking), which may be a good thing. Now they can concentrate on function instead of form, forget about the glitz, and compete by making their Web sites interesting and content-rich instead of just trying to be cool.

The Multimedia Experience

You'll find all sorts of file formats on the World Wide Web, including still pictures, video and animations, sounds, electronic documents, and 3D images. Any file format that you can play or display on your computer can be linked to a Web page.

When you click a link that takes you to one of these file formats, your browser handles the file, if it can. It displays the document or picture in the window in the normal way. If the file is a format that your browser can't handle, it has two options. Your browser may send the file directly to a program that *can* handle it (known as a *plug-in, viewer,* or *helper*), or it may ask you what to do. Chapter 6 deals with this topic.

Before I move on, though, here's a quick thought related to this issue:

> *The Internet is not a multimedia system!*

Remember that, and you'll be saved from a lot of frustration. This statement may seem a little strange after you've been bombarded by several years of advertising and media hype about the Internet. We've all seen the TV ads in which video rolls across a computer screen within a Web browser, as quickly as if it were being displayed on a TV screen. But the Internet does *not* work that quickly, and many of its problems seem to arise from people trying to treat it as if it does.

As a multimedia system, the Internet is primitive, mainly because it's so slow. If it's "lights, cameras, action" that you're after, use the TV or go see a movie; the Internet can't compete. The Internet, despite what you may have heard, is primarily a text-based system. (What's the fastest growing area on the Internet? Email publishing!) Even the Web is primarily text. All the hype in the world won't change that. What will change that is much faster connections from people's homes to the Internet, faster Web servers, and faster and more reliable backbone connections across the Internet. But don't hold your breath, because you'll turn blue before these things appear on the scene.

The Least You Need to Know

- The Web is far more diverse than it was a year or two ago; it's much more than just text with pictures.
- You'll find lots of tables and forms.
- Framed documents allow an author to split a document into multiple pieces, each of which is displayed in its own frame.
- Java, JavaScript, and ActiveX are Web programming languages that enable authors to bring their pages to life. The new programmer's toy is Dynamic HTML.
- Client pull is a system by which a browser automatically requests updates to a page. Server push is a system by which a server automatically sends updates.
- A wide range of multimedia formats must be displayed in viewers or plug-ins; you'll learn about those in Chapter 6.

Chapter 6

Web Multimedia

In This Chapter

- How does a browser handle different file formats?
- Finding plug-ins and viewers
- Types of plug-ins and viewers you may want
- Installing plug-ins
- Installing viewers in Netscape
- Installing viewers in Internet Explorer

As the Web gets older, and as people start using it more, it's storing more and more types of computer files. You'll find animations, videos, pictures of various formats, sounds that play once they've transferred to your computer, sounds that play *as* they transfer to your computer, "slide" presentations, and all sorts of other weird and wonderful things. Think of these formats as the *multimedia* content of the Web—literally "multiple media." But as I explained in the previous chapter, the Internet is not a true multimedia system. Yes, it has many types of media, but they tend to move rather slowly!

Today's Web browsers are designed to handle any computer file format. When you click a link to a file, that file is transferred to your computer, and your browser can then use it in one of three ways:

- *On its own.* The file format may be one that the browser can handle directly. Web browsers can play or display Web pages (.HTM or .HTML), text documents (.TXT), some graphics formats (.GIF, .XBM, .JPG, and .JPEG), and some sound formats.

- *With a plug-in.* The browser may open a *plug-in*, a special add-on program that plays or displays the file within the browser window.
- *With a viewer (or helper).* The browser may send the file to a *viewer* or *helper*, which is a separate program that recognizes the file format. That program then opens a window in which the file is played or displayed.

When you first get your browser, it probably won't recognize all the file formats you'll encounter. When the browser comes across a file format that it doesn't recognize, it will ask you what to do; you can then install a new plug-in or viewer to handle that file type, or simply save the file on your hard disk.

Two Types of Multimedia Inclusions

There are basically two ways to include a multimedia file in a Web page. The author may include the file as a *live, embedded,* or *inline object* (a file that is automatically transferred to your computer along with the Web page). For instance, an embedded file may play a background sound or display a video within the Web page. On the other hand, the author can include the file as an *external file*; you click a link, and that file alone (without a Web page) is transferred to your computer.

Which Plug-Ins Are Installed?

In Netscape Navigator, you can quickly find out which plug-ins are installed by choosing **Help, About Plug-ins**. You'll see a page showing you each plug-in and its filename. You'll also find a link to the Inline Plug-Ins page, where you can download more. In recent versions of Internet Explorer, you can select **Help, Product Updates**, and you'll see a Web page that lists a number of recommended plug-ins and shows you whether those plug-ins are already installed.

What's Available?

Scores of plug-ins and viewers are available; you just have to know where to find them. A good starting point for Netscape Navigator plug-ins is the Netscape Navigator Components page; select **Help**, **About Plug-ins**, and then click the **For More Information on Netscape Plug-ins, Click Here** link near the top of the page, or go to `http://home.netscape.com/comprod/products/navigator/version_2.0/plugins/index.html`. You can find links to viewers and plug-ins that will work in Internet Explorer by selecting **Help**, **Product Updates** or going to `http://www.microsoft.com/ie/ie40/download/rtw/x86/en/download/addonnt.htm`.

About now you're probably wondering whether you should use a plug-in or a viewer. In general, you'll probably prefer working with plug-ins because they allow the browser to display or play the file. In effect, a plug-in extends the capabilities of the browser, allowing it to work with a file type that it couldn't use before. A viewer, on the other hand, is a completely separate program; the Web browser remains at the previous Web page while the multimedia file is sent to the viewer. Of course, there may be cases in which a viewer is a better program and has more features than the equivalent plug-in. You may want to experiment and find out which is the more capable of the two.

Which Do You Need? Which Do You Want?

You don't need all the available viewers and plug-ins. There are hundreds already—almost 180 plug-ins for Netscape Navigator alone—and more are being added all the time. So unless you are independently wealthy and don't need to waste time working, you probably won't have time to install them all (and you probably don't have the disk space you'd need). To help you determine which plug-ins and viewers you should get, I've broken them down into a few categories and the most common file formats. You may not want to get them until you need them, though.

Music and Voice (Very Useful)

Some of the most useful plug-ins and viewers are those for music and voice. In particular, you may want RealAudio, TrueSpeech, and StreamWorks. (RealAudio is the most popular, and therefore the most useful, of these sound formats.)

Most sound formats can't play until they have been completely transferred to your disk drive (you twiddle your thumbs for 10 minutes, and then listen). The RealAudio, TrueSpeech, and StreamWorks formats play sounds as they are being transferred, though. They're used by radio stations and music libraries, for example, so you can listen to the news from National Public Radio (`http://www.npr.org`) or music from the Internet Underground Music Archives (`http://www.iuma.com`). The following illustration shows Netscape Navigator using RealAudio to play a file from the NPR site.

> Check This Out...
>
> **You Already Have Viewers**
>
> In many cases, you may already have viewers for certain file formats. For instance, if you use Windows, you can use the Windows Media Player as a viewer for MIDI files. If you use the Macintosh and have Microsoft Word, you can use Word as the viewer for Word .DOC files.

During your Internet travels, you are likely to come across these other sound formats:

➤ *.AU, .AIF, .AIFF, .AIFC, and .SND.* These common sound formats are used on UNIX and on the Macintosh. Your browser can probably play these formats without an additional plug-in or viewer.

➤ *.WAV.* This is the Windows sound format. Your browser can probably play files in this format without an additional plug-in or viewer.

- ➤ *.MID and .RMI.* These are MIDI (Musical Instrument Digital Interface) formats. You may need to add a plug-in or viewer for these. (Netscape Navigator, since version 3, comes with a preinstalled plug-in that will work with MIDI files.)

The MIDI formats are not common, but they are of interest to people who, well, are interested in MIDI. Many MIDI sites on the Web have sound clips. (MIDI is a system used to create music using computers and other electronic toys.)

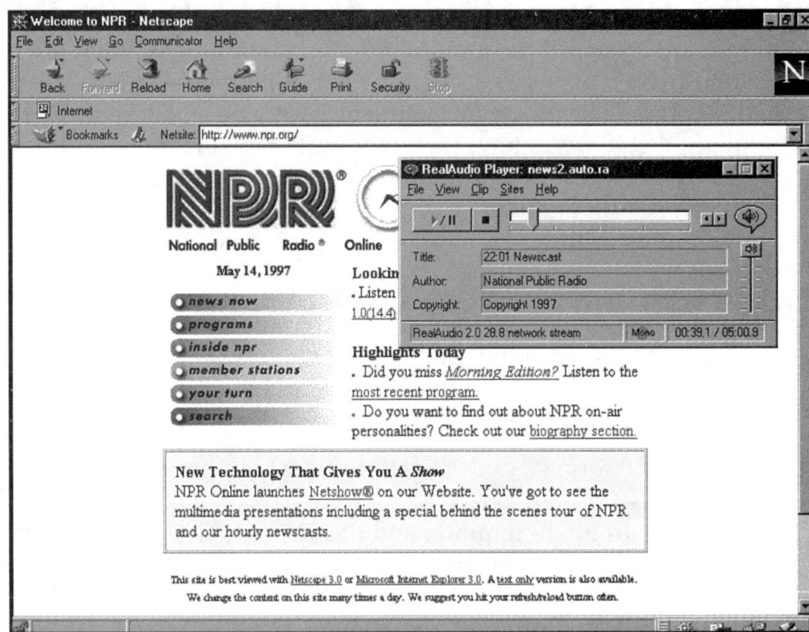

The RealAudio viewer playing the newscast from NPR.

Other Document Formats (Also Very Useful)

Viewers and plug-ins are also available for a number of document formats that you'll find on the Web. In particular, the Adobe Acrobat Reader is useful. You'll also find viewers and plug-ins that display Microsoft Word, Envoy, and PostScript documents.

Adobe Acrobat is a hypertext format that predates the Web. It enables an author to create a multipage hypertext document that is contained in a single .PDF file and that can be read by any Acrobat Reader, regardless of the operating system it is running on. Many authors like to use Acrobat because it gives them more control over the layout than they get when creating Web pages. It's also often used by companies that want to allow people to download forms from their Web sites; you can open the form in Adobe Acrobat Reader and then print it, and it will look exactly as the company intended (it's difficult to create high-quality forms using Web pages). For instance, most Internal Revenue Service forms are available in .PDF format. You can see an example of an Acrobat file in the following figure.

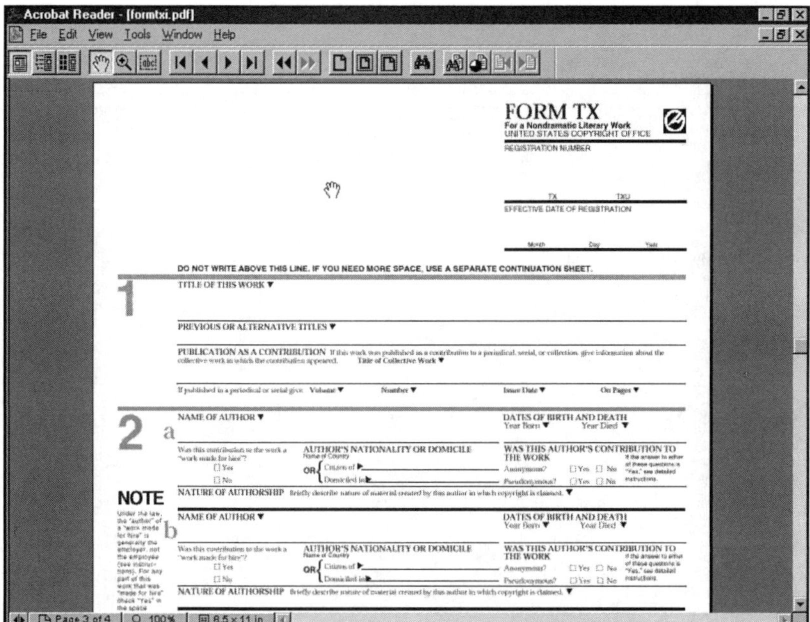
Acrobat Reader - [formtxi.pdf]

File Edit View Tools Window Help

FORM TX
For a Nondramatic Literary Work
UNITED STATES COPYRIGHT OFFICE
REGISTRATION NUMBER

TX TXU
EFFECTIVE DATE OF REGISTRATION

Month Day Year

DO NOT WRITE ABOVE THIS LINE. IF YOU NEED MORE SPACE, USE A SEPARATE CONTINUATION SHEET.

1 TITLE OF THIS WORK ▼

PREVIOUS OR ALTERNATIVE TITLES ▼

PUBLICATION AS A CONTRIBUTION If this work was published as a contribution to a periodical, serial, or collection, give information about the collective work in which the contribution appeared. Title of Collective Work ▼

If published in a periodical or serial give: Volume ▼ Number ▼ Issue Date ▼ On Pages ▼

2 a NAME OF AUTHOR ▼ DATES OF BIRTH AND DEATH Year Born ▼ Year Died ▼

Was this contribution to the work a "work made for hire"? ☐ Yes ☐ No AUTHOR'S NATIONALITY OR DOMICILE Name of Country OR { Citizen of ▶ Domiciled in ▶ WAS THIS AUTHOR'S CONTRIBUTION TO THE WORK Anonymous? ☐ Yes ☐ No Pseudonymous? ☐ Yes ☐ No

NOTE NATURE OF AUTHORSHIP Briefly describe nature of material created by this author in which copyright is claimed. ▼

b NAME OF AUTHOR ▼ DATES OF BIRTH AND DEATH Year Born ▼ Year Died ▼

Was this contribution to the work a "work made for hire"? ☐ Yes ☐ No AUTHOR'S NATIONALITY OR DOMICILE Name of Country OR { Citizen of ▶ Domiciled in ▶ WAS THIS AUTHOR'S CONTRIBUTION TO THE WORK Anonymous? ☐ Yes ☐ No Pseudonymous? ☐ Yes ☐ No

NATURE OF AUTHORSHIP Briefly describe nature of material created by this author in which copyright is claimed. ▼

Page 3 of 4 100% 8.5 x 11 in

A form from the United States Copyright Office saved in an Adobe Acrobat file and displayed in the Adobe Acrobat viewer.

3D Worlds (Greatly Overrated!)

There are a number of viewers and browsers that display 3D (three-dimensional) images. Netscape Navigator has a plug-in called Live3D or Cosmo Player (depending on the version of Navigator that you are using), which may have been installed when you installed the browser. Internet Explorer has a plug-in called Microsoft VRML Viewer, which probably won't be installed with the browser—you'll have to add it later. You can download other 3D plug-ins or viewers, too.

VRML These 3D images are in a format known as VRML: Virtual Reality Modeling Language.

Do you need a 3D plug-in or viewer? Probably not. Once you've seen a couple 3D sites, the novelty will quickly wear off. This is another of those much-touted technologies that hasn't yet lived up to the hype. Three-dimensional images load slowly and move slowly. They are, in my opinion, unnecessary gimmicks. Perhaps one day they'll be an integral part of the Web, but for now they're little more than toys.

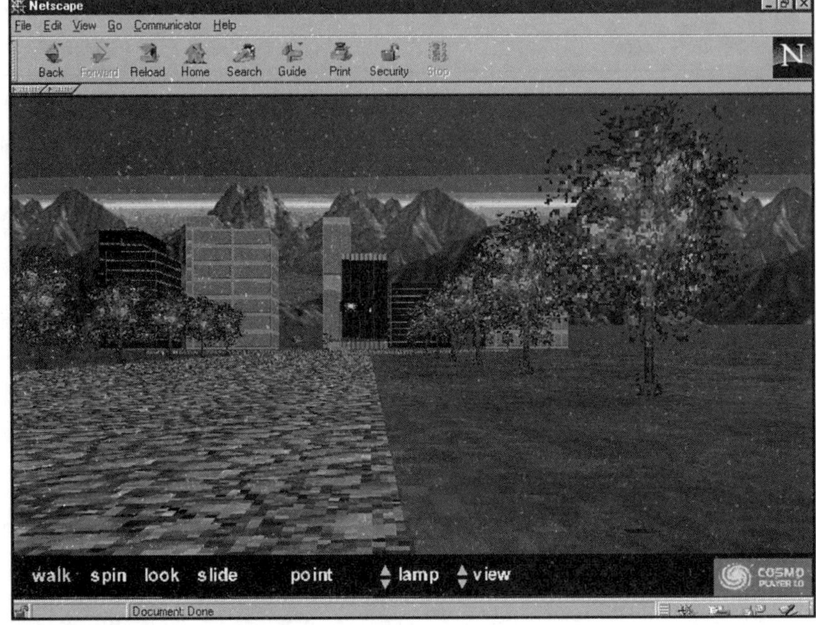

You can walk around these buildings and maybe even into them. This technology is cute, but slow (and not terribly exciting once you've done it once or twice).

Video (If You Can Wait)

Video is fairly popular on the Web, but it has serious drawbacks. The main problem is speed. It can take hours for anything big to transfer, and if it's small, what's the point? After waiting an eternity to watch a five-second cut from a movie, I was left with the question "Was that really worth it?" ringing in my head.

Video is another of those things that requires a fast connection. If you are on a corporate network you are probably okay—assuming the video clip is stored on a fast server and the Internet is not as sluggish as molasses on a cold day—but if you are using a modem to connect to a service provider, you'll find video to be very slow.

Still, if you want to try video you can find many viewers and plug-ins. The most common formats are the Windows .AVI and QuickTime formats (which may be built into your browser already) and MPEG. A new format, .VIV, is a compressed .AVI file that provides streaming video. Recently, a video format from RealNetworks has become popular (RealNetworks is the RealAudio company), too, with some news sites using it. Netscape 3.0 comes with a built-in .AVI plug-in, but other .AVI plug-ins and viewers have more features.

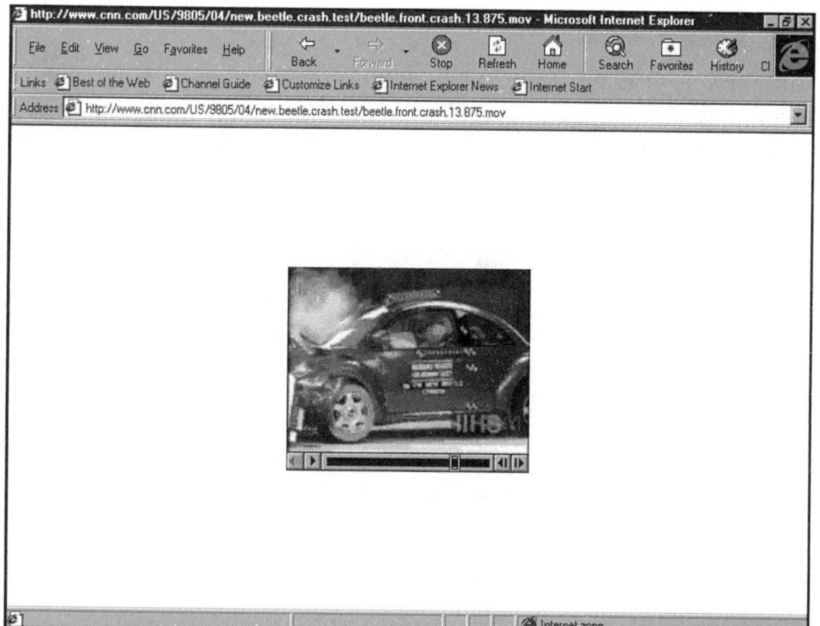

A VW Beetle crash test video from the CNN news site, displayed in the QuickTime viewer inside Internet Explorer.

Streaming Video

I mentioned RealAudio earlier; RealAudio is a streaming audio format, which means it plays as it transmits. That's the new thing in video, too. Not too long ago, you'd have to wait for a video file to transfer completely before you could play it. Now streaming video viewers and plug-ins are turning up; these viewers and plug-ins play the video as it transmits.

Animations (Here and There)

You'll find many animation plug-ins and viewers, but only a few formats are commonly used on the Web. Although it's popular these days for any software company with a proprietary file format to create a plug-in for it, very few Web authors are using animation, and only a few of the available formats are commonly used. Probably the most common animation formats are Macromedia's Authorware and Director animations, which can be viewed using the Shockwave plug-in. (How does animation differ from video? Think of video as a film; think of animation as a cartoon.)

Another very common form of animation is .GIF animation. The .GIF format is one of the basic image formats used on the Web, and GIF animations are created by layering several images. These animations require no plug-in or viewer, though; if a browser can display images, it can probably display GIF animations.

Other Weird File Formats

You'll find plug-ins and viewers available for all sorts of unusual file formats. Some plug-ins are not programs designed for handling particular file formats that you may come across while cruising the Web—they are more like special utilities designed to extend the features of the Web browser. For instance, there are Netscape plug-ins available for these tasks:

- *Carbon Copy.* This Netscape plug-in lets you control a PC across the Internet.
- *Chemscape Chime.* This is a plug-in for 2D and 3D chemical models.
- *EarthTime.* This plug-in displays eight different times from cities around the world.
- *ISYS Hindsight.* This plug-in keeps a record of every Web page you've seen and even allows you to search the text in those pages.
- *Look@Me.* This plug-in allows you to view another user's computer screen across the Web and see what's going on. (Assuming that person *wants* you to see what's going on, of course.)
- *Net-Install.* This plug-in is designed to automate the transfer and installation of software across the Internet.

Looking for Samples? A good place to find samples of these various multimedia formats is the Netscape plug-ins page that I mentioned earlier. For each plug-in or viewer, you'll find links to Web sites using the file format handled by that program.

As I mentioned earlier, any file type can be sent to a viewer of some kind. However, only a handful of file types are commonly used (the ones I mentioned earlier as the common formats). You'll only want to install other plug-ins and viewers if the particular file type happens to be used at the Web sites that you frequent.

You don't necessarily need to install these plug-ins or viewers right away. You can wait until you stumble across a link to one of the file formats. If your browser doesn't recognize the format, it will ask you what to do with the file. If you want to access the file, you will need to install the appropriate viewer or plug-in at that time.

Installing a Plug-in

Installing a plug-in is easy. Simply transfer the installation file from the Web and place it in a download directory (see Chapter 11, "Finding Stuff"). Then run the file (double-click it, for instance) to run the installation program. The installation program may run immediately, or you may find that a series of files are extracted from the one you downloaded, in which case you have to run a SETUP.EXE file to start the installation program. Follow the instructions to install the file. After you have installed the plug-in, your browser will be able to automatically call the plug-in anytime it needs it.

By the way, your browser may sometimes tell you when you need a plug-in. For instance, if you see the dialog box shown in the following figure (or something similar), you have displayed a Web page with an embedded file format that requires a plug-in. You can click the **Get the Plugin** button, and the browser will open another window and take you to a page with information about plug-ins.

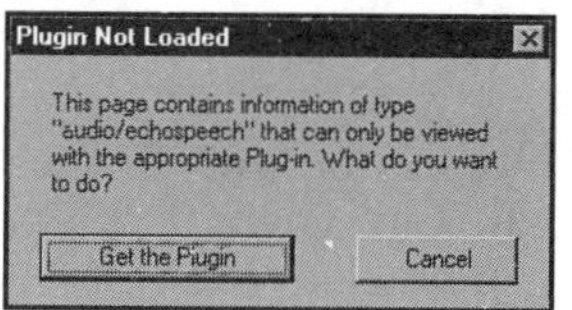

This Netscape dialog box opens when you click a link that loads a file requiring a plug-in you don't have.

Installing a Viewer

Installing a viewer is a little more complicated than installing a plug-in, but it's still not rocket science. There are generally two different types of viewer installations. One is the type used by the early versions of Netscape and by the Macintosh and UNIX versions of Netscape. In this type of installation, you tell the browser which viewer to work with for each file type. You also add information about a particular viewer to a list of viewers that the browser refers to when it needs to handle the appropriate file type.

The other method is that used by the Windows versions of Internet Explorer and by the Windows versions of Netscape Navigator 4 and later. These use the Windows file associations to set up viewers. For instance, by default Windows associates .WAV files with the Sound Recorder program. That means if you double-click a .WAV file in File Manager, Sound Recorder opens and plays the file. Internet Explorer and Navigator 4 use the same system-wide file-association system to determine which program should be used when it comes across a file type.

The next section gives you a look at installing a viewer in a Windows version of Internet Explorer, which is very similar to what you would do in the Windows version of Netscape Navigator 4. The section after that covers installing a viewer in a Windows version of Netscape Navigator 3, which is similar to the way installation is handled in other, non-Windows versions of Navigator and in some other browsers.

Installing a Viewer in Internet Explorer

When you install a viewer in Internet Explorer, you're not merely modifying Internet Explorer's internal settings; you are modifying the Windows file-association settings. When you click a file type that Internet Explorer doesn't recognize, it opens the dialog box shown in the following figure. (This dialog box is similar to what you saw from Netscape.) Because Explorer doesn't recognize the file type, you have to tell it what to do. Click the **Open It Using an Application on Your Computer** option button, and then click **OK.** Explorer transfers the file and then tries to open it.

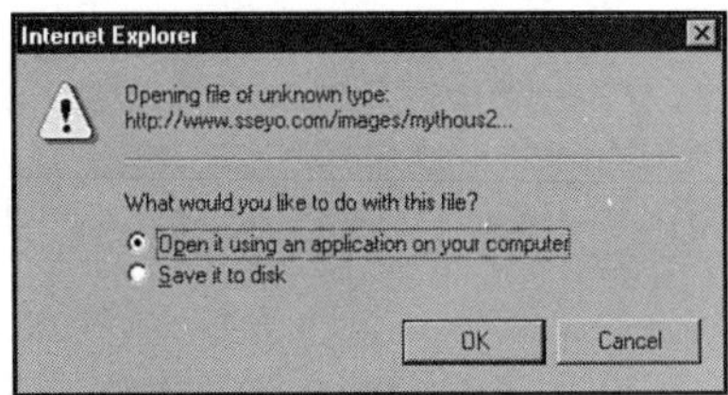

If Explorer doesn't recognize a file, you will see this dialog box.

You'll then see the Open With dialog box, shown next. Type a name for this type of file into the text box at the top. Then, if you can find the viewer you want to use in this list, click it and click **OK**. If you can't find it, click the **Other** button. In the Open dialog box that appears, select the viewer you want to use.

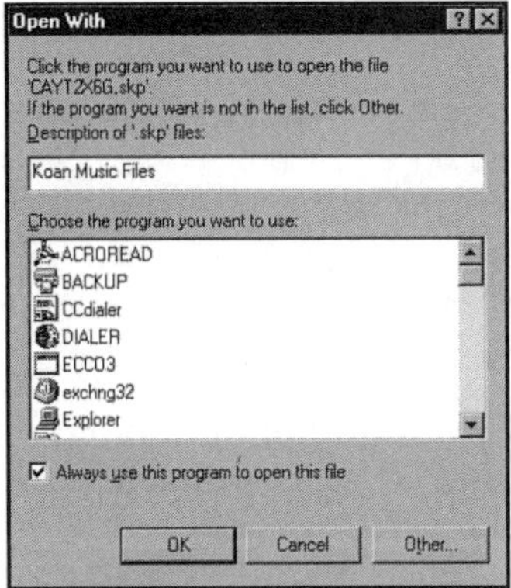

Enter a name for the file type, and then choose the application you want to use as a viewer.

Installing a Viewer in Explorer Beforehand

You can also install an Internet Explorer viewer before you need it. You do this using the File Types system, which you can access from the Windows Explorer file-management utility or, in some versions of Internet Explorer and in Netscape Navigator 4, from within the browser.

Open Windows Explorer, and then select **View**, **Options** (or **View**, **Folder Options** in some versions), and then click the **File Types** tab. You'll see an Options dialog box similar to that shown in the following figure. (In some versions of Internet Explorer you'll be able to access this dialog box in the same way, though more recent versions don't allow this. In Netscape Navigator 4 for Windows, select **Edit, Preferences**, and then open the **Navigator** category and click the **Applications** subcategory. The Navigator dialog boxes will be slightly different from those shown here, but similar enough for you to be able to follow along.)

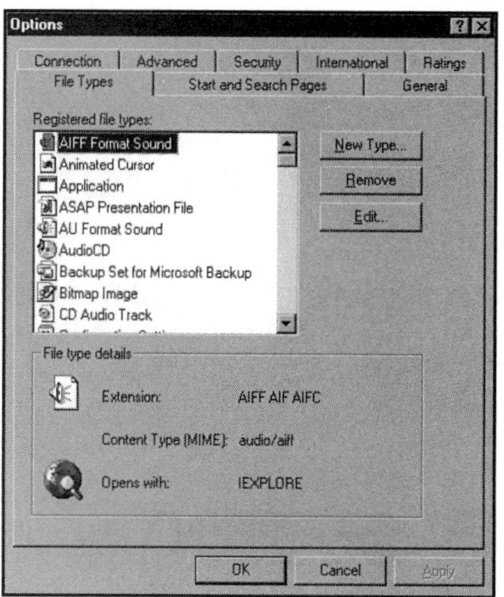

You can add viewers to Internet Explorer using the Options dialog box.

To add a new viewer, click the **New Type** button, and then fill in all the information in the dialog box that appears. Enter the description (whatever you want to call it), the file extensions used by that file type, and the MIME type. Click the **New** button and type **open** in the first text box you see. Then click the **Browse** button and find the application you want to use as the viewer.

What's MIME?

MIME stands for multipurpose Internet mail extensions. Although originally intended for email transmission of files, MIME is used on the Web to identify file formats. You can find detailed information about MIME and a large list of MIME types at `http://www.cis.ohio-state.edu/hypertext/faq/usenet/mail/mime-faq/top.html` or at `http://home.netscape.com/assist/helper_apps/mime.html`.

Installing a Viewer in Netscape

This section explains how to configure a viewer in the Windows version of Netscape Navigator 3. The process is similar in other versions of Netscape and even in other browsers. Rather than modifying the list of Windows file associations, you're modifying a list belonging to the browser.

Suppose you came across a link that looked interesting, and you clicked it. Netscape displayed the Unknown File Type dialog box, shown next. This means that Netscape doesn't recognize the file, so you have to tell it what to do.

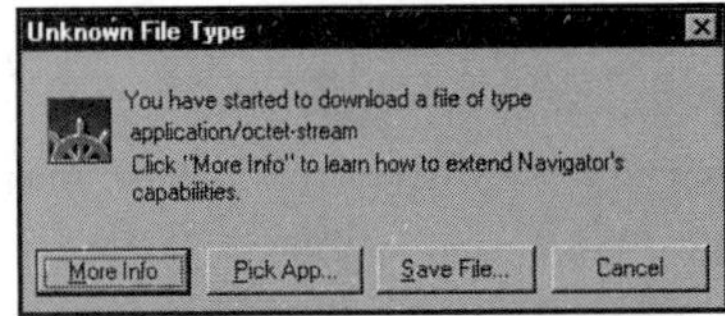

The Unknown File Type dialog box opens if you click a link to a file that Netscape doesn't recognize.

If you want, you can click the **More Info** button. Netscape will open another browser window and display an information document with a link to a page from which, perhaps, you can download a plug-in. Let's assume that you already know there is no plug-in for this particular file type or that for some other reason you want to configure a viewer. Click the **Pick App** button, and you'll see the dialog box in the following figure.

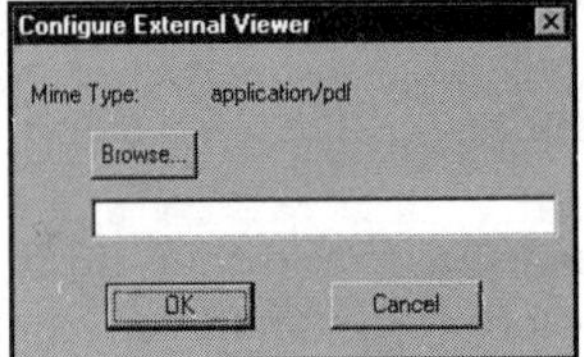

The Configure External Viewer dialog box lets you define which viewer should handle the file type.

Click the **Browse** button and then find the program that you know can handle this type of file. Double-click the program, and it is placed into the Configure External Viewer dialog box. Then click **OK**. That's it! You've just configured the viewer. The file referenced by the link you clicked will now be transferred to your computer and sent to the program you defined as the viewer. The viewer will then display the file (assuming, of course, that you picked the right viewer).

Setting Up Netscape Navigator Beforehand

What's That Button For? In case you're wondering, the Unknown: Prompt User option button is the default setting for formats that haven't been set up with a viewer. If you click a file for which you've configured this setting, Netscape will ask you what to do with the files of this type when they are transferred to your browser.

You can also set up Netscape Navigator's viewers before you ever get to a site that uses unusual file formats. Choose **Edit, Preferences**, and then open the **Navigator** category and click the **Applications** subcategory. Or, if you're using an early version of Navigator, choose **Options**, **General Preferences**, and then click the **Helpers** tab. You'll see the dialog box shown next.

The big list shows all the different file types (well, most of them; you can add more using the **Create New Type** button). To configure a viewer for one, click it in the list and then click one of the **Actions.** You can tell Netscape to **Save to Disk** if you want, but if you intend to configure a viewer, click **Launch the Application** instead. Then click the **Browse** button to find the application you want to use as the viewer.

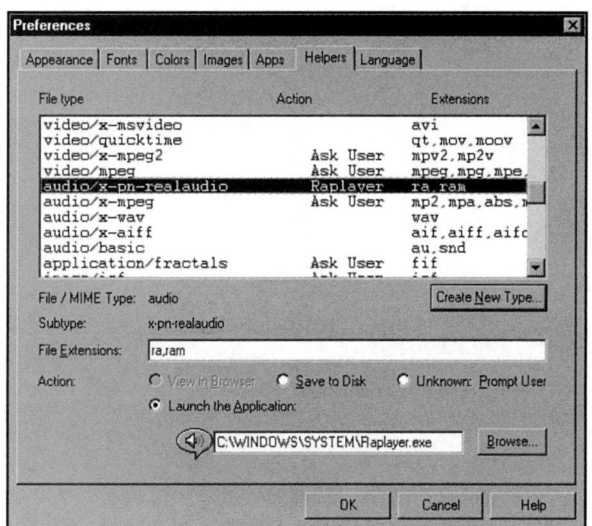

You can preconfigure viewers in Netscape's Preferences dialog box.

The Least You Need to Know

- A browser can handle many file formats: HTML, text, graphics, and sounds of various kinds. If a browser encounters a file format that it can't handle, it tries to pass the file to a viewer or plug-in.
- Viewers and plug-ins are designed to play or display file types that browsers can't handle. The difference between the two is that a plug-in temporarily converts the browser window into a viewer, but a viewer is a completely separate program that opens without changing the browser window in any way.
- There are hundreds of viewers and plug-ins for scores of file types. Most of these file types are rarely used, however.
- Plug-ins are more convenient than viewers are. However, if you find a viewer that has more features than the plug-in, use it.
- If your browser comes across a file type that it doesn't recognize, it asks you what to do. You can then install a plug-in or specify a viewer.

Part 2
There's Plenty More

The Internet is far more than just the Web, although you might not be able to tell that from the media coverage. There's a system called push, *for example, which is a sort of Web automation tool. But there are other important systems that have nothing to do with the Web. The Internet has hundreds of thousands of discussion groups (newsgroups and mailing lists), a file library system called FTP, and a once popular menu system known as Gopher. And, of course, there's chat. No, it's not really chat—instead of talking, you type—but many people find it to be a great way to while away an hour or ten. And you'll learn about a system (Voice on the Net) that enables you to make international phone calls for just pennies an hour! You might even use Telnet, a relatively little used system that allows you to log on to computers around the world. Even if you don't use all of the services covered in this part of the book, you're almost certain to find something useful.*

Chapter 7

Newsgroups: The Source of All Wisdom

In This Chapter

- What is a newsgroup?
- What can you find in newsgroups?
- Finding out what newsgroups exist
- What is Usenet?
- Choosing a newsreader

In this chapter, I'm going to introduce you to one of the Internet's most dangerous services: newsgroups. Many people find these discussion groups to be addictive. Get involved in a few groups and, if you have an addictive personality, you'll soon find that the rest of your life is falling apart as you spend hours each day swapping messages with people all over the world, on subjects such as bushwalking in Australia, soap operas, very tall women, or very short men.

If you don't have an addictive personality, newsgroups can be interesting, stimulating, and extremely useful. Anyway, being addicted to newsgroups is better than being addicted to booze or drugs. In this chapter, you'll find out what newsgroups are; in the next chapter, you'll find out how to use them.

What's a Newsgroup?

Let me answer the question, "What's a newsgroup?" with another question: Are you familiar with bulletin board systems (BBSs)? Electronic BBSs work much like the corkboard-and-thumbtack type of bulletin board. They're computerized systems for leaving both public and private messages. Other computer users can read your messages, and you can read theirs. There are tens of thousands of small BBSs around the world, each of which has its own area of interest. In addition, many computer companies have BBSs through which their customers get technical support, and many professional associations have BBSs so their members can leave messages for one another and take part in discussions.

An information service such as CompuServe or America Online is essentially a collection of many bulletin boards (called *forums* in CompuServe-speak or *message boards* on AOL). CompuServe has a few thousand such BBSs. Instead of having to remember several thousand telephone numbers (one for each BBS), you can dial one phone number and access any number of BBSs on the service.

As you've already seen, the Internet is a collection of networks hooked together. It's huge, and consequently it has an enormous number of discussion groups. In Internet-speak, these groups are called *newsgroups*, and there are thousands of them on all conceivable subjects. Each Internet service provider subscribes to a selection of newsgroups—perhaps just 5,000 or 10,000, but sometimes as many as 40,000, maybe even more. I just checked with one of the service providers I use, and it has more than 50,000 newsgroups available.

A New Way to Serve Newsgroups

Some service providers are using a fancy new news server system that allows them to provide tens of thousands of newsgroups, yet use minimal resources. Rather than transfer all the messages in all the newsgroups to the service provider's computers, a list of groups is transferred (most of the actual newsgroup messages are not). It's not until a user actually tries to read messages from a newsgroup that the messages are transferred across the Internet to the service provider, and then from the service provider to the user. This system is known by the delightful phrase, *dynamic sucking feed.*

What do I mean by *subscribe*? These newsgroups are distributed around the Internet by a service called Usenet; consequently, they're often referred to as Usenet groups. Usenet distributes around 30,000 groups (the number keeps changing), but not all service providers get all of the groups. A service provider can choose which groups it wants to receive, in essence *subscribing* to just the ones it wants. Although almost 30,000 internationally distributed newsgroups exist (along with thousands more local groups), most providers get only a few thousand of them.

If your service provider subscribes to a newsgroup, you can read that group's messages and post your own messages to the group. In other words, you can work only with groups to which your service provider has subscribed. You read newsgroup messages by using a *newsreader*, a program that retrieves messages from your service provider's *news server*.

If you've never used a newsgroup (or another system's forum, BBS, or whatever), you may not be aware of the power of such communications. This sort of messaging system brings computer networking to life, and it's not all computer nerds sitting around with nothing better to do. (Check out the Internet's alt.sex newsgroups; these people are not your average introverted propeller-heads!) In my Internet travels, I've found work, made friends, found answers to research questions (much quicker and more cheaply than I could have by going to a library), and read people's "reviews" of tools I can use in my business. I've never found a lover or spouse online, but I know people who have (and anyway, I'm already married). Just be careful not to get addicted and start spending all your time online.

Public News Servers

If your service provider doesn't subscribe to a newsgroup you want, ask the management to subscribe to it. If they won't, you *might* be able to find and read it at a public news server. Try looking at these sites for information about public servers:

`http://www.yahoo.com/News/Usenet/Public_Access_Usenet_Sites/`

`http://www.reed.edu/~greaber/query.html`

`http://www.geocities.com/SiliconValley/Pines/3959/usenet.html`

You can also read newsgroups through a Web site, at `http://www.supernews.com/`.

So What's Out There?

You can use newsgroups for fun or for work. You can use them to spend time "talking" with other people who share your interests—whether that happens to be algebra (see the alt.algebra.help group) or antique collecting (rec.antiques). You can even do serious work online, such as finding a job at a nuclear physics research site (hepnet.jobs), tracking down a piece of software for a biology project (bionet.software), or finding good stories about what's going on in South Africa for an article you are writing (za.events).

Check This Out...

News? True to its UNIX heritage, the Internet uses the word *news* ambiguously. Often, when you see a reference to news in a message or an Internet document, it refers to the messages left in newsgroups (not, as most people imagine, to journalists' reports on current affairs).

The following newsgroups represent just a tiny fraction of what is available:

alt.ascii-art. Pictures (such as Spock and the Simpsons) created with ASCII text characters.

alt.comedy.british. Discussions on British comedy in all its wonderful forms.

alt.current-events.russia. News of what's going on in Russia right now. (Some messages are in broken English, and some are in Russian, but that just adds romance.)

alt.missing-kids. Information about missing kids.

bit.listserv.down-syn. Discussions about Down's syndrome.

comp.research.japan. Information about computer research in Japan.

misc.forsale. Lists of goods for sale.

rec.skydiving. A group for skydivers.

sci.anthropology. A group for people interested in anthropology.

sci.military. Discussions on science and the military.

soc.couples.intercultural. A group for intercultural couples.

If you are looking for information on just about any subject, the question is not "Is there a newsgroup about this?" The questions you should ask are "What is the newsgroup's name?" and "Does my service provider subscribe to it?"

Can You Read It?

The many newsgroups out there take up a lot of room. A service provider getting the messages of just 3,000 newsgroups may have to set aside tens of megabytes of hard disk space to keep up with it all. So service providers have to decide which ones they will subscribe to. Nobody subscribes to all the world's newsgroups because many are of no interest to most Internet users, and many are not widely distributed. (Some are of regional interest only; some are of interest only to a specific organization.) So system administrators have to pick the ones they want and omit the ones they don't want. Undoubtedly, some system administrators censor newsgroups, omitting those they believe have no place online.

I Want to Start One! Do you have a subject about which you want to start a newsgroup? Spend some time in the news.groups newsgroup to find out about starting a Usenet newsgroup, or talk to your service provider about starting a local newsgroup.

I've given you an idea of what is available in general, but I can't specify what is available to you. You'll have to check with your service provider to find out what they offer. If they don't have what you want, ask them to get it. They have no way of knowing what people want unless someone tells them.

Okay, Gimme a List!

The first thing you may want to do is find out what newsgroups your service provider subscribes to. You can do that by telling your newsreader to obtain a list of groups from the news server; I'll talk more about newsreaders later.

What if you don't find what you are looking for? How can you find out what's available that your provider does not subscribe to? There are lots of places to go these days to track down newsgroups. I like Liszt (`http://www.liszt.com/news/`), which currently lists more than 30,000 newsgroups, and Tile.Net (`http://www.tile.net/`), which you can see in the following figure. Both Liszt and Tile.Net also list thousands of mailing lists; Tile.Net also lists FTP sites. You can try the Usenet Info Center (`http://sunsite.unc.edu/usenet-i/`) or the Finding Newsgroups and Mailing Lists page (`http://www.synapse.net/~radio/finding.htm`). You can also search at any Web search site (which you'll learn about in Chapter 11, "Finding Stuff"). For instance, try Yahoo! (`http://www.yahoo.com/News/Usenet/Newsgroup_Listings/`).

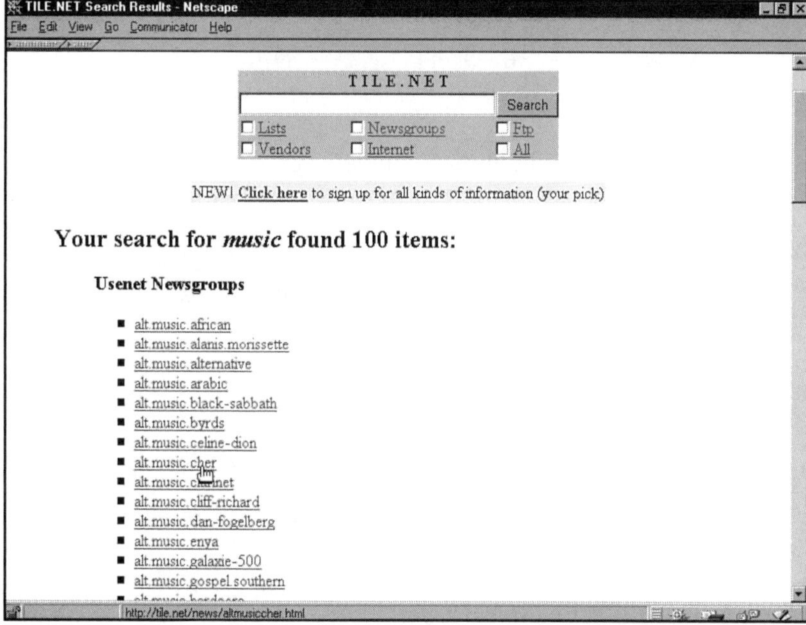

Tile.Net is a good place to find out what's available on Usenet.

Where Does It All Come From?

Where do all these newsgroups come from? People all over the world create newsgroups on their computers. Any system administrator can create a newsgroup, and many do. Each host has newsgroups of local interest that contain information about the service provider's services, local politics, local events, and so on.

Moderated Groups As you'll see when you refer to some of the directories of newsgroups, some newsgroups are *moderated*, which means someone reads all the messages and decides which ones to post. The purpose is to keep the newsgroup focused and to prevent the discussions from "going astray." Of course, it may look a little like censorship, depending on what you want to say.

A large number of newsgroups, although not all of them, are part of the Usenet system. Like the Internet, Usenet is a network of networks. No one owns it, and it doesn't own anything itself. It is independent of any network, including the Internet (in fact, it's older than the Internet). Usenet is simply a series of voluntary agreements to swap information.

What's in a Name?

Newsgroup names look much like host addresses: a series of words separated by periods. The reason for this format is that, like host names, newsgroup names are set up in a hierarchical system (although instead of going right-to-left, they go left-to-right). The first name is the top level. These are the primary top-level Usenet groups:

comp. Computer-related subjects.

news. Information about newsgroups, including software you can use to read newsgroup messages and information about finding and using newsgroups.

rec. Recreational topics, including hobbies, sports, the arts, and so on.

sci. Discussions about research in the "hard" sciences, as well as some social sciences.

soc. A wide range of social issues, such as discussions about different types of societies and subcultures, as well as sociopolitical subjects.

talk. Debates about politics, religion, and anything else that's controversial.

misc. Stuff. Job searches, things for sale, a forum for paramedics. You know, stuff.

Not all newsgroups are true Usenet groups. Many are local groups that Usenet distributes internationally (don't worry about the difference, it doesn't matter). Such newsgroups are part of the alternative newsgroup hierarchies. They have other top-level groups, such as these:

alt. "Alternative" subjects. These are often subjects that many people consider inappropriate, pornographic, or just weird. In some cases, however, the newsgroup is simply interesting reading, but someone created the newsgroup in an "unauthorized" manner to save time and hassle.

bionet. Biological subjects.

bit. A variety of newsgroups from BITnet.

biz. Business subjects, including advertisements.

clari. Clarinet's newsgroups from "official" and commercial sources; mainly UPI news stories and various syndicated columns.

courts. Newsgroups related to law and lawyers.

de. Various German-language newsgroups.

fj. Various Japanese-language newsgroups.

gnu. The Free Software Foundation's newsgroups.

hepnet. Discussions about high energy and nuclear physics.

ieee. The Institute of Electrical and Electronics Engineers' newsgroups.

info. A collection of mailing lists formed into newsgroups at the University of Illinois.

k12. Discussions about kindergarten through 12th-grade education.

relcom. Russian-language newsgroups, mainly distributed in the former Soviet Union.

vmsnet. Subjects of interest to VAX/VMS computer users.

You'll see other groups, too, such as the following:

brasil. Groups from Brazil (Brazil is spelled with an "s" in Portuguese).

Birmingham. Groups from Birmingham, England.

podunk. A local interest newsgroup for the town of Podunk.

thisu. This university's newsgroup.

Okay, I made up the last two, but you get the idea. You'll run into all sorts of different hierarchies, with new ones appearing all the time. To see a list of virtually all the top-level group names in both Usenet and alternative newsgroups, go to `http://www.magmacom.com/~leisen/master_list.html`.

Reaching the Next Level

The groups listed in the previous section make up the top-level groups. Below each of those groups are groups on another level. For instance, under the alt category is a newsgroup called alt.3d, which contains messages about three-dimensional imaging. It's part of the alt hierarchy because, presumably, it was put together in an unauthorized way. The people who started it didn't want to go through the hassle of setting up a Usenet group, so they created an alt group—where anything goes—instead.

Another alt group is alt.animals, where people gather to talk about their favorite beasties. This group serves as a good example of how newsgroups can have more levels. Because animals are such a diverse subject, one newsgroup isn't enough. Instead of posting messages to the alt.animals group, you can choose your particular interest. The specific areas include the following:

alt.animals.dolphins

alt.animals.felines.lions

alt.animals.felines.lynxes

alt.animals.felines.snowleopards

alt.animals.horses.icelandic

alt.animals.humans

These are just a few examples of the many newsgroups available. If you're into it, chances are good there's a newsgroup for it.

All areas use the same sort of hierarchical system. For example, under the bionet first level, you can find the genome level, with such newsgroups as bionet.genome.arabidopsis (information about the Arabidopsis genome project), bionet.genome.chrom22 (a discussion of Chromosome 22), and bionet.genome.chromosomes (for those interested in the eucaryote chromosomes).

I'm Ready; Let's Read

Now that you know what newsgroups are, you'll probably want to get in and read a few. Newsgroup messages are stored in text files, saved on your service provider's computer system. You'll read the messages using a newsreader to help you filter through all the garbage.

If you are with an online service, you already have a built-in newsreader. These range from the good (MSN's newsreader is pretty capable) to the absolutely awful (CompuServe's was horrible last time I looked; maybe its next software upgrade will fix that). If you are with a service provider, they may give you a newsreader, or it may be already installed on your computer. For example, Netscape Navigator and some versions of Internet Explorer have built-in newsreaders, and Windows 98 comes with Outlook Express (see the following figure), which includes a newsreader. Or you may have one of many other newsreaders, such as WinVN, Gravity, and Free Agent on Windows or NewsWatcher and Nuntius on the Mac. There are loads of commercial newsreaders around, many of which are included with commercial software products such as Internet Chameleon, SuperHighway Access, and Internet in a Box.

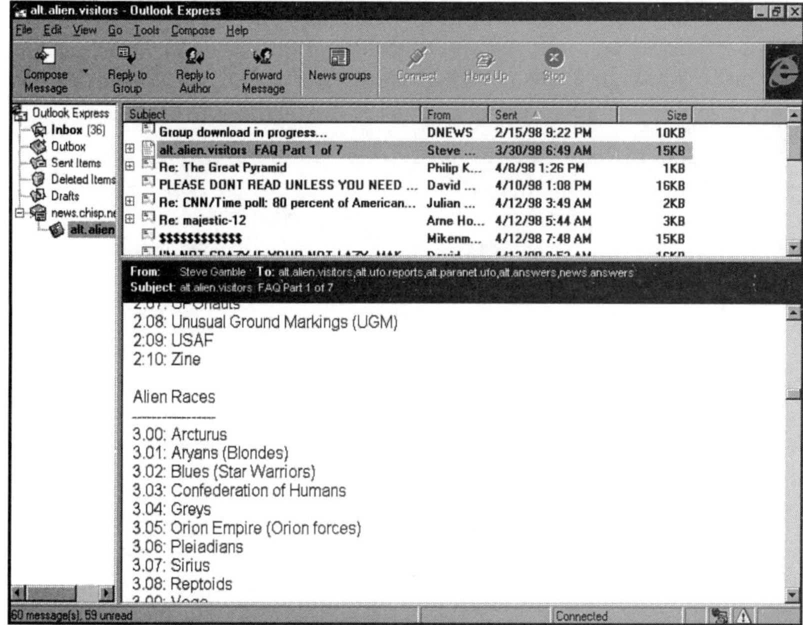

Outlook Express, which is included with Windows 98, displays the list of messages in the top pane and the selected message in the lower pane.

Techno Talk

Still Using UNIX?

If you are using a command-line interface, send email to `ciginternet@mcp.com`, with news in the Subject line to receive the newsgroup chapters (Chapters 15 and 16) from the first edition of *The Complete Idiot's Guide to the Internet*, which explain how to use a UNIX-based newsreader.

I'm going to use the Outlook Express newsreader for my examples in the next chapter. If you have something different, the commands you use will vary, but the basic principles will remain the same. Of course, different programs have different features, so you might want to try out a few programs to see what you like.

The Least You Need to Know

- A newsgroup is an area in which people with similar interests leave public messages, a sort of online public debate or discussion.
- There's a newsgroup on just about every subject you can imagine. If there isn't, there probably will be soon.
- Newsgroup names use a hierarchical system, and each group may have subgroups within it.
- The major online services have built-in newsreaders. If you are with a service provider, it may have given you a newsreader.
- Some available newsreaders include Gravity, Free Agent, and WinVN on Windows or NewsWatcher and Nuntius for the Mac.

Chapter 8

Your Daily News Delivery

In This Chapter

- Starting your newsreader
- Reading and responding to messages
- Marking messages as read
- Rot13: encoded messages
- Sending and receiving binary files
- Special newsreader features

This chapter explains how to work in the newsgroups. As I mentioned in the preceding chapter, I'm going to use the Outlook Express newsreader for my examples, but many other newsreader programs are available. Although each program is a little different, they all share certain characteristics. Check your program's documentation for the specific details and to learn about any extra features it includes. Even if you don't have Outlook Express, I suggest that you read this information because it provides a good overview of the functions available in most newsreaders.

If you are using an online service, you may be using that service's system to work in the newsgroups. For instance, in MSN you'll see links or icons all over the place representing collections of newsgroups. Many of MSN's BBSs (the term MSN uses for forums or subject areas) contain icons that represent links to newsgroups. Click the icon to go to the newsgroups. The most recent MSN software uses the Outlook Express newsreader or the

Microsoft Internet News newsreader (an earlier version of Outlook Express). You can find information about newsgroups from the main MSN window by selecting the **Communicate** link, then **Internet Center (Newsgroups)**, and then **Newsgroups**. If you're using an old version of the MSN software, you can use the Go To word **Internet** to go to the Internet BBS. In CompuServe, use **GO INTERNET**; in AOL, use the keyword **Internet** to find more information about starting the newsreaders.

A Quick Word on Setup

I want to quickly discuss setup and subscribing. If you are with an online service, there's nothing to set up; it's all done for you. If you are with a service provider, though, you may have to set up the newsreader.

First, your newsreader must know the location of your news server. Ask your service provider for the hostname of the news server (the news server is the system the service provider uses to send messages to your newsreader); the hostname may be `news.big.internet.service.com`, or `news.zip.com`, or something like that. Then check your newsreader's documentation to see where to enter this information.

The other thing you may have to do is subscribe to the newsgroups you are interested in. I've already said that your service provider has to subscribe to newsgroups; that means that the provider makes sure the newsgroups are available to its members. However, the term *subscribe* has another meaning in relation to newsgroups. You may also have to subscribe to the newsgroup to make sure that the newsgroup you want to read is available to your newsreader. Not all newsreaders make you subscribe in order to read a newsgroup. For instance, you don't have to worry about subscribing if you use MSN's newsreader or if you are reading newsgroup messages through a newsgroup "gateway" Web site such as Supernews (`http://www.supernews.com/`). Many newsreaders, however, require that you fetch a list of newsgroups from your service provider (the newsreader has a command you'll use to fetch and display the list and may even offer to do so the first time you start the program) and then subscribe to the ones you want to read. Subscribing is no big deal; you simply choose which ones you want. Until you subscribe, though, you can't see the messages.

Check This Out...

Pick Your Own Newsreader

Some of the online services have rather weak newsreaders. But if your online service allows you to get to the Internet through a TCP/IP connection, you may be able to install another newsreader, such as Gravity, Free Agent, NewsWatcher, or Nuntius. However, to do so, you may have to connect to one of the public news servers that I mentioned in Chapter 7, "Newsgroups: The Source of All Wisdom." The online services often have special news servers that are not designed to be accessed by TCP/IP; they're designed to be accessed with the service's own program. Check with your service's technical support staff.

Starting and Subscribing

The following figure shows the Outlook Express newsreader, which comes with Windows 98. The first time you use the program a dialog box opens, asking for all the configuration information. Then the Newsgroups dialog box opens (shown in the following figure) and begins grabbing a list of newsgroups from your service provider's news server.

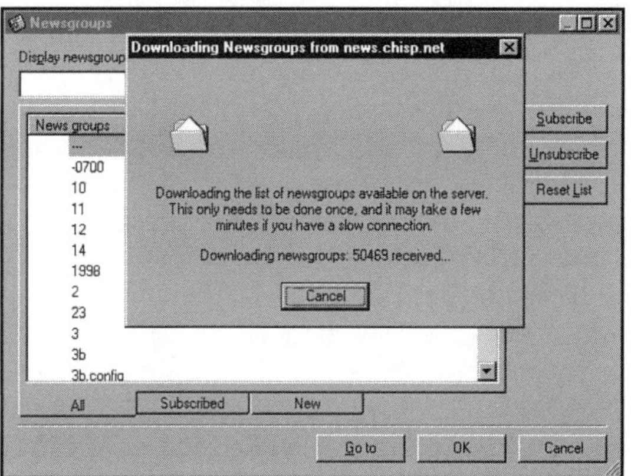

The Outlook Express Newsgroup dialog box, where you can view a list of all the newsgroups your service provider has subscribed to; at the moment, the system is downloading a list of newsgroups from the server.

Once you have the list, you can decide which newsgroups you want to read. (Remember that this is a list of only the newsgroups that your service provider has subscribed to, not a full list of all the groups distributed by Usenet. For information about finding newsgroups not included in this list, see Chapter 7.) In Outlook Express, you click the group you want to read, and then click the **Subscribe** button, or simply double-click the name. (You can also use the text box at the top; type a name or part of a name to move to that part of the list.)

Check This Out...

Where Are the Alt. Groups?

If you are with an online service, you may find that you can't initially read the alt. groups and perhaps some others as well. Your online service may regard these groups as a trifle "naughty," in which case you have to apply for permission to read them. Go to your online service's Internet forum or BBS to find out how to activate these groups, or refer to the parental control information.

When you close the dialog box, you'll see a list of the newsgroups you subscribed to in a pane on the left side of the window. You can subscribe to more later by clicking the **Newsgroup** button or by selecting **Tools**, **Newsgroups** to see the dialog box again (to refresh the list, click the **Reset List** button). You can also open the dialog box, click the **New** tab, and then click the **Reset List** button to see a list of newsgroups that your service provider has added since you last collected the list.

Click one of the newsgroups you've subscribed to in the left pane, and the top pane will display a list of messages from that newsgroup (see the next figure). It may take a little while for these messages to transfer, especially if your service provider is using the dynamic sucking feed I mentioned in the last chapter. (If so, you'll see a message header that says `Group download in progress.`)

Many newsgroups are empty—they rarely, if ever, contain messages—so you won't always see message "headers" in the top pane. Most newsreaders will have some kind of indicator showing how many messages are in the newsgroup (see the numbers in parentheses in the following illustration). If there are only a few messages, it's quite possible that all the messages are promotional messages completely unrelated to the subject of the newsgroup, perhaps advertising get-rich-quick schemes or pornographic Web sites.

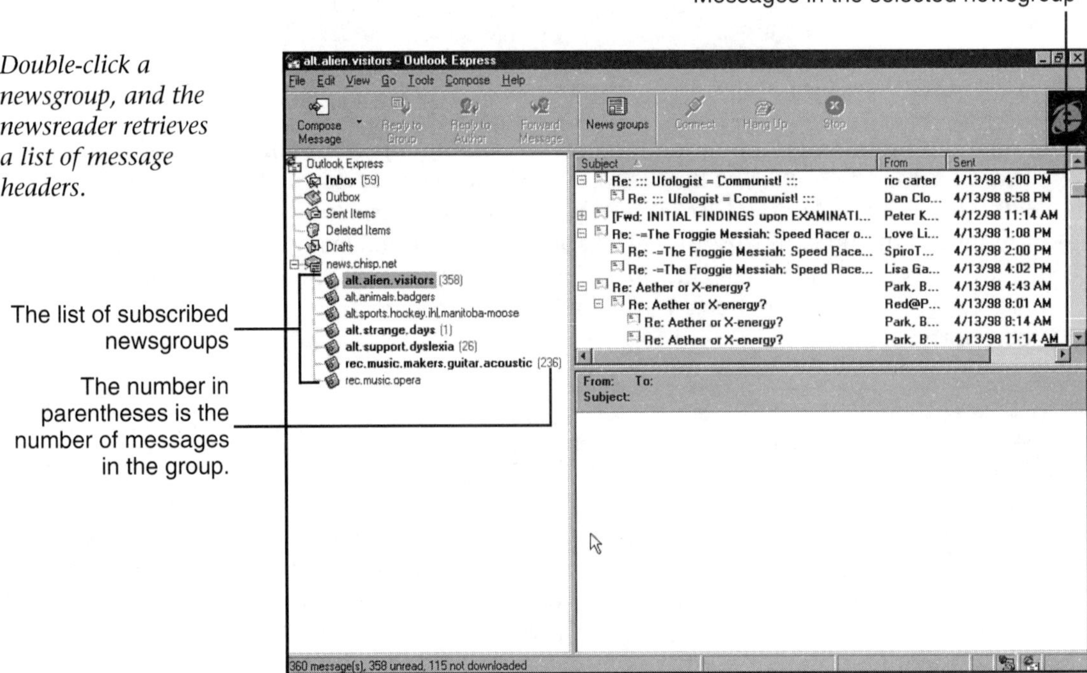

Double-click a newsgroup, and the newsreader retrieves a list of message headers.

Not All the Messages

You may not see all the messages listed at once. Some newsreaders enable you to specify a number to retrieve each time (in the program's Options or Preferences dialog box). So if the newsgroup is very busy, only a portion of the messages will be listed; you'll have to use another command to retrieve the rest.

Taking a Look

Notice that some messages are indented below others, and that there's a small – icon next to the messages. This icon indicates that the message is part of a *thread* (known as a *conversation* in some newsreaders). So what's a thread? Suppose you post a message to a newsgroup that isn't a response to anyone; it's just a new message. Then, a little later, someone else reads your message and replies. That message, because it's a reply, is part of the thread you began. Later, someone else sends a response to *that* message, and it becomes part of the thread. (Note, however, that there's generally a long lag time—a day or more—between the time someone sends a message to a newsgroup and the time that message turns up in everyone's newsreader.)

If you click the little – icon, the thread closes up, and you see only the message at the beginning of the thread. The icon changes to a + icon. Click the + icon to open up the thread again. (A message that has a – icon but does not have messages indented below it is not part of a message thread.) Most newsreaders (but not all) support threading and many other functions in a very similar manner.

To read a message, click the message's header (some newsreaders make you double-click). The newsreader retrieves the message and places it in the bottom pane of the window, as you can see in the figure on the next page.

The Messages Are Gone!

The first time you open a newsgroup, all the messages from that newsgroup currently held by your service provider are available to you. How long a message stays in the newsgroup depends on how busy that newsgroup is and how much hard disk space the service provider allows for the newsgroup messages. Eventually all messages disappear. You don't necessarily see all the newsgroup's messages the next time you use your newsreader, though. When you return to the newsgroup later, you may see all the messages *except* those marked as read.

Why didn't I just say "all the messages except those that you have read?" Well, the newsreader has no way of knowing which messages you've read—it can't see what you are doing. Instead, it has a way of marking messages that it thinks you've read, and it generally provides you with a way to mark messages as read, even if you haven't read them (in effect, providing a way for you to tell the newsreader that you don't want to see the messages).

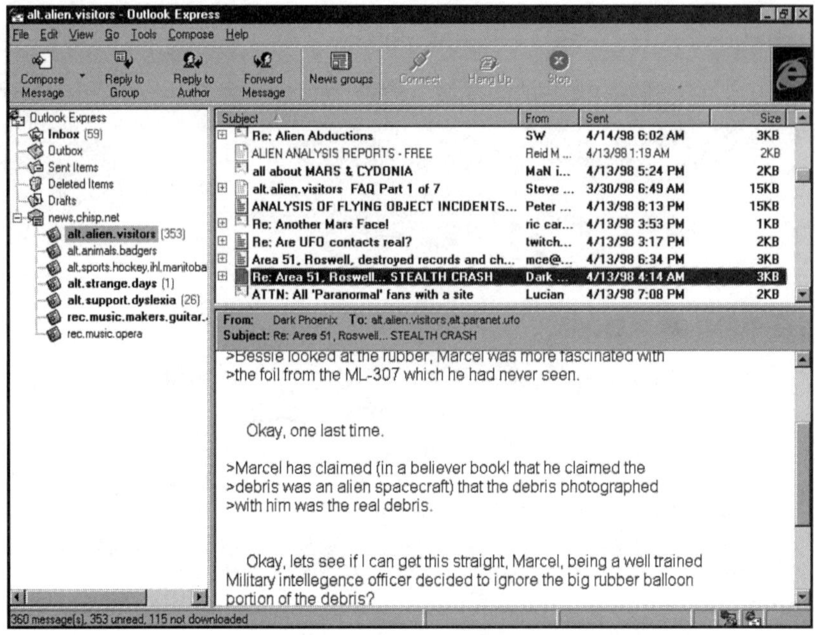

This message is from the alt.alien.visitors newsgroup.

Marking Your Messages

Most newsreaders mark a message as read when you open the message. Some newsreaders enable you to quickly scan messages without marking them as read. Outlook Express, for instance, has a setting in the Options dialog box labeled **Message is read after being previewed for x second(s)**. So you can set this option to, say, 10 seconds, allowing you to read a little bit of a message and move on, leaving the message marked as unread.

In addition, newsreaders often allow you to mark the messages as read even if you have not read them. This capability might come in handy to tell the newsreader that you don't want to see certain messages when you come back to the newsgroup in a later session. Suppose you get a couple of messages into a conversation and realize that it's pure rubbish (you'll find a lot of messages that have virtually no usefulness to anyone!). Mark the entire thread as read, and you won't see the rest of the messages the next time you open the newsgroup window. Or maybe the messages are worthwhile (to someone), but you quickly read all the messages' Subject lines and find that nothing interests you. Mark them all as read so you see only new messages the next time.

You can generally mark messages as read in several other ways as well. Here's what you can do in Outlook Express, for instance:

- ➤ Click a message header and select **Edit**, **Mark As Read**.
- ➤ Click a message header and select **Edit**, **Mark Thread As Read to** mark the entire thread as read.

- Right-click a message header and select **Mark As Read** or **Mark Thread As Read** from the shortcut menu.
- Choose **Edit**, **Mark All As Read** to mark all the current newsgroup's messages as read.

Different newsreaders handle read messages differently. Some newsreaders remove them from the list, so you only see the unread messages listed. Gravity, an excellent and popular Windows newsreader (`http://www.microplanet.com/`), does this. If you don't want the newsreader to remove the read messages, you can change the view by choosing **Newsgroup**, **Filter Display**, **Read Articles** to see just messages you've read, or **Newsgroup**, **Filter Display**, **All Articles** (or by selecting these from the drop-down list box in the toolbar) to make Gravity show the read message headers in gray text. Other newsreaders might use special icons or gray text to indicate messages that you've read.

Articles In keeping with the "news" metaphor, newsgroup messages are often known as *articles*.

Outlook Express, on the other hand, displays all the messages, read and unread. But you can select **View**, **Current View**, and then choose an option. Choosing **Unread Messages**, for instance, would make Outlook work like Gravity; it would display only the messages you haven't yet read.

Check This Out...

I Want the Message Back!

If you need to bring a message back, your newsreader probably has some kind of command that enables you to do so. For example, Gravity has the **Newsgroup**, **Filter Display**, **Read Articles** command that I just mentioned. But if your service provider no longer holds the message you want to see—that is, if the message has been removed from the service provider's hard disk to make more space for new messages—you're out of luck. So if you think there's a chance you may want a message later, save it using the **File**, **Save As** or equivalent command.

Many newsreaders even have commands for marking messages as unread. Perhaps you've read a message, but want to make sure it appears the next time you open the newsgroup. You can mark it as unread so that it will appear in the list the next time you open the newsgroup. In Outlook Express, for instance, select **Edit**, **Mark As Unread**.

Moving Among the Messages

You'll find a variety of ways to move around in your messages. As you already know, you can double-click the ones you want to view (some newsreaders use a single click). In addition, you'll find commands for moving to the next or previous message, the next or previous thread, and, perhaps, the next or previous unread message or thread. In Outlook Express, these commands are on the View, Next menu.

Many newsreaders also provide a way for you to search for a particular message. Outlook Express has several Find commands in the Edit menu, which allow you to search for a message by the contents of the From line or the Subject line. Outlook Express also enables you to search through the text of the currently selected message. Some other newsreaders have much more sophisticated utilities. In Gravity, for example, select **Search**, **Search** to access a dialog box in which you can search for text in the From or Subject lines or even within the text of the messages; you can also specify whether to search the selected newsgroup or all the subscribed newsgroups. You can even tell Gravity whether to search only those messages already transferred to the newsreader or to search messages still held by the news server.

Saving and Printing

If you run across a message that you think might be useful later, you can save it or print it. Simply marking it as unread isn't good enough because newsgroups eventually drop all messages. So sooner or later it won't be available.

Most newsreaders have a File, Save As (or File, Save) command or toolbar button. Most also have a File, Print command or button. Of course, you can always highlight the text, copy it to the Clipboard, and then paste it into another application, such as a word processor or email program.

Your Turn: Sending and Responding

There are several ways to send messages or respond to messages. For example, you can use any of the techniques listed here in Outlook Express. (Although Outlook Express is typical, and many newsreaders use these same command names, some newsreaders may use different names.)

- You can send a message that isn't a response (that is, you can start a new thread). In Outlook Express, for instance, select **Compose**, **New Message** or click the **Compose Message** toolbar button.
- You can reply to someone else's message (the reply is often known as a follow-up). Choose **Compose**, **Reply to Group** or click the **Reply to Group** button.
- You can reply to someone privately via email (that is, send a message that *doesn't* appear in the newsgroup). Select **Compose**, **Reply to Author** or click the **Reply to Author** button.
- Reply to both the author and the newsgroup at the same time. Select **Compose**, **Reply to Newsgroup and Author**.
- You can send a copy of the message to someone else. Select **Compose**, **Forward** or click the **Forward Message** button.

Sending messages to a newsgroup—or via email in response to a message—is much the same as working with an email window. You type the message and then click some kind of **Send** or **Post** button.

What's This Gibberish? Rot13

Now and again, especially in the more contentious newsgroups, you'll run into messages that seem to be gibberish. Everything's messed up, and each word seems to be a jumbled mix of characters, almost as if the message is encrypted. It is.

What you are seeing is *rot13*, a very simple substitution cipher (one in which a character is substituted for another). Rot13 means "rotated 13." In other words, each character in the alphabet is replaced by the character 13 places further along. Instead of A you see N, instead of B you see O, instead of C you see P, and so on. Got it? So to read the message, all you need to do is substitute the correct characters. Easy. (Or *Rnfl*, as I should say.)

For those of you in a hurry, there is an easier way. Most newsreaders have a command that quickly does the rot13 for you. For instance, in Outlook Express, you can select **Edit, Unscramble (rot13)**, and, like magic, the message changes into real words. If you don't run across rot13 messages and want to see what rot13 looks like, use the command to take a normal message and convert it to rot13 message (which is what I did for the following figure). How do you create one of these messages to send to a newsgroup? You'll often find a rot13 command in the window in which you create a message. For instance, in Gravity's message composition window, there's an **Options, Scramble (rot13)** command. For some reason, Outlook Express, although it can unscramble messages, doesn't let you use rot13 when sending messages.

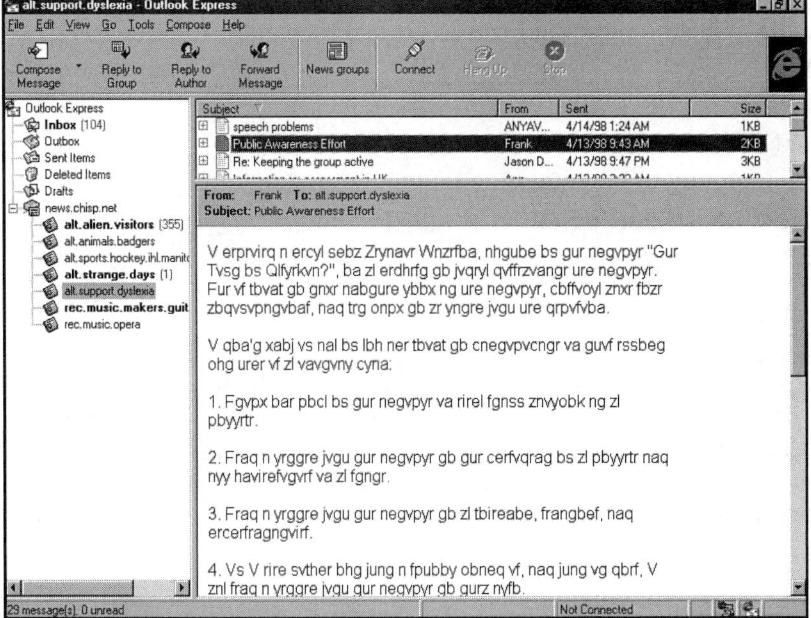

An example of a rot13 message.

You might be wondering why a person would encode a message with a system that is so ridiculously easy to break. People don't rot13 (if you'll excuse my use of the term as a verb) their messages as a security measure that's intended to make them unreadable to anyone who doesn't have the secret key. After all, anyone with a decent newsreader has the key. No, using rot13 is a way of saying "if you read this message, you may be offended; so if you are easily offended, *don't read it*!" Rot13 messages are often crude, lewd, or just plain rude. When a message is encoded with rot13, the reader can decide whether he wants to risk being offended.

Pictures (and Sounds) from Words

The newsgroups contain simple text messages. You can't place a character into a message that is not in the standard text character set. So if you want to send a computer file in a newsgroup message—maybe you want to send a picture, a sound, or a word processing document—you must convert it to text. Some of the newer newsreaders help you do this, either by automating the process of attaching MIME-formatted files to your messages or by uuencoding files and inserting them into your messages. (I discussed this issue in relation to email, back in Chapter 2, "The Premier Internet Tool: Email.") Some newsreaders will even convert such files on-the-fly and display pictures inside the message when they read the newsgroup messages; others will automatically convert the file to its original format.

If you were using Outlook Express, for example, you could follow these steps to send a file:

1. Open the message composition window using the **Compose, New Message** command or the **Compose, Reply to Newsgroup** command.
2. Choose **Insert, File Attachment** or click the **Insert File** toolbar button (the little paper clip). You'll see a typical File Open dialog box, from which you can choose the file you want to send.
3. Select the file and click **OK**. The name of the attached file appears in the bottom pane of the message composition window (see the following figure).
4. Send the message (click the **Post** button or select **File, Send Message**). The name of the file appears in the message header when you view the messages in that particular newsgroup.

What method was used to send this message? MIME or uuencode? Outlook Express doesn't make this clear. Some newsreaders let you quickly specify which method to use; Gravity, for instance, enables you to select **uuencode** or **MIME** from a drop-down list box at the top of the window. In Outlook Express, the method of transmission is hidden away. By default, the program uses uuencode when sending to newsgroups (that's the standard method of sending files to newsgroups). If you want to use MIME, you have to go back to the main Outlook Express window, choose **Tools**, **Options**, click the **Send** tab, click the **Settings** button next to **News Sending Format: Plain Text**, and click the **MIME** option button. Convenient, eh? (It doesn't matter too much when sending messages to newsgroups, but Outlook Express uses the same method for email messages, which is very inconvenient because you may want to switch between MIME and uuencode now and again.)

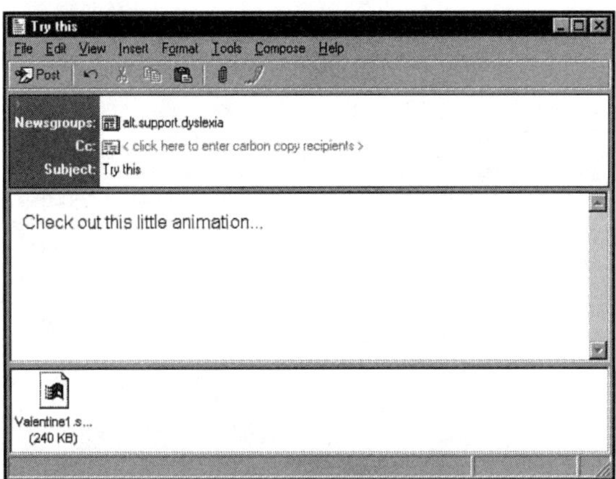

Most newsreaders let you send uuencoded or MIME files to a newsgroup.

When a message with an attached file is posted to a newsgroup, what do participants of that newsgroup see? If the attached file is an image, as many are, some newsreaders will display the picture inside the message. Others may display the message text, something like that shown in the following figure.

Techno Talk

No Built-in Converter?

If you are using a newsreader that doesn't have a built-in conversion system, you can save the message on your hard disk and then use a conversion program such as Wincode (a Windows program that converts uuencode), munpack (a DOS program that converts MIME), or Yet Another Base64 Decoder (a Macintosh program that converts both uuencode and MIME).

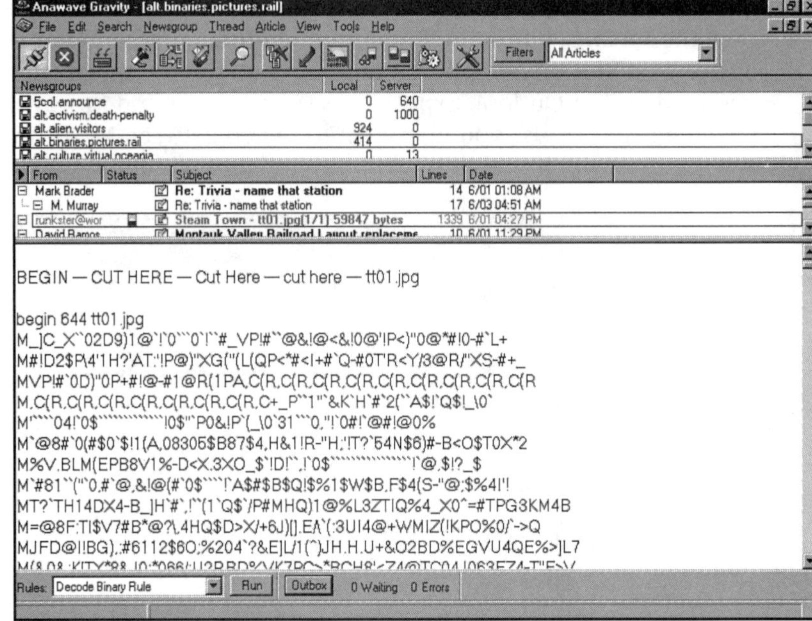

This message contains an attached file. The jumbled text is the file, converted to text. The text must be converted back before you can view the file.

Even if your newsreader doesn't initially display the image within the message, it may be able to convert the image file. In particular, newsreaders can often convert .GIF, .JPEG, and perhaps .BMP files to their original formats. In the case of Gravity, for instance, you can click the **View Image** button or select **Article**, **View**, and Gravity converts the file for you and then places it in a viewer window (as you can see in the following figure). Outlook Express will display the image by default. You can tell it *not* to display images by choosing **Tools**, **Options**, clicking the **Read** tab, and clearing the **Automatically Show Picture Attachments in Messages** check box.

A few newsreaders can even decode several messages together. If someone posts a large picture split into several pieces, for instance (as people often do), the newsreader may automatically retrieve all the pieces and paste them together.

The Fancy Stuff

Some newsreaders have useful extra features. For example, the newsreader may be able to automatically "flag" messages if the header contains a particular word. Or you may be able to set up the newsreader to automatically remove a message if the header contains a particular word. Outlook Express has a filtering system that you can use to automatically throw away some messages, depending on who sent the message or what the subject is, if it's older than a specified time, or if it's longer than a specified length (choose **Tools**,

Newsgroup Filters). Some other newsreaders have much better filtering systems. Gravity, for instance, can throw the message away, display a special alert message, or save the message in a text file according to what appears in the header or body text.

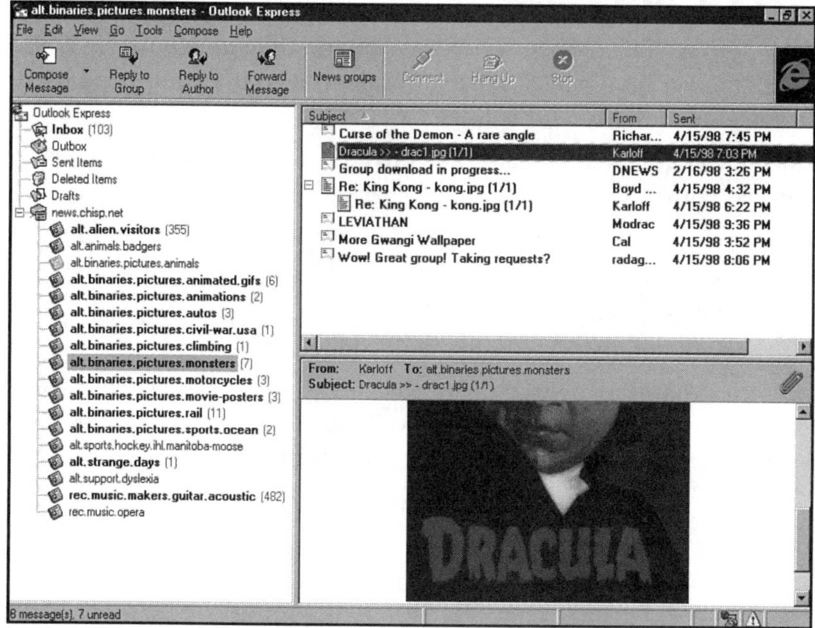

In this case, the message window displays an image that's been inserted into a message.

Many newsreaders display links in the newsgroup messages. You can click e-mail addresses or Web URLs that appear in messages to automatically open the mail window or your browser. Outlook Express can set up a little slide show, displaying one image after another in messages that contain multiple images.

Newsreaders can do a lot of different things, so you may want to experiment to find out what's available in the newsreader you have; if you spend a lot of time in newsgroups, you may want to go searching for the most capable newsreader.

A Word of Warning

Newsgroups can be addictive. You can find messages about anything that interests you, angers you, or turns you on. If you are not careful, you can spend half your life in the newsgroups. You sit down in the morning to check your favorite newsgroups, and the next thing you know you haven't bathed, eaten, or picked up the kids from school.

Hang around the newsgroups, and you'll find people who are obviously spending a significant amount of time writing messages. These people are usually independently wealthy (that is, they work for large corporations who don't mind paying for them to talk politics over the Internet or who don't know that they are paying them to do so). If you have a job, a family, and a life, be careful!

The Least You Need to Know

- To begin using the newsgroups, start your newsreader, and then download a list of newsgroups from the server. You may also have to subscribe to the groups you want to read; each newsreader does this a little differently.
- A good newsreader lets you view a "thread" or "conversation," which shows how messages relate to each other.
- Rot13 is a special encoding system that stops people from accidentally stumbling across offensive messages. Many newsreaders have a rot13 command that converts the message to normal text.
- You can include binary files in messages using uuencode or MIME.
- Many newsreaders these days can decode uuencode and MIME attachments. If your newsreader doesn't, you'll need a utility such as Wincode or munpack (for Windows and DOS) or Yet Another Base64 Decoder (for the Macintosh). Or you can get a better newsreader.

Chapter 9

Yak, Yak, Yak: Chatting in Cyberspace

In This Chapter

- What are chat and talk?
- Chat sessions and public auditoriums
- Using the online service chat rooms
- Using a graphical chat program
- Working with IRC (Internet Relay Chat)
- Real uses for chat

One of the most important—yet least discussed—systems in cyberspace is chat. It's important because its immense popularity has been a significant factor in the growth of online services (not so much the Internet as a whole). It is, perhaps, the least discussed because the fact is that many people use the chat systems as a way to talk about sex and even to contact potential sexual partners. In this chapter, you'll take a look at chatting in cyberspace, in Internet Relay Chat (the Internet's largest chat system) as well as in the online services. You'll also learn that there's plenty more than sex-related chat.

Chatting and Talking

What is chat? Here's what it's *not:* a system that allows you to talk out loud to people across the Internet or an online service. That sort of system does exist, but a chat system does not use voice; it uses the typed word. Communications are carried out by typing messages.

What's the difference between chat and email, then? With email, you send a message and then go away and do something else. You come back later—maybe later that day, maybe later that week—to see whether you have a response. Chat is quite different: it takes place in *real time,* to use a geek term. (What other kind of time is there but real time, one wonders.) In other words, you type a message, and the other party in the chat session sees the message almost instantly. He can then respond right away, and you see the response right away. It's just like, yes, a chat—only you are typing instead of talking.

Chat Can Have Voice

The problem with the Internet is that you make a statement today, and tomorrow it's wrong. Right now the use of voice in chat sessions is rare. Voice *is* being added to chat, though, and you can expect chat sessions to gradually come to resemble the real thing, as people type less and talk more. However, as wonderful as that may sound, it presents a problem. Many IRC (Internet Relay Chat) users are working at big companies, sitting in their little cubicles, typing away and looking busy. Their bosses may think they are working hard, but they are gabbing on IRC, and voices would just give away the game!

There's also an Internet system known as *talk,* which also isn't talking. Talk is a system in which one person can "call" another on the Internet and, once a connection has been made, can type messages to the other person. It's very similar to chat once the two parties are connected, but the manner in which you connect is different. With chat, you have to go to a chat "room" to chat with people; with talk, you simply open the talk program, enter the email address of the person you want to connect to, and click a button to call that person (who may not be available, of course).

To further complicate the issue, some Voice on the Net programs incorporate these talk programs, but they sometimes call them *chat* systems! For instance, Netscape Communicator's Conference program (known as CoolTalk in earlier versions of Netscape Navigator) has a little program that you can use to type messages to another person, but it's called the Chat tool.

Chat is one of those "love it or hate it" kind of things. Many people just love it; they even find it addictive, spending hours online each night. Personally, I can do without it. It's an awkward way to communicate. I can type faster than most people, yet I still find chat rather clunky. I've been the guest in chat question-and-answer sessions in both MSN and CompuServe and at a Web site called TalkCity, and quite frankly my experiences with chat sessions have not exactly been the high points of my life. The sessions tended to be chaotic at worst, simply slow at best. You run into too many people trying to ask questions at once (some chat systems are not designed to allow someone to control the flow of questions very well), lots of typos, long pauses while you wait for people to type and they wait for you, and so on. I'm no chat fan, but chat certainly appeals to millions of people.

> Check This Out...
>
> **Sex?** Should I be talking about sex in this book? My editors have suggested that I avoid sexual subjects for fear of offending people. Chat, however, is a case in which it's hard to avoid the sexual. Certainly many people go to chat rooms for nonsexual purposes. But be warned that many (possibly most?) are there to meet members of the opposite sex (or the same sex in some cases) for sexual purposes.

Two Types of Sessions

Chat sessions are categorized into two types: private and group. Generally, what happens is that you join a *chat room*, in which a lot of people are talking (okay, typing) at once. Then someone may invite you to a private room, where just the two of you can talk without the babble of the public room. These private rooms are often used for cybersex sessions, although of course they can also be used for more innocent purposes, such as catching up on the latest news with your brother-in-law in Paris, discussing a project with a colleague, or talking about a good scuba-diving spot in Mexico.

Public chat rooms are often used as a type of auditorium or lecture hall. A famous or knowledgeable person responds to questions from the crowd. Michael Jackson and Buzz Aldrin, for instance, have been guest "speakers" in chat forums, as have many other world-famous people.

Score One for the Online Services

I'm going to mostly discuss the online services in this chapter because they generally have the most popular, and in some ways the best, chat systems. Chat has been extremely important to the growth of the online services, so they've made an effort to provide good chat services. Chat on the Internet, though, is still relatively little used and in many ways not as sophisticated. (That's changing as many new chat programs designed for the Internet, often running through the Web, are being introduced.)

If you use CompuServe or AOL, you can get to the chat rooms by using the GO or keyword **chat**. Most forums have conference rooms for chatting too, but they are often empty. If you use The Microsoft Network, you'll find chat rooms scattered all over the place; almost every forum (or BBS as they're known in MSN-speak) has a chat room. Click the chat link and either Microsoft Chat will open, or, in a few cases, a simple chat program appears inside the Web page. (The latest MSN system is based on Web pages displayed inside Internet Explorer.) If you're still using the older software, you can go to a Chat BBS by opening the **Communicate** menu and selecting **Chat Central.**

If you have Windows 98, you'll find that the Microsoft Chat program is available from the Start menu: **Start, Programs, Internet Explorer, Microsoft Chat.** This program is currently set up to work with a couple of chat servers: `chat.msn.com` is available only to Microsoft Network members, but `publicchat.msn.com` is open to anyone, even nonmembers—if you can connect to the Internet, you can open Microsoft Chat and connect to this chat server.

Using Internet Relay Chat (IRC) on the Internet is a little more complicated than using the online services. I cover IRC later in this chapter.

Chatting in AOL

In AOL, click the **People** button, and then select **People Connection** from the menu that opens (if you're not using the latest version of the software, you may have to use the keyword **chat**, or click the **People Connection** button in the Welcome window). You'll go straight to a chat window (see the next figure). Use the **List Chats** button to see all the available chat rooms. There are about a dozen categories and hundreds of individual rooms.

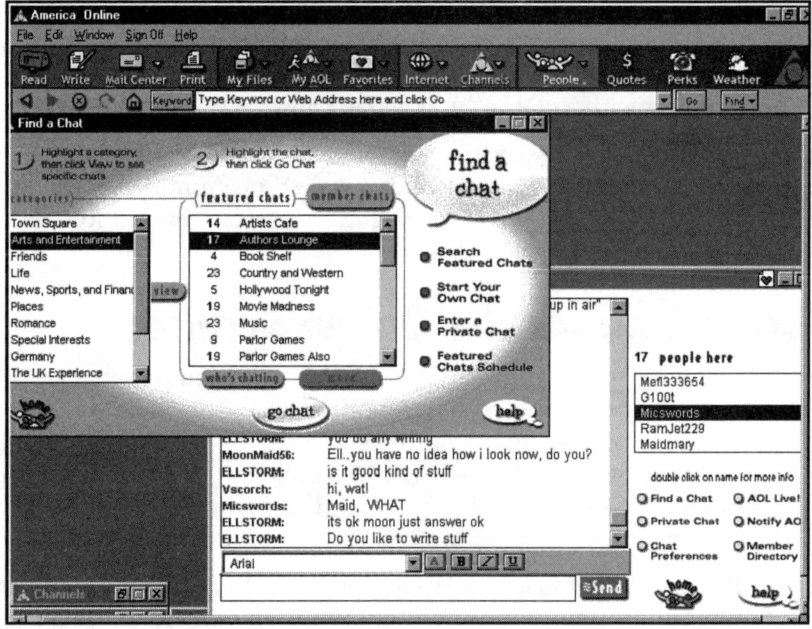

AOL's chat room system: lots of glitz, very busy.

AOL's system enables you to create private rooms so that you and your friends (or family or colleagues) can use that room without interference. If you want to talk to only one person, you just double-click the person's name in the People Here box and click the **Message** button. If the person responds, you get your own private message window for just the two of you. You can see in the following figure that this message box has special buttons that allow you to modify the text format.

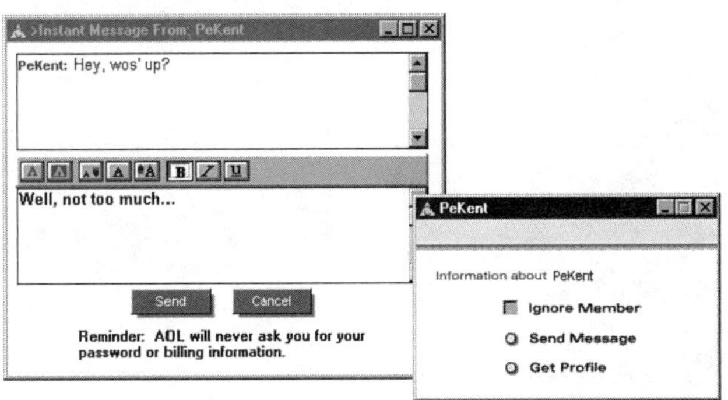

AOL provides you with a little message window in which you can carry on private conversations.

CompuServe's Chat Rooms

To use a CompuServe chat room, you can go to just about any forum or to the Chat forum, where you'll find loads of chat sessions. Most forums have a number of conference rooms, but unless some kind of presentation has been scheduled, they may all be empty. You can be sure to find people to chat with in the Chat forum, though (**GO CHAT**, or click the big **Chat** button in the main menu).

CompuServe's chat system has been completely revamped just recently, and the old CB radio analogy has completely gone (CompuServe used to call their chat system a CB system, after the Citizen Band radio systems that were so popular in the 1970s). You'll start by picking a chat category (General Chat, Adult Chat, Conferences and Special Events, and so on). Then click the **Chat** button to see a list of chat rooms. Double-click a room to open the chat window, or click a room and then click the **Participate** or **Observe** button to take part in the chat room's discussion or just "listen in." (See the following figure.)

The list of rooms shows you how many people are in each room; this might be helpful if you want to pick a quiet one or get right into the action. As you can see in the figure, you can "listen" by reading other people's messages. Whenever you want to jump in, you can type your own message in the lower panel of the window; press **Enter** to send the message, or click the **Send** button. You can invite people to private rooms, too; click the **Who's Here** button to see a list of members, and then click the person you want to speak with and click **Private Chat**.

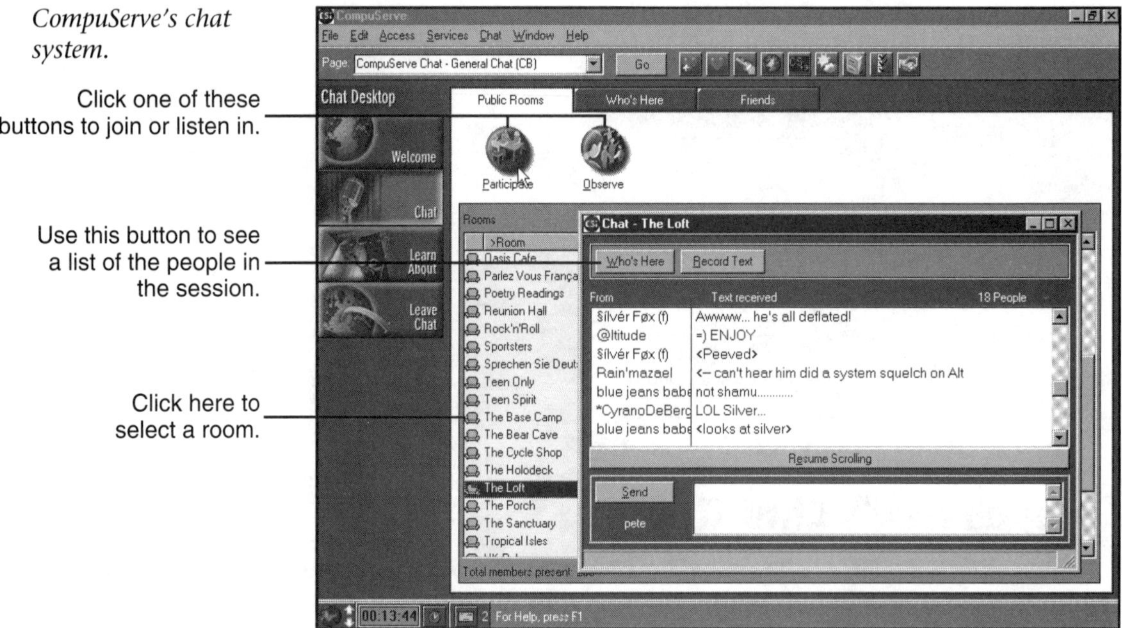

CompuServe's chat system.

Microsoft Chat and MSN

Microsoft Network uses a program called Microsoft Chat. Microsoft has included this program in Windows 98 as well, so even if you don't have an MSN account, you can still use Microsoft Chat.

To open Microsoft Chat, select **Start, Programs, Internet Explorer, Microsoft Chat**. You'll see a dialog box that lets you select the server you want to work with. If you're an MSN member, you can use either of the servers (there are currently only two). If you're not an MSN member, select `publicchat.msn.com`; although this chat server is hosted by MSN, anyone can enter its chat rooms. When you select **OK**, you'll see a list of rooms. Just double-click the one you want to enter. If you're an MSN member, you can also enter a chat room directly from one of MSN's forums; lots of chat rooms are scattered around, and clicking a link will open Microsoft Chat.

MSN's chat system used to be rather weak; it simply didn't have all the features available on other online system chat rooms. However, the latest version of Microsoft Chat is very good, providing all sorts of useful features. You can send files and sounds, include links to Web sites and email addresses (recipients just have to click a link to activate it), hold private conversations with chat room members, and so on. If you want to set up a private chat you can do that, too; you have to create a room, and then invite the person to that room. It's not quite as convenient as, say, AOL, in which you can invite someone to a room and the room is automatically created if the invitee accepts. But still, Microsoft

Chat has a number of handy features; you can make your new room invisible to all but those you invite, make the room accessible by invitation only, and even define an access password.

Microsoft Chat has two chat modes: text and Comic Chat. Comic Chat is a type of chat system that uses **avatars** (which we'll look at under "Pick Your Avatar," later in this chapter), which are little pictures that represent participants. Both systems use the same basic program, but anyone can choose to view the chat in text or Comic Chat mode. You can see an example of the text mode in the following figure; I've included a picture of Comic Chat mode later in this chapter.

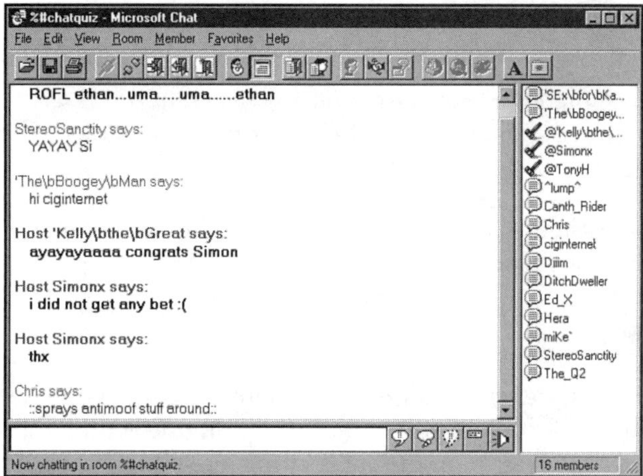

MSN's chat system can work in two modes: text only and Comic Chat. You can see the Comic Chat mode later in this chapter.

Commands to Look For

Although the details for using each chat system differ, a number of features are similar in most systems. For example, these features are generally similar (even though the names may vary):

- Who or People Here shows a list of people currently participating in the chat session.
- Invite enables you to invite a participant in the current chat to a private chat room. (On AOL, you send the person an Instant Message.)
- Ignore or Squelch enables you to tell the program to stop displaying messages from a particular user. This command is very useful for shutting up obnoxious chat-room members. (You'll find a lot of them!) It's also a good tool for "tuning out" conversations you don't want to hear.
- Profile allows you to view information about a particular participant, including whatever information that person decided to make public. Some systems allow more

information than others, but the information might include a person's email address, interests, real name, and even phone number and address in some systems (although most participants choose *not* to include this information).

- Change Profile or Handle gives you access to the place where you'll change your own information. Some systems let you change your profile from within the Chat program, but on others you may have to select a menu option or command elsewhere.
- Record or Log or Capture usually lets you record a session. (Of course, in most cases you'll want to forget the drivel—oh, there I go again!)
- Preferences enables you to set up how the system works: whether to tell you when people enter or leave the room, for example.
- Kick or Ban are available on some systems if you set up the chat room yourself. Kick allows you to remove someone from the chat room; Ban stops the person from getting back in.

No matter which chat system you use, read the documentation carefully so you can figure out exactly how to get the most out of it.

Pick Your Avatar

The latest thing in chat is the use of graphical systems in which you select an *avatar*, an image that represents you in the chat session. The first figure on the following page shows a room with several avatars, each representing a real-life person, in Club Chat. Selecting an avatar is a simple matter of clicking a button in the top-left portion of the window, and then choosing from a drop-down list box. Then you can type a message in the text box at the bottom and click the **Send** button. You can also choose from a small selection of sounds ("Aaaah," "Joy," "Doh," and other such intellectual utterings).

So far I've heard mixed reactions to these graphical chat systems. Some people say they are awful; some say they're nothing special; some say it's just stuff to get in the way of the chat. Others really like them. Experiment and decide for yourself.

The major online services have avatar chats. For example, Microsoft Network's Comic Chat is a form of avatar chat (see the second figure on the following page). Other avatar chats are available on the Web. Try one of these sites, which have links to a number of chat sites that use avatars:

The Palace (`http://www.palacespace.com/`)

WorldCHAT (`http://www.worlds.net/`)

Although you can reach these sites on the Web, you have to download a special Chat program and then reconnect using that program.

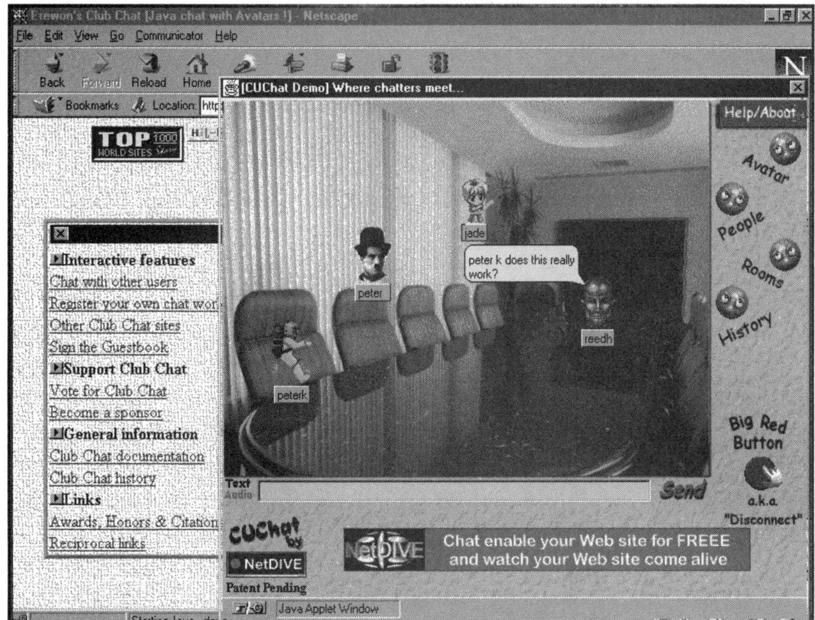

Playing with avatars in Club Chat.

MSN's Comic Chat in action. You can pick your own avatar and even change the avatar's expressions by clicking the box in the lower-right corner.

They're Everywhere!

These avatar chats are now sprouting on the Internet like weeds in my backyard. The Palace software, for instance, allows people to set up their own chats at their own Web sites—and many people have done so already. For more information, see the Palace site (`http://www.palacespace.com/`) or look at Yahoo's 3D Worlds information (`http://www.yahoo.com/Recreation/Games/Internet_Games/Virtual_Worlds/3D_Worlds/`).

Web Chat's Coming Up Fast

Most chat participants are still using chat systems running on the online services, but it may not always be that way. Hundreds, perhaps thousands, of Web-based chat systems have sprung up and in some cases are quite good. There are chat sites set up for celebrity "visits," education-related issues, gay chat, skateboarding chat, and more. If you're a chat fan and have been hiding out in the online service chat rooms, perhaps it's time to take a look at the World Wide Web and see what's available. (Here's a good place to start: `http://www.yahoo.com/Computers_and_Internet/Internet/World_Wide_Web/Chat/`.)

Chat Versus Discussion Group There's a little confusion on the Web about the difference between chat rooms and discussion groups. Some Web sites advertising "chat" actually have Web forums. If the discussion isn't "real time"—you type something, someone immediately responds, you type back—then it's not chat.

Web chat systems vary from the very clunky—your message is displayed within a Web page, which must be constantly rewritten to see the conversation—to the very good. The better sites, such as TalkCity (`http://www.talkcity.com/`), have their own chat programs that you must download before you enter the chat room. These are true chat systems, with the same sort of features as the chat rooms in the online services. You can see an example of the Talk City chat program in the following figure.

Internet Relay Chat: Productivity Sinkhole?

I'll admit I haven't spent a lot of time in Internet Relay Chat (IRC). That's mainly because what few visits I have made have been so uninspiring that I can't think of a good reason to return. But there I go again, slamming a chat system. Many thousands of people really *do* like IRC, so let's take a look at how to use it.

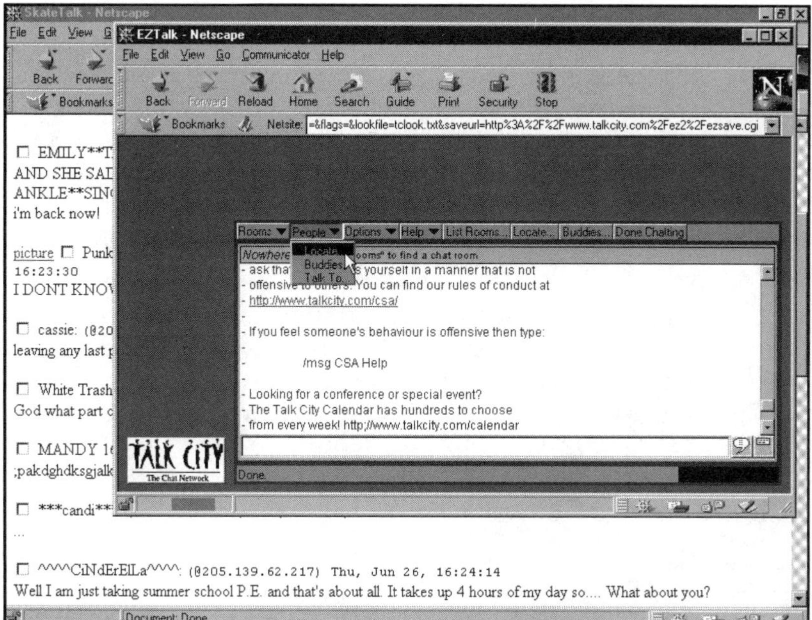

Talk City, one of the Web's more sophisticated chat sites. In the background, you can see a more primitive Web-page type chat system.

Techno Talk

Command-line User?

If you don't have a graphical user interface, you cannot use the fancy IRC programs, of course. You'll have to use a command-line interface to IRC, which is very awkward, but thousands of other people have managed, and you can, too. For help doing this, you can get the IRC chapter from my out-of-print book *The Complete Idiot's Next Step with the Internet* by sending email to `ciginternet@mcp.com` and putting the word **irc** in the Subject line (leave the message body blank).

Step 1: Get the Software

The first thing you'll need is an IRC *client program*. That's the program you'll use to send and receive IRC communications. If you are using a Mac, try Ircle, a well-known IRC program for that operating system. On Windows, you might try mIRC or PIRCH.

Go to a software archive and download a copy of some kind of IRC program. Then follow the documentation's instructions to set up the program and spend some time reading everything there is to read. Unfortunately, IRC can be a little complicated, if only because it has so many features.

Step 2: Connect to a Server

Nicknames

Your nickname is the name by which you will be iden-tified in the chat ses-sions. Notice that you can remain anonymous in a chat session by entering in-correct information into the Real Name and Email Address boxes.

The next thing you have to do is connect to an IRC server somewhere. IRC servers are programs run on someone's computer out on the Internet and act as "conduits," carry-ing information between IRC participants. These servers are the equivalent of the online services' chat forums. At a server, you'll find hundreds of IRC channels that you can choose from.

Find the command that you must use to connect to a server. With mIRC, for instance, the dialog box in the following figure opens automatically when you start the program. You can get back to it later (to select a different server, for example) by choosing **File**, **Setup**.

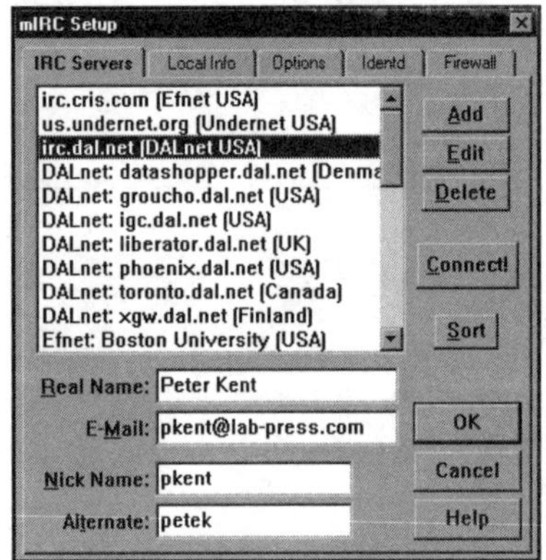

Here's where you choose a server to connect to and enter your personal information in mIRC.

Select the server you want to use, click the **Connect** button, and away you go. You're connected to the server, and a dialog box appears, listing some of the channels (see the next figure). This listing is by no means all the channels; most servers have hundreds. This box holds a list of the ones you are interested in (actually it's initially a list of channels that the programmer thought you might like to start with, but you can add more). To get into one of these channels, double-click it.

If you'd like to see a complete listing of all the channels, close the dialog box, type **/list** in the text box at the bottom of the main window (which is where you type your messages and any IRC commands), and press **Enter**.

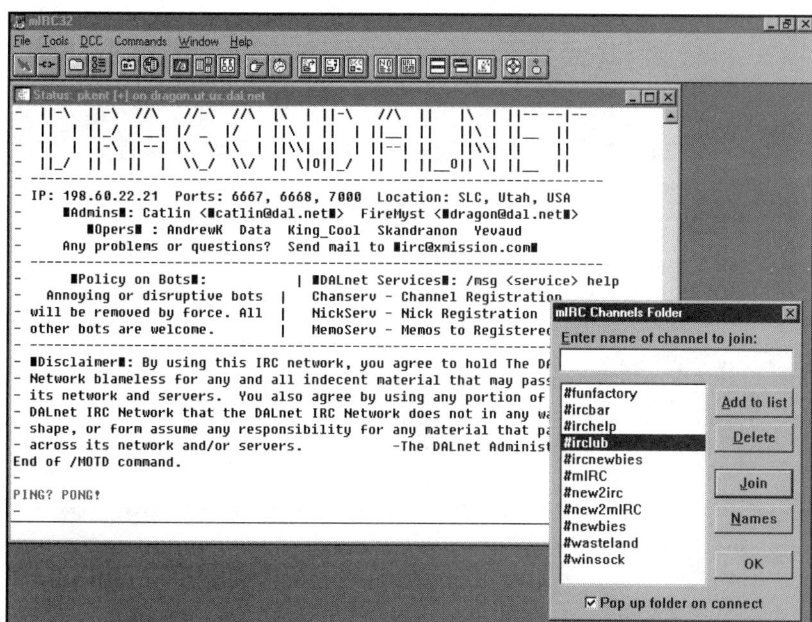

You've connected, and you're ready to join a channel.

Know the Commands

IRC commands begin with a slash (/), and there are loads of them. Most IRC programs hide the commands from you to some degree, providing menu commands instead, but they don't replace all of them. Some things can only be done using the original typed IRC command.

In mIRC, the **/list** command opens a window in which all the channels are listed. This window may take a while to open because there are so many channels. As you can see in the title bar in the first figure on the following page, this server has 744 channels! If you want to enter one of these channels, all you have to do is double-click it.

Once you are in a channel, just start typing; it's much like chatting in any other chat system. In the second figure on the following page, you can see a chat in progress. As usual, you type your message in the little box at the bottom, and you view what's going on in the big panel. The participants are listed on the right side. You can invite one to a private chat by double-clicking a name. You can right-click to see a pop-up menu with a series of commands such as Whois (which displays information about the user in another window).

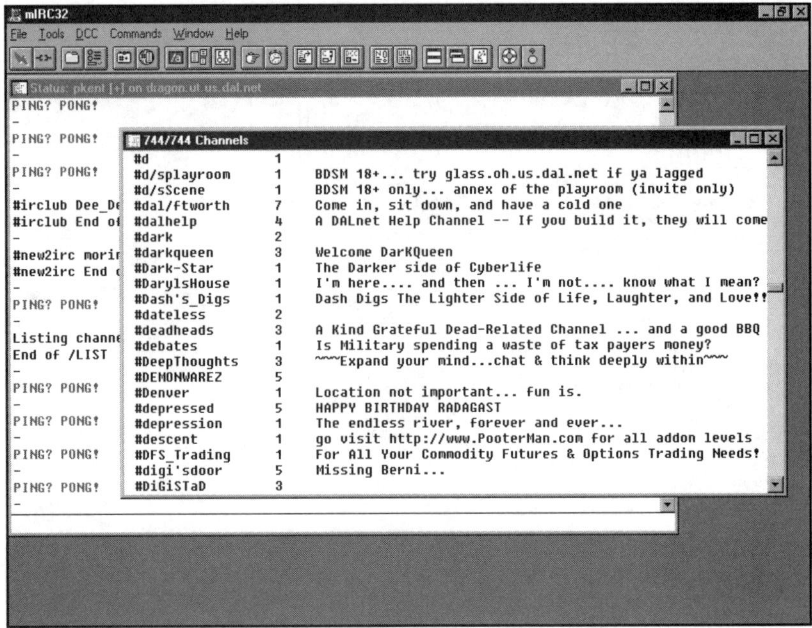

mIRC's channel listing: Are 744 channels enough for you?

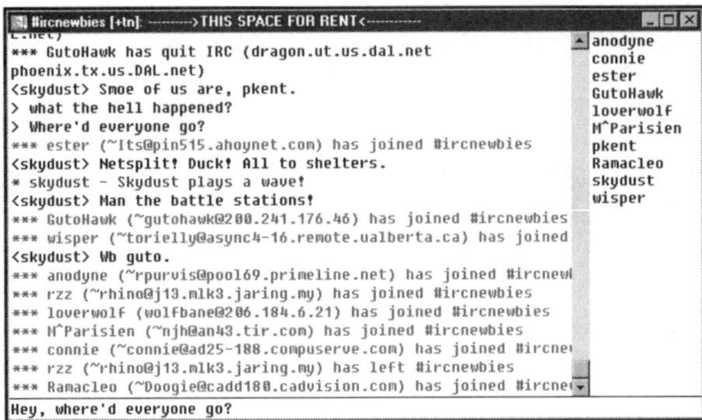

Here's where you chat in mIRC.

There's a lot to learn about IRC. IRC programs are a little complicated because IRC has so many features. For example, you can transmit computer files to other users; people often send pictures to each other. You can also add a special program that reads (with a voice, that is) incoming messages from other chat members, and you can ban, kick, and ignore users (if you open a channel, you have some control over who you let in) and plenty more.

Spend some time playing around with the program you choose to see what it can do, and read the documentation or help files carefully. It's complicated stuff, but once you learn what one program can do, you can pick up how to use one of the others very quickly.

How Many Conversations Can You Keep Going?

IRC is almost a game. People get into multiple chat sessions at once. They chat in the main window, and then they have a few private chat sessions in other windows. That's why it takes them so long to respond sometimes!

What Is It Good For? Real Uses for Chat

It could be argued that chat systems are a complete waste of perfectly good electrons. (*I* wouldn't claim that, of course, but I'm sure many people would.) The chat is often little better than gibberish. "Hey, dude, how goes it? ...Cool man, you?...Yeah, doing well; you chatted with that babe CoolChick, yet?...No, she cute?" Blah...blah...blah. This is neither educational nor particularly interesting.

I should note that not all chats are quite so inane. Chats allow people of like interests to get together in cyberspace, reaching across continents to discuss issues that interest them in a way that would be prohibitively expensive using any other technology. (I've proposed a stupidity tax to make the totally stupid chats prohibitively expensive once again.)

There are other worthwhile uses, too. This list points out a few such scenarios:

- Technical support can be given using chat rooms. This use will become more important as more software is distributed across the Internet. For instance, a small company that, in the past, may have provided support only within the United States can now provide support to the entire world by using chat.
- Companies can use chat systems for keeping in touch. An international company with salespeople throughout the world can arrange weekly "meetings" in a chat room. Families can do the same so that they can keep in touch even when they're separated by thousands of miles.
- Groups that are planning international trips might want to try chat rooms. For instance, if a scout group is traveling to another country to spend the summer with another group, a chat room could provide a way for the leaders to "get together" beforehand to iron out final details.
- Colleges can use chat. Many colleges already provide courses over the Internet, using the Web to post lessons and using email to send in completed assignments. In addition, teachers can use chat to talk with students, regardless of the geographic distance between them.

However, having said all that, chat may eventually be superseded by what's known as Voice on the Net, a system that allows you to place "phone calls" across the Internet and even have conference calls. International phone rates have dropped tremendously in the last couple of years, making connecting by typing less attractive than it used to be.

What About Talk?

I mentioned *talk* earlier in this chapter, and then pretty much ignored it. Talk, you'll remember, is a system that allows two people to get together and chat privately online; no need to go to a chat site, you just open your talk program and begin typing.

In the UNIX world—and in the early days, the Internet was firmly entrenched in the UNIX world—talk is widely available and frequently used. (There are two popular UNIX talk programs, imaginatively named *talk* and *ntalk*.) But very few Internet users have installed talk on their Windows or Macintosh systems—in fact, most have no idea what this system is.

You can still find talk programs, though. In fact, talk seems to be undergoing a renaissance, as a number of good talk programs have been introduced recently and promoted by large companies. America Online recently launched *AOL Instant Messenger*, a talk system that allows any Internet user to talk with any other Internet user. AOL members already have Instant Messenger installed (as long as they're using the latest AOL software). Other Internet users can download the software from the AOL Web site (`http://www.aol.com/`).

Yahoo! has a similar program, called *Yahoo! Pager*. You'll need a Yahoo! email account to use this system, but the account is free. (Yahoo! is apparently attempting to justify its $5.4 billion market capitalization by launching services and programs that used to be created by shareware programmers working in basements.) You can download this system from `http://pager.yahoo.com/pager/` (you can see Yahoo! Pager in the following illustration). Remember, though, that whatever system you choose, the people you want to talk to have to use the same system.

Other talk programs are available; you can find them in the software sites mentioned in Appendix C. I used to recommend that people try out a few and see which they prefer, and then tell their friends to download the same one. But it's probably a good idea to work with one of the major systems, such as AOL Instant Messenger or Yahoo! Pager, because they're now in wide use.

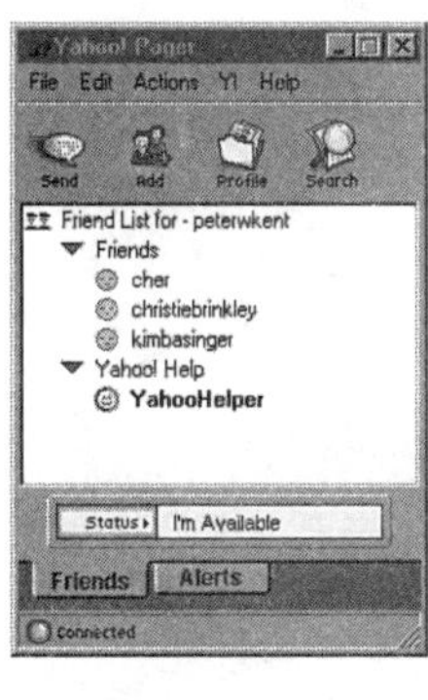

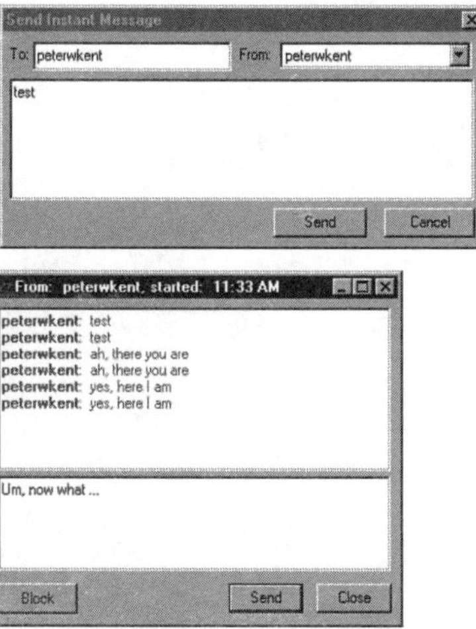

Yahoo! Pager allows you to send a message to one of your friends; when the friend receives the message, a chat window opens and you can continue in a chat session. I don't have any friends, so I'm talking to myself in this illustration.

The Least You Need to Know

- A *chat* system allows participants to take part in public discussions or to move to private "rooms" if they prefer. A *talk* system is a direct link between participants in a conversation, without the need for a public chat room.
- Neither chat nor talk uses voices; you type messages and send them to and from.
- Chat sessions are often very crude and sexually orientated; if you're easily offended, pick your chat room carefully.
- All the online services have popular chat systems. Many Web sites have chat rooms, too.
- If you want to use Internet Relay Chat, you'll have to download an IRC program from a shareware site and then connect across the Internet to a server.
- You can use chat rooms to keep in touch with friends, family, or colleagues or to meet new people.

Chapter 10

What on Earth Are All Those File Types?

In This Chapter

- About the directory (folder) system
- Picking a download directory
- File extensions and file types
- File types you'll run into
- What are compressed files?
- Working with compressed and archive files
- Avoiding viruses

It's possible to work with a computer for years without really understanding directories and file types. I know people who simply save files from their word processor (the only program they ever use) "on the disk." *Where on the disk?* Well, you know, on the hard disk. *Yes, but where? Which directory?* Well, you know, where the program saves the files.

You can get away with this lack of knowledge if you use only one program and don't use it too much. But if you plan to spend any time on the Internet and plan to make the most of your time there, you'll need to understand a bit more about files and directories. You'll come across a plethora of file types, and it helps if you understand what you are looking at.

About Download Directories

I don't want to spend a lot of time explaining what a directory is. This is very basic computing stuff, and if you don't understand it you should probably read an introduction to computing (such as *The Complete Idiot's Guide to PCs* by Joe Kraynak). However, I'll quickly explain it, and that may be enough.

You can think of a directory as an area on your hard disk that stores computer files. You might think of it as a file folder in a filing cabinet. The hard disk is the filing cabinet, holding dozens, maybe hundreds, of folders (directories). In some graphical user interfaces, such as recent versions of Microsoft Windows and the Macintosh, directories are actually called *folders*. (But I've been using the term *directory* too long to give it up now.)

If you look inside a filing cabinet and open a file folder, what do you find? Documents—those are the individual files. You may also find another folder within the first folder. That's a *subdirectory*. So directories can contain files and other directories, and those directories can contain more files and more directories (more subdirectories), and so on. Thus you have what is known as the directory tree. (The following figure shows what this "tree" looks like.) The point of this system is to help you organize your files. It's not uncommon for today's computers to have thousands of files, tens of thousands even. If you don't organize this lot logically, you'll end up with a mess that will make the Gordian knot look simple.

Directories Are Not Areas of the Hard Disk!

Before you email me saying that a directory is *not* an area on your hard disk, let me say *I know that!* It just *appears* to be an area on your hard disk. Computer files are spread across the disk in an apparently illogical and disorganized manner—a piece of a file here, a piece there. The directory system is a visual way to organize the files to make the hard disk easier to use.

The disk says, "I have a directory here that contains these files." But that's a lie, because the files are scattered all over the place. But it doesn't matter. It's rather like a child who *swears* that he has tidied up his room, that his socks are in the dresser and his shoes are in the closet. They're not, of course; everything's scattered over the floor. But you really don't want to look inside because it will just upset you. So you accept it and think in terms of where things *should be* within the room, without wanting to see the truth. Don't worry about the technical details; directories contain files, and that's all you need to know.

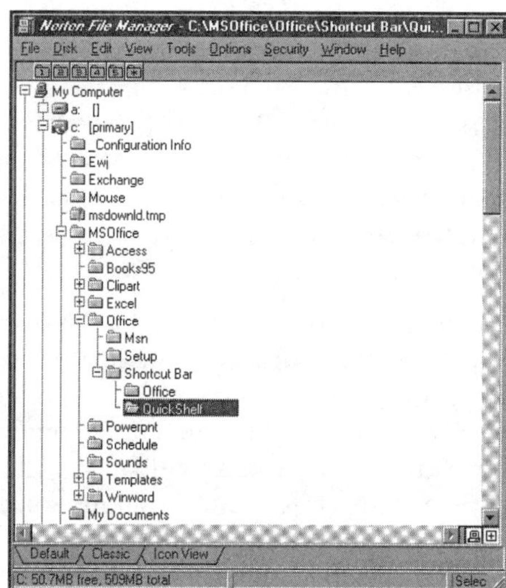

Folders within folders within folders make up the directory tree, shown here in the Norton File Manager program.

A *download directory* is a directory into which you download a file. Let's say that you are using your Web browser to download a shareware program. Where is that file saved? By definition, it's downloaded into the download directory. What is the download directory named? It may be called DOWNLOAD, but it could be anything; the download directory is whichever directory you tell the program to put the file in.

The directory chosen by the browser as the download directory is not always the best place to put the file. In many cases, it's a lousy choice. Internet Explorer, for instance, wants to place downloaded files on the Windows *desktop*. (In Windows 95, 98, and NT, the desktop is a special subdirectory of the WINDOWS or WINNT directory; anything placed inside that directory will appear on the desktop, which is the area of your computer screen that is visible when all the programs have been closed.) That's often a bad place to put it; if you download a lot of things, your desktop will soon be as cluttered as my office. (And believe me, that's not good.) Of course, you can always move the file to another directory later, but in that case, why not put it where you want it in the first place?

Also, many of the files that you will download are archive files; these files are sort of file "containers." Although an archive file is a single file, it has other files within it, perhaps hundreds of them. When you extract those files, they are generally placed in the same directory. After you extract those files, you no longer have one easily recognized file on your desktop (or in whichever download directory the program chose). You now have dozens or more new files there. Do this with several download files, and you'll soon become confused; which file came from which archive?

Pick a Download Directory Sensibly

When you download files from the Web, FTP, Gopher, your online service, or wherever, think sensibly about where you place the files. Many users create a special directory called *download*. Some programs even do this automatically: Many FTP programs, for instance, create a directory called *download* to be used as the default location for downloaded files. You can place all the downloaded files directly into that directory. Later you can decide what you want to do with each file.

I prefer to go one step further. When I download a file, I think about where I'll eventually want the file. For instance, if it's a document file related to a book I'm working on, I save it directly into one of the directories I've created to hold the book. If it's a program file, I'll have to create a directory to hold the program at some point, so why not create a directory for the program right now and download the file directly into that directory? (Depending on which operating system and program you are using, you may be able to create the directory while you are telling the program where to save the file; or you may have to use some kind of file-management program to create the directory and *then* save the file.)

Learn about directories. Make sure you understand how to find your way around the directory tree (or folder system, as it's known in some operating systems). And make sure you save files in such a manner that you can find them when you need them.

A Cornucopia of File Formats

Many computer users don't understand the concept of file formats because they never really see any files. They open their word processors, do some work, and then save the file. They may notice that when they give the file a name, the program adds a few letters such as .DOC or .WPD at the end, but they don't think much about it. If you're going to be playing on the Net, though, you need to understand just a little about file formats because you'll have to pick and choose the ones you want.

Hidden File Extensions

Windows 95, 98, and NT4 hide the file extensions from you. I think this is particularly stupid, but then, Microsoft didn't ask me before deciding to do this. To see file extensions, open Windows Explorer and select **View, Options**. Then, under the **View** tab, clear the check box labelled **Hide MS-DOS File Extensions for File Types That Are Registered**.

All computer files have one thing in common: They all save information in the form of zeros and ones. The difference between a file created by one word processor and another, or between a file created by a word processor and one created by a graphics program, is in what those zeros and ones *mean*. Just as two languages can use the same basic sounds and string them together to create different words, different programs use the zeros and ones to mean different things. One program uses zeros and ones to create words, another to create sounds, another to create pictures, and so on.

The File Extension

How, then, can computer programs identify one file from another? They can often look for a familiar sequence of zeros and ones at the beginning of a file; if they find it, they know they have the right file. But there's also something called a *file extension* that identifies files, and it has the added advantage of being visible to mere mortals. A file extension is a piece of text at the end of a filename, preceded by a period, that is used to identify the file type. For example, look at this sample filename:

THISDOC.TXT

The extension is the .TXT bit. This extension means the file is a plain text file; any program that can read what is known as ASCII text can open this file and read it.

Different Extensions, Same Format

Some files are identified by two or more file extensions. For instance, the .JPEG extension is often used on UNIX computers to identify a form of graphics file commonly used on the Web. But because Windows 3.1 and DOS can't display four-character extensions, this type of file is often seen with the .JPG extension, different extension, but the same file format. You'll also find .HTM and .HTML files, .TXT and .TEXT files, and .AIF and .AIFF files (sound files).

Now, in most operating systems (including DOS and Windows), file extensions are three characters long; on some operating systems, extensions are three or four characters. Normally, each file has only one file extension. Some operating systems, such as UNIX and Windows 98, for example, allow multiple extensions and extensions with more than three characters, such as THISDOC.NEWONE.TEXT. However, this sort of thing is becoming rare on the Internet these days, and you'll generally run into only simple three- and four-character extensions.

Macintosh files, by the way, don't require a file extension; rather, an identifier is built into the file, visible to the computer but not to the computer operator. However, note that Macintosh files stored on the Internet often *do* have an extension— .hqx or .sea, for instance. This extension is to make them readily identifiable as Macintosh files by human beings. (I find it amusing that the Mac's programmers, for all the talk of making their computers easy to use, didn't realize how important file extensions are to mere humans.)

You might be thinking that there are probably three or four file formats you need to know about. No, not quite. Try four or five dozen. The following table gives you a list to get you started.

File formats you should know

File Format	Type of File It Identifies
.ARC	A PKARC file (a DOS compression file).
.AU, .AIF, .AIFF, .AIFC, .SND	Sound files often used on Macintosh and UNIX systems; Netscape and Internet Explorer can play these sounds.
.AVI	Video for Windows.
.BMP, .PCX	Common bitmap graphics formats.
.DOC	Microsoft Word files, from Word for the Macintosh, Word for Windows, and Windows WordPad.
.EPS	A PostScript image.
.EXE	A program file or a self-extracting archive file.
.FLC, .FLI, .AAS	Autodesk Animator files.
.GIF	Graphics files often found in Web pages.
.gzip and .gz	UNIX compressed files.
.HLP	Windows Help files.
.HTM, .HTML	The basic Web document format.
.hqx	A BinHex file, a format often used to archive Macintosh files. Programs such as StuffIt Expander can open these files.
.JPG, .JPEG, .JPE	JPEG graphics files, also often found in Web pages.
.JFIF, .PJPEG, .PJP	A few more variations of the .JPEG file format.
.MID, .RMI	MIDI (Musical Instrument Digital Interface) sounds.
.MMM	Microsoft Multimedia Movie Player files.
.MOV, .QT	The QuickTime video format.
.MP2	An MPEG audio format.
.MPEG, .MPG, .MPE, .M1V	The MPEG (Motion Pictures Expert Group) video formats.
.PDF	The Portable Document Format, an Adobe Acrobat hypertext file. This format is becoming a very popular means of distributing electronic documents.
.pit	The Macintosh Packit archive format.
.PS	A PostScript document.
.RAM, .RA	RealAudio. This sound format plays while it's being transmitted. Click a link to a RealAudio file, and it begins playing within a few seconds (you don't have to wait until the entire file is transferred).

File Format	Type of File It Identifies
.RTF	Rich Text Format. These word processing files work in a variety of Windows word processors.
.sea	A Macintosh self-extracting archive.
.SGML	A document format.
.shar	A UNIX shell archive file.
.SIT	The Macintosh StuffIt archive format.
.tar	A UNIX tar archive file.
.TIF	A common graphics format.
.TSP	TrueSpeech, a sound format similar to RealAudio.
.TTF	Windows TrueType font files.
.TXT, .TEXT	A text file.
.WAV	The standard Windows "wave" sound format.
.WPD	A WordPerfect document file.
.WRI	Windows Write word processing files.
.WRL	A VRML (Virtual Reality Modeling Language) 3D object.
.XBM	Another graphics file that can be displayed by Web browsers (although it's not used very often these days).
.XDM	The StreamWorks WebTV and WebRadio format. This is similar to RealAudio, but it allows the real-time playing of video in addition to sound.
.XLS	A Microsoft Excel spreadsheet file.
.Z	A UNIX compressed file.
.z	A UNIX packed file.
.ZIP	A PKZIP archive file (a DOS and Windows compression file), used by many Windows (and even some Macintosh) compression utilities.
.zoo	A zoo210 archive format available on various systems.

Is that all? By no means! Netscape currently claims that it has 176 plug-ins. Although many of these duplicate the functions of other plug-ins, handling the same file types, this number still represents a lot of different file formats. There are all sorts of file formats out there; to be honest, though, you'll only run across a few of them. You may never even run across some of the ones I included in the table; for instance, the .ARC format, which used to be very common in the shareware world, is now quite rare.

File Compression Basics

As you can see from the preceding table, a number of these file formats are archive or compressed formats. These are files containing other files within them. You can use a special program to extract those files; or in the case of a "self-extracting archive," the file can automatically extract the files within it.

Is It Possible?

This is similar to Dr. Who's Tardis, which has much more space *inside* than would be allowed within a box of that size according to normal physics. And no, I don't plan to explain how it's done. Suffice it to say that, thanks to a little magic and nifty computing tricks, these programs make files smaller.

Why do people bother to put files inside archive files? Or even, in some cases, a single file within an archive file? Two reasons. First, the programs that create these files often compress the files being placed inside, so the single file is much smaller than the combined size of all the files inside. You can reduce files to as little as 2% of their normal size, depending on the type of file and the program you use (although 40% to 75% is probably a more normal range). Bitmap graphics, for instance, often compress to a very small size; program files and Windows Help files can't be compressed so far. If you want to transfer a file across the Internet, it's a lot quicker to transfer a compressed file than an uncompressed file.

The other reason to use these systems is that you can place files inside another file as a sort of packaging or container. If a shareware program has, say, 20 different files that it needs in order to run, it's better to wrap all these into one file than to expect people to transfer all 20 files one at a time.

Archive Versus Compressed

What's the difference between an archive file and a compressed file? They're often the same thing, and people (including me) tend to use the terms interchangeably. Originally, however, an archive file was a file that stored lots of other files: it archived them. An archive file doesn't have to be a compressed file; it's just a convenient place to put files that you are not using. A compressed file must, of course, be compressed. These days, archive files are usually—although not always—compressed files, and compressed files are often used for archiving files. So there's not a lot of difference between the two anymore. There's one notable exception, though. The .tar files you may run across, UNIX tape archive files, are *not* compressed. However, .tar archive files are often compressed using the gzip format (you'll see something like filename.tar.gz).

Which Format?

Most compressed DOS and Windows files are in .ZIP format, a format often created by a program called PKZIP (but the file format is not owned by anyone, so other programs create .ZIP files, too). There are other compressed formats, though; you may also see .ARJ (created by a program called ARJ) and .LZH (created by LHARC) now and again, but probably not very often. PKZIP won the compression war.

In the UNIX world, .Z, .gz, and .tar files are common archive formats. On the Macintosh, you'll find .sit (StuffIt) and .pit (Packit) compressed formats, as well as .hqx (BinHex) archive files. This table gives you a quick rundown of the compressed formats you'll see.

Common compressed file formats

Extension	Program That Compressed It
.ARC	DOS, PKARC (an older method, predating PKZIP and rarely seen these days)
.EXE	A DOS or Windows self-extracting archive
.gz	Usually a UNIX gzip compressed file (although there are versions of gzip for other operating systems, they're rarely used)
.hqx	Macintosh BinHex
.pit	Macintosh Packit
.sea	A Macintosh self-extracting archive
.shar	UNIX shell archive
.sit	Macintosh StuffIt
.tar	UNIX tar
.Z	UNIX compress
.z	UNIX pack
.ZIP	PKZIP, WinZip, and many others
.zoo	zoo210 (available on various systems)

It goes without saying (but I'll say it anyway, just in case) that if you see a file with an extension that is common on an operating system other than yours, it may contain files that won't be good on your system. Macintosh and UNIX software won't run on Windows, for instance. However, that's not always true. The file may contain text files, for instance, which can be read on any system. So there are cross-platform utilities; for example, some Macintosh utilities can uncompress archive files, such as .ZIP files, that are not common in the Macintosh world, and some .ZIP utilities running in Windows can extract files from .gz and .tar files. For instance, some versions of Stuffit Expander, a Macintosh utility, can open .ZIP files, and WinZip, a Windows program, can open .gz and .tar files.

Those Self-extracting Archives

Various programs, such as PKZIP and ARJ, can create files that can be executed (run) to extract the archived files automatically. These files, called self-extracting archives, are very useful for sending a compressed file to someone when you're not sure if he has the program to decompress the file (or would know how to use it). For instance, PKZIP can create a file with an .EXE extension; you can run such a file directly from the DOS prompt just by typing its name and pressing **Enter** or by double-clicking the file in the Windows Explorer file-management program. When you do so, all the compressed files pop out. In the Macintosh world, .sea (self-extracting archive) files do the same thing. Double-click an .sea file, and the contents are automatically extracted.

In the Meantime
How can you download and extract one of these compression utilities from a shareware library before you have a program that will extract an archive file? Don't worry; the programmers thought of that! These utilities are generally stored in self-extracting format, so you can download them and automatically extract them by running the file.

If you find a file in two formats, .ZIP and .EXE for instance, you may want to take the .EXE format. The .EXE files are not much larger than the .ZIP files, and you don't need to worry about finding a program to extract the files. If you take a .ZIP file, you must have a program that can read the .ZIP file and extract the archived files from within. You may already have such a program. Some Windows file-management programs, for instance, can work with .ZIP files. Otherwise, you'll need a program that can extract from the compressed format.

Your Computer Can Get Sick, Too

Downloading all these computer files can lead to problems: computer viruses. File viruses hide out in program files and copy themselves to other program files when someone runs that program. Viruses and other malevolent computer bugs are real, and they do real damage. Now and then you'll even hear of service providers having to close down temporarily after their systems become infected.

Unfortunately, security on the Internet is lax. The major online services have strict regulations about virus checks. Members generally cannot post directly to public areas, for instance; they post to an area in which the file can be checked for viruses before it's available to the public. But on the Internet it's up to each system administrator (and there are hundreds of thousands of them) to keep his own system clean. If just one administrator does a bad job, a virus can get through and be carried by FTP, the Web, or email all over the world. The large shareware archives are probably quite careful, but there are tens of thousands of places to download software on the Internet, and some of those are probably a little careless.

Viruses Under the Microscope

The term *virus* has become a catchall for a variety of digital organisms, such as

- Bacteria, which reproduce and do no direct damage except using up disk space and memory.
- Rabbits, which get their name because they reproduce very quickly.
- Trojan horses, which are damaging programs embedded in otherwise useful programs.
- Bombs, which are programs that just sit and wait for a particular date or event (at which time they wreak destruction); these are often left deep inside programs by disgruntled employees.
- Worms, which are programs that copy themselves from one computer to another, independent of other executable files, and clog the computers by taking over memory and disk space.

However, having said all that, I also must say that the virus threat is overstated—probably by companies selling antivirus software. We've reached a stage where almost any confusing computer problem is blamed on computer viruses, and technical support lines are using it as an excuse not to talk with people. "Your computer can't read your hard disk? You've been downloading files from the Internet? You must have a virus!" Most computer users have never been "hit" by a computer virus. Many who think they have probably haven't; a lot of problems are blamed on viruses these days. So don't get overly worried about it. Take some sensible precautions, and you'll be okay.

Tips for Safe Computing

If you are just working with basic ASCII text email and perhaps FTPing documents, you're okay. The problem of viruses arises when you transfer programs, including self-extracting archive files, or files that contain mini "programs." (For instance, many word processing files can now contain macros, special little programs that may run when you open the file.)

If you do plan to transfer programs, perhaps the best advice is to get a good antivirus program. They're available for all computer types. Each time you transmit an executable file, use your antivirus program to check it. Also, make sure you keep good backups of your data. Although backups can also become infected with viruses, if a virus hits, at least you can reload your backup data and use an antivirus program to clean the files (and some backup programs check for viruses while backing up).

Rule of Thumb

Here's a rule of thumb to figure out if a file is dangerous: "If it does something, it can carry a virus; if it has things done to it, it's safe." Only files that can carry out actions (such as script files, program files, and word processing files from the fancy word processors—such as Word for Windows—that have built-in macro systems) can pose a threat. If a file can't do anything—it just sits waiting until a program displays or plays it—it's safe. Pictures and sounds, for instance, may offend you personally, but they won't do your computer any harm. (Can self-extracting archives carry viruses? Absolutely. They're programs, and they run—you don't know that they're self-extracting archives until they've extracted, after all.)

The Least You Need to Know

- Don't transfer files to your computer without thinking about *where* on your hard disk they should be. Create a download directory in a sensible place.
- Files are identified by the file extension, typically a three-character (sometimes four-character) "code" preceded by a period.
- Compressed and archive files are files containing other files within. They provide a convenient way to distribute files across the Internet.
- Self-extracting archives are files that don't require a special utility to extract the files from within. Just run the file, and the files within are extracted.
- Viruses are real, but the threat is exaggerated. Use an antivirus program, and then relax.
- The virus rule of thumb is this: "If it does something, it can carry a virus; if it has things done to it, it's safe."

Part 3
Getting Things Done

Now that you've learned how to use the Internet's services, it's time to learn some important general information about working on the Net. This place is so huge, you might have trouble finding what you need; I'll show you where to look. You'll also need to learn how to stay safe on the Internet. You've heard about the problems that go along with using credit cards on the Internet, about kids finding pornography, and so on—we'll examine the truth and the lies.

In addition to covering all those issues, I'll answer all sorts of questions I've heard from Internet users, from how to get rich on the Internet to why those $500 Internet boxes may not be such a great buy. I'll also tell you about a couple dozen ways that people use the Internet. Maybe you'll find something worth pursuing, or you'll think of an idea of your own. And you'll even find out where the Internet is going in the future.

Chapter 11

Finding Stuff

In This Chapter

- Finding people
- Searching the Internet with search engines
- Using Internet directories
- Searching newsgroups
- Other Internet services

By now you must have realized that the Internet is rather large: tens of millions of users, millions of files in FTP sites, millions and millions of Web pages, Telnet sites, Gopher servers, newsgroups, mailing lists—this thing is huge. How on earth are you ever going to find your way around?

Finding what you need on the Internet is surprisingly easy these days. Dozens of services are available to help you find your way around. That's what this chapter is about: finding what you need and where you need to go.

Finding People

The most complicated search task is finding people on the Internet. There are millions of Internet users and no single Internet directory. Unlike the online services, which have directories you can search to find someone you want to contact, there's no one place to search on the Internet. But that's not so surprising. After all, there's no single directory for the world's telephone system, and the Internet is comparable—it's thousands of connected networks that span the world. So how are you going to find someone?

Still Working at a Command Line?

If you are using the command-line interface, send an email message to **ciginternet@mcp.com** and type **who** in the Subject line of the message (leave the body blank). In return, you'll receive the chapters on finding people from the first edition of *The Complete Idiot's Guide to the Internet*.

Quite frankly, the easiest way to find someone's email address is to talk to that person or talk to (or email) a mutual acquaintance. You can spend hours looking for someone in the Internet's various directories. If you know of someone else who might have the information, or know the person's telephone number, you can save yourself some time and trouble by tracking down the email address that way. If you can't contact the person directly, or can't think of someone else who knows the person you're after, you'll have to dig a little deeper.

Directories, Directories, and More Directories

There are a lot of directories on the Web. (No, I don't mean directories on a computer's hard disk this time; now when I say *directories*, I mean it as in the telephone directory or directory assistance.) A good place to start is at your browser's people search page. For instance, if you're using Netscape Navigator 4, click the **Guide** button and select **People** from the drop-down menu. In Navigator 3, click the **People** button in the Directory Buttons bar. If you're not using that browser, you can go directly to Netscape's People page (`http://guide.netscape.com/guide/people.html`). Each time you go to this page, Netscape displays one of several directories (WhoWhere?, Four11, Bigfoot, InfoSpace, and WorldPages). The first figure on the following page shows the Bigfoot directory. You can search the directory Netscape displays, or you can choose one of the others.

Another good directory to use is Yahoo! People Search (go to `http://www.yahoo.com/search/people/`), which you can see in the second figure on the following page. This directory of people on the Internet is surprisingly good. I searched for my own name and found myself, along with about 90 other Peter Kents. (I hadn't realized there were so many of us.) You can search for a name and, using the advanced settings, narrow the search by including a city and state, or you can search for a telephone number. Note, however, that these directories are often quite out-of-date. I found a couple of old listings for myself; one of the email addresses had not worked for about three years.

If you don't find the person you need in Yahoo! People Search, don't worry; there's still a chance you'll find him. Yahoo!'s `http://www.yahoo.com/Reference/White_Pages/` page has links to dozens more directories; when I looked a moment ago, I found links to almost 150 different directories, some of which had links to dozens more, including directories at colleges, celebrity directories, many regional directories, and so on.

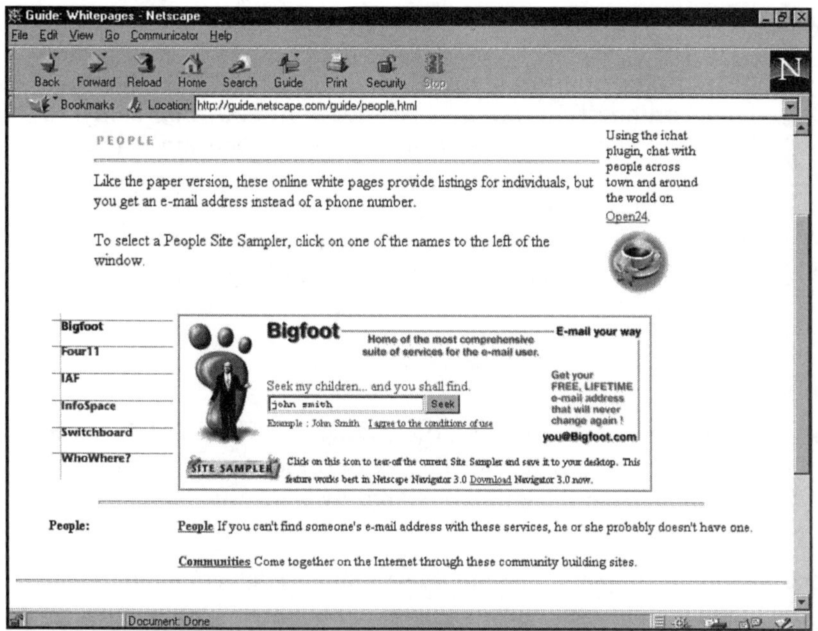

Netscape's People page automatically picks a directory for you.

The Yahoo! People Search form.

Other Search Engines, Too
Yahoo! is not the only *search engine* you can use to find directories. We'll look at more search engines later in this chapter, and many of them will have links to directories you can use to find people, too.

I'm not going to go into more detail about these directories. A year or two ago, it was quite difficult to find people on the Internet (when I searched for myself for the first edition of this book, I had a lot of trouble finding myself—and I knew where I was!). These days there are so many directories of people that, with a bit of time and trouble, you have a good chance of finding the person you need (even if he doesn't have Internet access—you can often track down a phone number more easily than an email address).

Using the Search Sites

You want to find information about something or other. Where do you start? The best place is probably at the Web search sites. There are dozens of these sites, and I'm always surprised what I can turn up in just a few minutes of searching. There are basically three ways to use these search sites:

- You can view a directory from which you can select a subject category and subcategories; then you'll see a list of links to related pages.
- You can search an index of subjects; type a keyword into a form, and then click a **Search** button to carry out a search. You'll see a list of links to Web pages related to the subjects you typed into the search form.
- You can search an index of pages. Some search engines let you search for words within Web pages. AltaVista, for example, claims that it has an index of most of the words on *30 million* Web pages, at over a million Web sites! (At least, it used to claim that, but it's growing all the time, and it doesn't seem to state a specific number anymore.) You'll see a list of pages that contain the words you typed into the form.

Which type of search should you use? The first or second method should normally be your first choice. Services such as AltaVista are very useful, but because they don't categorize the pages—they search for words within the pages instead of searching the subjects of the pages—they often give you more information than you can ever handle. The other services categorize pages (and sometimes even describe or review pages), so they are generally easier to use. Save places like AltaVista for "plan B," when you can't find what you're looking for on your first attempt.

Finding the Search Sites

Getting started is easy. Most Web browsers these days have a button that takes you straight to a search page of some kind (generally a form that lets you search a choice of search sites). For example, both Netscape and Internet Explorer have a Search button.

The Best?

Which is the best Web search site? There is no "best." Even though I really like Yahoo!, I sometimes use others. Each one is different and works in a different way, which means each one will give you a different result. Try a few and see which you like, or check to see how others rate them.

Here are a few search sites you can use. I've started with Yahoo! because that's where I prefer to start. Of course, after you've used a few search sites, you may find that you have a different preference.

- *Yahoo!*. http//www.yahoo.com
- *Lycos*. http//www.lycos.com/
- *InfoSeek*. http//www.infoseek.com/
- *HotBot*. http//www.hotbot.com/
- *AltaVista*. http//www.altavista.digital.com/
- *Inktomi*. http//inktomi.berkeley.edu/

What's the difference between a Web directory and a Search engine? A directory provides categorized lists of Web pages from which you can select a category, and then a subcategory, and then another subcategory, and so on until you find the site you want. A search engine lets you use a program with which you'll search a database of Web pages. With a search engine, you type a keyword and click a **Search** button or press **Enter**. The search engine then searches the database for you. Some sites such as Yahoo! contain both directories and search engines.

Browser Tip

Here's a quick way to search for something: Search directly from your browser's Location text box. If you're using Netscape Navigator, enter two words into the Location box. For instance, if you want to search for information about hiking in Iceland, type **iceland hiking**. (If you just want to search for one word, enter it twice, as in **iceland iceland**.) Press **Enter**, and Netscape picks a search engine for you from its selection (InfoSeek, Excite, and Lycos) and sends the search keywords to the search engine. If you're using Internet Explorer, type **find** followed by the word you want to search for: **find iceland**, for instance.

How Do I Use the Search Engines?

Internet *search engines* enable you to search a database. Take a quick look at InfoSeek (`http://www.infoseek.com/`) in the following figure as an example. Start by typing a search term into the text box. You can type as little as a single word, but you may want to get fancy—in which case you should read the instructions. You'll find a link at InfoSeek, probably labeled Tips or Huh?, that takes you to a document that describes exactly what you can type. Read this document; it gives you many suggestions and hints for using the search engine. (Most search engines have a link like this to background information.)

As you will learn in the information document, you can enter these types of things at InfoSeek:

- *Words between quotation marks.* Entering words this way tells InfoSeek to find the words in the exact order you type them: "the here and now."
- *Proper names.* Make sure these names are capitalized correctly: Colorado, England, or Gore, for instance.
- *Words separated by hyphens.* Entering words this way tells InfoSeek to find both words as long as they are close together in the document: diving-scuba, for instance.
- *Words in brackets.* Entering words this way tells InfoSeek to find the search words if they appear together, but not necessarily in the order you've entered them: [diving scuba], for example.

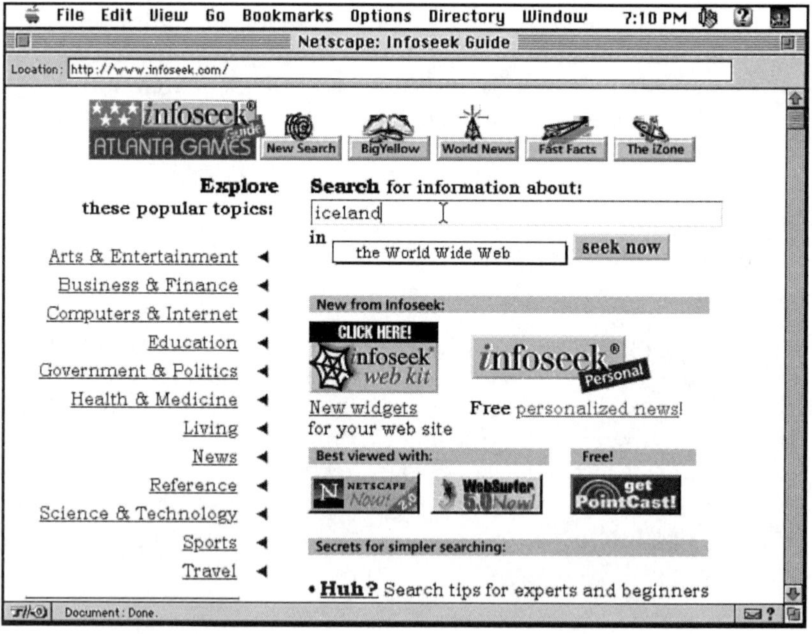

Infoseek, a Web search engine.

Each search engine is a little different and allows you to use different sorts of search terms. You can always search by entering a single word, but the more you know about each search engine, the more efficiently you can search.

When you first go to a search engine, look around for some kind of link to a Help document. When you finish reading the Help information, click the **Back** button to return to the InfoSeek page with the text box. Enter the word or phrase you want to search for, and then press **Enter** or click the **Search** button. Your browser sends the information to InfoSeek, and with a little luck you'll see a result page shortly thereafter (see the following figure). Of course, you may see a message telling you that the search engine is busy. If so, try again in a few moments.

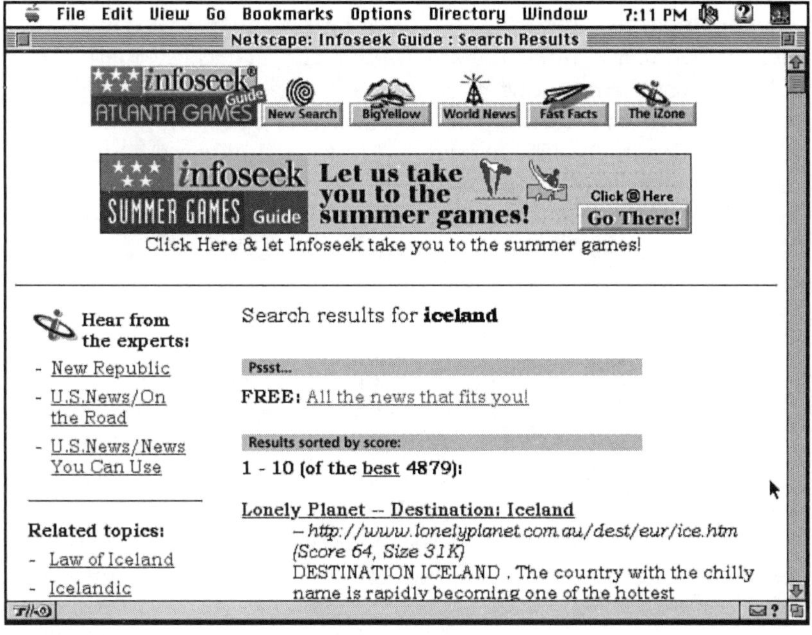

InfoSeek found a few links to Icelandic subjects for me.

As you can see in the figure, when I searched for "iceland," InfoSeek found 4,879 links to Web sites that contain information about Iceland. The document I'm viewing doesn't show me all the links, of course. It shows me the first 10 and provides a link at the bottom of the page that I can click to see the next 10. It found links to things such as *Travel Guides to Iceland, History of Iceland, Books on Iceland, Airlines,* and plenty more. If one of these links interests me, all I have to do is click the link and away I go, over the North Atlantic and into Iceland.

Browsing the Internet Directories

For a sample of Internet directories, take a look at Yahoo!. Go to `http://www.yahoo.com/`. Yahoo! has a search engine, so you can type a word into the text box if you want, but notice the category links: Art, Education, Health, Social Science, and so on. Each of these links points deeper into the Yahoo! system, a level lower down in the hierarchical system of document categories. To see how this system works, click **Recreation**, and you see a document from Yahoo! with a list of more categories: Amusement/Theme Parks@, Aviation, Drugs@, Motorcycles, and so on.

The @ sign at the end of some of these categories indicates that this entry is a sort of cross-reference: you will be crossing over to another category if you select this link. For instance, click **Drugs@**, and you'll see a page from the Health:Pharmacology:Drugs category. This page also contains links to other drug-related categories, along with links to Web pages that are related to recreational drugs (from alcohol to XTC), political and legal issues, pharmacology, and many other subjects.

You'll also notice that some links are shown with bold text and numbers in parentheses after them (such as **Nicotine (31)**), and links that are not bolded (such as Psychiatric Drug Therapy). The bold links take you farther down the hierarchy, displaying another document that contains more links. The number in parentheses after the link shows how many links you'll find in that document. The regular text links are links across the Internet to Web documents that contain the information you're looking for. Select **WWW Drug Links**, and you'll find yourself viewing a Web document with more links to drug pages.

Finding Specific Stuff

Now that you've seen how to search for general stuff, you're ready to learn about searching for specific stuff. Instead of going to a general search site, you can go to one of many sites that help you find specific things; you might want a site where you can search for stuff about books and publications on the Internet (`http://www.alexandria-home.com/directory.asp`), boat stuff (`http://boatingyellowpages.com/`), or kid stuff (`http://www.yahooligans.com/`), for example. You can find scores of these specialized search sites, with information about everything from lawyers to pets. A good place to find them is at `http://www.yahoo.com/Computers_and_Internet/Internet/World_Wide_Web/Searching_the_Web/Web_Directories/`. You can also find them at any of the other big search sites.

Finding Out What People Are Saying

Are people talking about you (do you hear voices in your head?). If you want to know what people are saying about you on the Internet, you can search newsgroup messages for particular words. You can search for your own name to find out what your friends—or enemies—are saying about you, or you can search for a subject if you are researching a particular topic.

There are a number of places you can search newsgroups. One of the best is DejaNews (`http://www.dejanews.com/`). Or try Yahoo!; go to `http://www.yahoo.com`. At the search page, click the link—currently the **Options** link—that takes you to the advanced search.

Then click the **Usenet** option button and enter your keywords. (As another alternative, you can use InfoSeek and click the **Newsgroups** option button before you search.) When the search site carries out the search, it displays a page of links to the matching messages. Click a link to read the message. Another great place to search is `http://www.reference.com/`, which helps you search newsgroups, mailing lists, and Web forums.

Set a Bookmark to Repeat the Search Later

Here's a handy little trick. If you've just done a search about a subject that you think you'll want to check back on later—to see what new information has appeared on the Internet—bookmark the search. I don't mean the search site, but the search itself. Go to the search site, carry out the search, and when you get the page displaying the search results, bookmark that page. The next time you want to search, all you have to do is select that bookmark. Your browser automatically sends the search statement to the search engine, which carries out the search and displays the result. (This trick works on most, although not all, search sites.)

FTP, Gopher, Telnet, and More

No, you are not finished. You can search for much, much more. Go back to the earlier chapters on FTP, Gopher, Telnet, newsgroups, and mailing lists, and you'll see that I gave you information about how to find things on those services. For instance, you can use Archie to search FTP sites, and you can use Tile.Net and other similar services to find mailing lists and newsgroups related to subjects that interest you. You can also use Jughead and Veronica to search Gopherspace. If you don't find what you need at any of the Web sites you learned about in this chapter, spend a little time searching the other services.

The Least You Need to Know

- There is no single directory of Internet users, so the easiest way to find someone is often to ask a mutual acquaintance.
- There are now lots of good directories. You may have to search a few, but there's a good chance that eventually you'll find the person you're looking for.
- A search engine is a program that searches for a word you enter.
- You can search indexes of keywords describing the contents of Web pages, or you can search the full text of the Web pages (millions of words in millions of pages).
- A directory is a categorized listing of Web links. Choose a category, then a subcategory, then another subcategory, and so on until you find what you want.
- Services such as DejaNews, Yahoo!, and InfoSeek let you search newsgroup messages. The result is a list of matching messages. Click a link to read a message.
- You can set a bookmark on a page that displays search results; to repeat the search quickly at a later date, all you have to do is select that bookmark.

Chapter 12

Staying Safe on the Internet

In This Chapter

- Keeping kids "safe"
- Protecting your email
- The identity problem
- Internet addiction
- Protecting your credit card
- Keeping out of trouble with your boss or spouse

There are many dangers on the Internet—most of them imagined or exaggerated. We're led to believe that our children will become corrupted or be kidnapped, our credit cards will be stolen, and we'll be arrested for copyright infringement. Although some of these dangers are real, keep in mind that you're sitting in front of a computer at the end of a long cable. Just how dangerous can that be? If you use a little common sense, it's not dangerous at all.

Your Kid Is Learning About Sex from Strangers

Sex, sex, sex. That's all some people can think of. The media's so obsessed with sex that sometimes the only thing that our journalists seem to notice are stories with a little spice in them. Consequently, the press has spent a lot of time over the past couple of years talking about how the Internet is awash in pornography. Well, it isn't.

I'll admit that there are pornographic images on the Internet, but in general you won't just trip over pornography. If you decide to take a look at the alt.binaries.pictures.erotica.pornstar newsgroup, for instance, just what do you expect to find?! You can hardly claim to be offended if you choose to enter such a locale. In some cases, the publicly accessible sex-related Web sites are quite "soft." Take a look at the *Hustler* or *Playboy* sites, and then run down to your local magazine store and take a look at them there. You'll find that the bookstore version is far more explicit than the Web version. (Believe me, I've done this little experiment—but only in the interest of research, you understand.)

You Can Do Your Own Research

Because this is a family book, I'm not going to go much further on this topic. If you care to research the subject of sex on the Internet further, just go to the search engines (see Chapter 11, "Finding Stuff") and search for **sex**. (But don't carry out this experiment and then blame me if you're offended by something you find!)

On the other hand, some very explicit stuff is available on the Internet. Since I wrote the third edition of this book in 1996, Web sites seem to have become more explicit. In 1996, the Computer Decency Act was holding people back—much of the really explicit stuff was hidden away on private Web sites. To get in you had to subscribe by providing a credit card number. Since then the Computer Decency Act has been struck down by the courts. There are still many private sites, but quite a lot of very smutty stuff is available at the free Web sites. Furthermore, some porn sites use email messages to bring in new customers; they send these messages to just about any email address they can find, so some of the recipients are children. A number of newsgroups carry extremely explicit sexual images and, in a few cases, images of violent sex. (Even though most things don't particularly shock me, I have to admit that I've been disgusted by one or two things I've seen in newsgroups.)

Although the press would have you believe it's hard to get to the Smithsonian Web site or to read a newsgroup about cooking without somehow stumbling across some atrocious pornographic image, this is far from the truth. You have to go looking for this stuff. The chance that you'll stumble across it is about as good as the chance that you'll run into Queen Elizabeth on your next trip to the supermarket. Unless, that is, you make a spelling mistake. Type **whitehouse.com** into a Web browser instead of **whitehouse.gov**, type **sharware.com** instead of **shareware.com**, or **nassa.com** instead of **nasa.com**, and you'll end up at a porn site. So when you make your fingers do the walking, walk slowly and carefully.

Don't Expect the Government to Help

If you have kids, you already know that they can be a big bundle of problems. The Internet is just one more thing to be concerned about. Still, you signed up for the job, and it's your responsibility.

Many people have suggested that somehow it's the government's responsibility to look after kids. (These are often the same people who talk about "getting the government off our backs" when it comes to other issues.) A few years ago the U.S. Congress passed the Computer Decency Act (CDA), which bans certain forms of talk and images from the Internet. This law definitely had an effect, and pornography was, for a while, harder to find on the Internet. But the CDA was a sloppily written piece of overreaction; it could be construed to ban all sorts of genuine public discourse, such as discussions about abortion. Consequently, the law was judged unconstitutional by a federal court in Philadelphia and later overturned by the U.S. Supreme Court.

The court in Philadelphia wrote that "Those responsible for minors undertake the primary obligation to prevent their exposure to such material." Hey, isn't that what I said? (I wrote most of this *before* the law was struck down. Looks like there could be a judicial career waiting for me!)

The bottom line is that the Computer Decency Act is history. Even if it's replaced by something else (various U.S. states are trying a variety of clumsy experiments), remember that the Internet is an international system. How is the U.S. government going to regulate Swedish, Finnish, Dutch, or Japanese Web sites? It's not. So what are you going to do to keep your kids safe?

It's Up to You; Get a Nanny

If you want to protect your kids, I suggest you spend more time with them at the computer or get a nanny. You can't afford a nanny, you say? Of course, you can. Lots of programs are available to help you restrict access to "inappropriate" sites. Programs such as Net Nanny (I'm not endorsing this one in particular; I just used it so I could put "Nanny" in the heading) contain a list of sites that are to be blocked; you can add sites from your own hate-that-site list, or you can periodically download updates from the Internet. Using these programs, you can block anything you want, not just pornography. As the Net Nanny site says, you can "screen and block anything you don't want running on your PC, such as bomb-making formulas, designer drugs, hate literature, Neo-Nazi teachings, car theft tips—whatever you're concerned about."

You can find Net Nanny at `http://www.netnanny.com/`. To find other such programs, search for the word "**blocking**" at Yahoo! or some other Web search site (or go directly to `http://www.yahoo.com/Business_and_Economy/Companies/Computers/Software/Internet/Blocking_and_Filtering/Titles/`). You'll find programs such as SurfWatch, CyberPatrol, CYBERSitter, NetShepherd, TattleTale, Bess the Internet Retriever, and Snag. (I'm serious, all these are names of real programs!)

If you use an online service, you'll also find that it probably offers some way of filtering out areas you don't want your kids to get to. America Online has had such filtering tools for a long time. MSN enables you to block the Internet's alt. newsgroups and other "adult" areas.

You'll also soon find blocking tools built into most Web browsers. Internet Explorer already has blocking tools. To use them, choose **View**, **Options** and click the **Ratings** or **Security** tab. You'll find an area in which you can turn a filtering system on and off. This system is based on the Recreational Software Advisory Council's ratings (although you can add other systems when they become available), and you can turn it on and off using a password. You can set it up to completely block certain sites or to allow access with a password (just in case you don't practice what you preach!). The following figure shows a site that's blocked except for password entry.

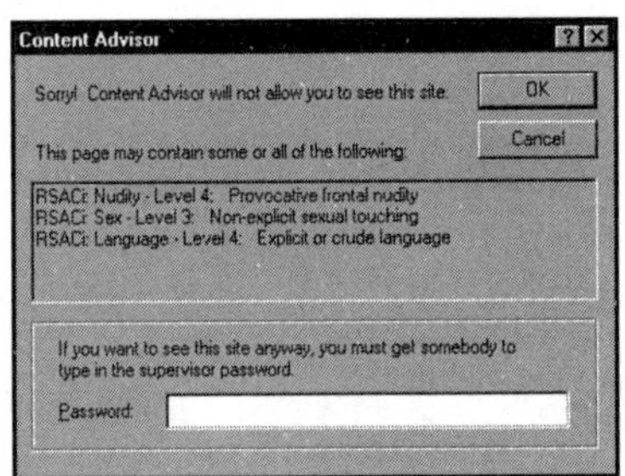

With Internet Explorer's Ratings turned on, your kids can't get in—but you can.

I've heard people criticize these blocking programs for two reasons: 1) because they're not perfect (of course, they're not) and 2) because they're an affront to the concept of free speech. Personally, I believe they are very useful and effective. I believe in supervising my kids, and these programs provide a supervision tool for a new era. They also provide a way for concerned parents to keep their kids away from sites they object to without locking people up and forcing adults to read nothing more than sixth-grade materials on the Web.

What About *TIME*?

Oh, so you read *TIME* Magazine's exposè on Internet porn, did you? It was complete nonsense and widely criticized as careless and inaccurate. *TIME* based the story on a flawed study, which looked at pornographic images on BBSs (individual "adult" computer systems hooked up to the phone lines). It then used the findings to suggest that the Internet was full of porn. *TIME* published a follow-up that didn't exactly apologize but that admitted the study was wrong. (It wasn't *TIME*'s fault, though; it was the fault of the "researcher," they said.) The author of the article has also publicly apologized. The original *TIME* article got front-page coverage; the follow-ups didn't, of course!

From a personal viewpoint (it's *my* book, after all), this whole sex-on-the-Internet is a whole lot of fuss about almost nothing. Sure, clean up the Internet—but what are you going to do about the schoolyard? Schools are hotbeds of filthy language and talk about sex, sprinkled with the occasional pornographic magazine and actual sex. I have the perfect solution, though. I call it "chemical supervision," and it entails giving kids drugs to reduce certain hormonal levels. Remember, you heard it here first.

Your Private Email Turned Up in the National Enquirer

Email can get you in a lot of trouble. It got Oliver North in hot water, and ordinary people have lost their jobs or been sued over things they've said in email. Several things can go wrong when you use email:

- The recipient might pass the email on to someone else.
- The message can be saved on a backup system and read by someone other than the recipient later.
- Someone could spy on you and read your email looking for incriminating comments.

The most likely scenario is that the recipient intentionally or thoughtlessly passes on your message to someone who you didn't count on seeing it. The second problem—that the message could be copied to a backup system—is what got Oliver North (and others) into trouble. Even if you delete a message and the recipient deletes the message, it may still exist somewhere on the network if the system administrator happened to do a backup before it was deleted. So if you are ever the subject of some kind of investigation, that message could be revived. A message goes from your computer, to your service provider's computer, to the recipient's service provider's computer, to the recipient's computer—at least four places from which it could be copied.

Finally, someone might be out to get you. Internet email is basic text, and a knowledgeable hacker with access to your service provider's system (or the recipient's service provider's system) can grab your messages and read them.

What do you do, then? The simplest solution is to avoid putting things in email that you would be embarrassed to have others read. The more complicated solution is to encrypt your email. A number of encryption programs are available that scramble your message using a public-key encryption system, and encryption systems are now being incorporated into email programs. Figure out how they work, and use them.

Digital Signatures You can also use public-key encryption systems to digitally sign documents. When you encrypt a message with the private key, it can only be decrypted with your public key. After all, your public key is public. But if it can be decrypted with your public key, it *must* have come from your private key. Therefore, it must have come from you.

If you don't have an email program with built-in encryption, you can find an add-on system. A good way to start is to search for the word "**encryption**" at any of the Web search sites (or try `http://www.yahoo.com/msn/Computers_and_Internet/Security_and_Encryption/`). There's a problem with these systems, though. Right now, they're complicated to use (the systems built into email programs are generally much simpler). PGP, for instance, can be very complicated; if you want to use it, I suggest that you get one of the "front-end" programs that make it easier to use, such as WinPGP. In addition, because few people use encryption anyway, if you want to use it, you'll have to arrange to use it first. Remember also that even if you encrypt your mail messages, they're not completely secure; you're still trusting the recipient not to pass on the decrypted message to someone else.

Prince Charming Is a Toad!

I'm not sure why I should have to explain this, but when you meet someone online, *you don't know who that person is!* Something about electronic communications makes people quickly feel as though they know the person with whom they are communicating, but they don't!

There are two problems here. First, cyberspace is not the real world. People communicate in a different way online. As another author told me recently, "I know people who seem to be real jerks online, but who are really nice people offline. And I've met people who seemed to be great online, but were complete jerks offline."

Then there's the misrepresentation problem. Some people flat out lie. A man who claims to be single may be married. A woman who claims to look like Michelle Pfeiffer may really look like Roseanne Barr. A 35-year-old movie executive who graduated from Harvard may actually be a 21-year-old unemployed graduate of Podunk Bartending School. It's easy to lie online when nobody can see you. Couple that with a natural tendency to feel like you know the people you meet online, and you have trouble.

Not everyone lies online though. As my friend Phyllis Phlegar wrote in *Love Online* (Addison Wesley), "Even though some individuals choose to be deceptive, many others see the online world as the ultimate place in which to be totally honest, because they feel safe enough to do so." (Phyllis met her husband online.) She also recognizes the dangers: "As long as the person or people you are talking to can't trace you, free-flowing communication between strangers is very safe." But if you're not careful and you give out information that can be used to trace you, Prince Charming may turn out to be the Black Prince. And if you do choose to meet someone in person after meeting that person online, be cautious.

She's a He, and I'm Embarrassed!

Chapter 9, "Yak, Yak, Yak: Chatting in Cyberspace," covers chat systems, which are great places to meet people. For many, they're a great place to meet people of the opposite sex (or of whichever sex you are interested in meeting). But keep in mind that sometimes people are not of the sex that they claim to be. I don't pretend to understand this, but some people evidently get a kick out of masquerading as a member of the opposite sex. Usually men masquerade as women, which could be construed as the ultimate compliment to womanhood or could simply be blamed on the perversity of men. Either way, there's a lot of it around, as the saying goes. (I recently heard chat systems described as being full of "14-year-old boys chatting with other 14-year-old boys claiming to be 21-year-old women." True, it's an exaggeration, but it illustrates the point well.) So if you hook up with someone online, bear in mind that she (or he) may not be quite who he (or she) says (s)he is.

Check This Out...

Profiles If you are a member of an online service, be careful about what you put in your profile. Most services allow you to list information about yourself—information that is available to other members. Omit your address, phone number, and any other identifying information!

You Logged On Last Night, and You're Still Online This Morning

The Internet can be addictive. I think three particular danger areas stand out: the chat systems, the Web, and the discussion groups (mailing lists and newsgroups). Apparently, chat is extremely addictive for some people. I've heard stories of people getting stuck online for hours at a time, until early in the morning—or early in the morning after that. I know of people who've met people online, spent hundreds of hours chatting, and finally abandoned their spouses for their new "loves."

The Web is not quite so compelling, but it's a distraction, nonetheless. There's just so much out there. If you go on a voyage of discovery, you *will* find something interesting. Start following the links, and next thing you know you've been online for hours. Discussion groups are also a problem. You can get so involved in the ongoing "conversations" that you can end up spending half your day just reading and responding.

What's the answer to Net addiction? The same as it is for any other addiction: self-discipline, along with some support. It also helps if you have a life in the real world that you enjoy. Fear probably helps, too (like the fear of losing your job or kids). If you need help, why not spend a bit more time online? Do a search for "**addiction**," and you'll find Web sites set up to help you beat your addiction. You might also take the Internet Addiction survey at The Center for On-Line Addiction (`http://netaddiction.com/`) to see whether you really have a problem.

Just Because You're Paranoid Doesn't Mean Someone Isn't Saying Nasty Things About You

A little while ago, someone started saying rather unpleasant things about me in a mailing list. What she didn't tell people was that she had a sort of vendetta going against me and had for some time. (No, I'm not getting into details.) Anyway, I saw her comments in one mailing list and was struck by a thought: There are tens of thousands of internationally distributed newsgroups and thousands more mailing lists! What else is she saying? And where?!

There's a way to find out what's being said about you (or someone or something else) in newsgroups and Web pages. This is something that may be very useful for anyone who is in the public eye in any way (or for people involved in feuds).

To see what's being said about you in a Web page, search AltaVista; this service lets you use a search engine that indexes all the words in a page, instead of just categorizing Web pages (Chapter 11 explains how to use search engines). To search a newsgroup, though, you'll need a program like DejaNews (`http://www.dejanews.com/`). In DejaNews, you type a name or word you want to search for, and the service searches thousands of newsgroups at once and shows you a list of matches (see the following figure). Click the message you are interested in to find out exactly what people are saying about you. (You can also search DejaNews from some of the other search engines, which have links to it.)

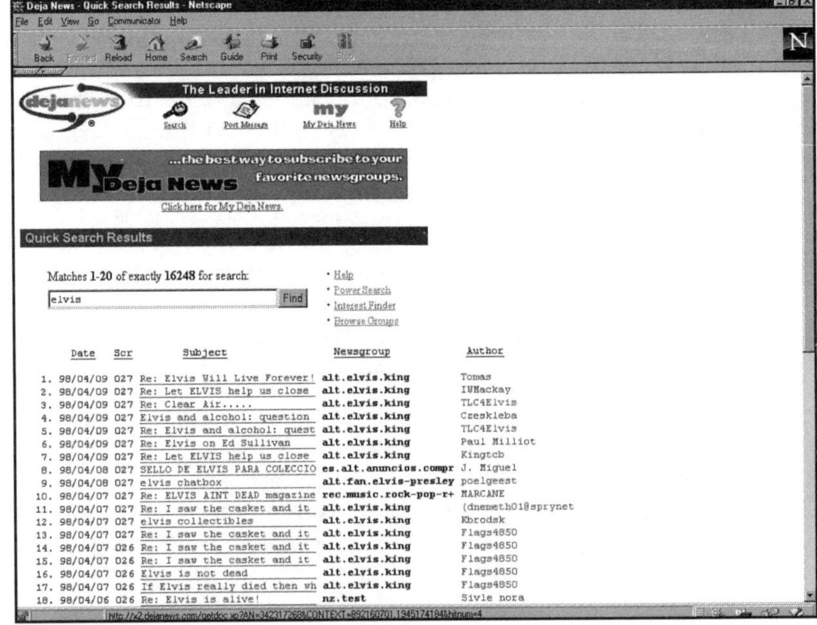

DejaNews provides a great way to search newsgroup messages. (Looks like Elvis has been busy.)

When I did this little search on my own name, I was surprised at what I found. I discovered information about a science-fiction conference at which I was to be a guest, and I found messages in which people recommended a book I'd written about PGP. I also discovered that there's a stunt man called Peter Kent (I found that in alt.cult-movies).

DejaNews is not the only such service; you can find a list of these services at `http://www.yahoo.com/News/Usenet/Searching_and_Filtering/`. How about mailing lists? Reference.com (`http://www.reference.com/`) indexes many mailing lists and some Web forums (and newsgroups). You can even set up a service that searches automatically for you once a week or so, and then emails you the result.

I Was "Researching" at Hustler Online, and Now I'm Unemployed

This title is more than a joke. Some people really have been fired for viewing "inappropriate" Web sites during work hours. This seems quite unfair to me; companies give people Web browsers, often unnecessarily. They provide a temptation, and then fire the people who succumb!

Of course, you can avoid such problems by staying away from the sites in the first place. But if you must go there, practice safe surfing by clearing the cache when you finish! (I discussed the cache in Chapter 4, "More About the Web.") When you visit a site, a copy of the Web page is saved on your hard disk in case you want to view it again at a later time. In effect, this creates a history of where you've been. And speaking of history, some browsers (such as Internet Explorer and Netscape Navigator 4) have excellent multisession history lists, which will also list every Web page you've seen!

To cover your tracks, clear the cache to remove the offending pages. Then clear the history list (either clear it completely, or remove just the offending entries). Netscape Navigator and Internet Explorer also keep a list of URLs you've typed into the Location bar, so if someone starts typing, say, `www.4work.com` at your computer, before the URL is completed the browser may automatically finish it for you by typing `www.4adultsonly.com`! (In any case, you may not want your boss to know that you've been visiting `4work.com` either—it's a job search site.)

> Check This Out...
>
> **It's Bugged!** Your boss can spy on your Internet activities using special software programs, regardless of whether you clear the cache and history list. So maybe you'd better just get back to work.

I Think Kevin Mitnick Stole My Credit Card Number!

Here's another Internet myth: Shopping on the Internet is dangerous because your credit card number can be stolen. The second part of the myth is correct. Yes, your number can be stolen. But the first part is nonsense. Using your credit card on the Internet is not unsafe. Let me give you a couple of reasons.

First, credit card number theft is quite rare on the Internet. It can be done, but only by a computer geek who really knows what he's doing. But why bother? Credit card numbers are not very valuable because it's so easy to steal them in the real world. For example, a little while ago I handed over my credit card to a supermarket clerk and then started bagging my groceries. The clerk put my card down while I wasn't looking. The woman behind me in the line moved forward and set her bag down on the counter. When I went to look for my card, it was gone. It wasn't until I (politely) asked her to move her bag that I found the card underneath. From the look on her face, I'm sure she knew where it was.

This sort of theft is very common. When you give your card to a waiter, a grocery-store clerk, or someone at a mail-order company, you don't think twice about it. But for some reason, people are paranoid about theft on the Internet. Banks know better, though. Internet-business author Jill Ellsworth found that credit card companies regard Internet transactions as safer than real-world transactions.

The second reason is that both Netscape and Internet Explorer, the two most used browsers, have built-in data encryption. Many Web sites now use special Web servers that also have built-in encryption. When a credit card number is sent from one of these browsers to one of these secure servers, the data is encrypted and is therefore unusable. The following figure shows how several Web browsers indicate a secure Web site. Notice the little padlock in the lower-right or lower-left corner of the window? Both Internet Explorer and Netscape Navigator 4 use a locked padlock to indicate that a site is secure. Netscape 2 and 3 displays a key image in the lower-left corner for the same purpose; if the key is broken, the site is not secure. Navigator 4 also puts a yellow line around the padlock toolbar icon.

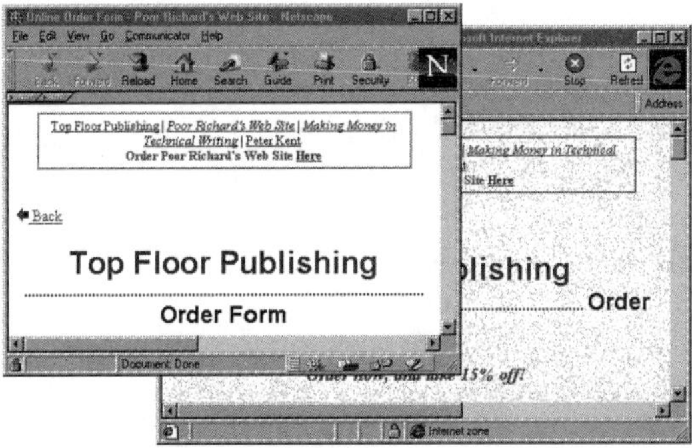

When you see a locked padlock or a key in the status bar, you can send your credit card without worry.

As for Kevin Mitnick, cyberthief extraordinaire, there's a lot of confusion about what he did. He broke into systems and stole information en masse. (He didn't steal individual numbers as they flew across the Internet.) No matter how you pass your credit card number to a vendor, the most dangerous time is *after* they've received the number—and there's little you can do about that.

My Wife Found My Messages in alt.sex.wanted

A lot of people are saying a lot of odd things on the Internet. Undoubtedly, each day thousands of people with very poor judgment make millions of statements that could get them in trouble. This little problem has long been recognized. And for some time now there's been an (almost) perfect way around it: You post messages anonymously.

One way to do that is to configure your email or newsgroup program with incorrect information (with another name and email address, for instance). When you send the message, the header contains that incorrect information instead of the true data. That tactic will fool most list members, but it's not completely safe; the header also contains information that allows the message to be tracked by a system administrator (or the police), and in any case falsifying the header in your email is likely to upset people and may even be illegal soon.

A better method is to sign up for a free email account on the Web. A lot of companies now provide such email accounts (you can find a list at `http://www.yahoo.com/Business_and_Economy/Companies/Internet_Services/Email_Providers/Free_Email/`; Yahoo! even gives away email accounts). Why do they do this? So they can sell advertising. Anyway, many of these systems allow you to sign up for an account anonymously. Sure, you have to provide information about yourself, but it doesn't have to be real.

To use email, you log on to your Internet account through whatever service provider or online service you happen to use. Then you go to the mail system's Web site and log on to your mail account. You can now send and read your email. Each message that goes out is sent from the Web site, not from your service provider or online service. So there's nothing in the header that directly identifies you.

How safe is this email service? Someone reading your message won't be able to find you without the help of the system administrators at the email service and your service provider or online service. So this service is pretty safe for day-to-day anonymity, but perhaps not so safe if you are doing something that might offend the government or police of the country in which those services are found.

Another method is to use an anonymous remailer, a system that posts the messages for you, stripping out all information that can be used to track you down. In other words, you send the message to the remailer with information about which newsgroup or person it should be posted to, and the remailer sends the message on, sans identity.

You can find these services by searching for remailers at a search site (or go to a list of remailers at `http://www.cs.berkeley.edu/~raph/remailer-list.html` or Yahoo!'s Anonymous Remailers page: `http://www.yahoo.com/Computers_and_Internet/Security_and_Encryption/Anonymous_Mailers/`). But note that these systems are not perfect. They depend on the reliability of the person running the service and, in some cases, on that person's willingness to go to prison. If the police come knocking at his door, the administrator might just hand over his records. (This has happened; at least one anonymous remailer has handed over information.) Another problem with remailers is that they go one way only. You can send, but not receive.

Another Problem Who runs the anonymous remailers? If you were a smart computer cop, wouldn't it occur to you to set up your own anonymous remailer? It already has occurred to various police forces, so you can't be absolutely sure that the anonymous remailer you are using isn't merely a trick to track down people saying things that they "shouldn't" say.

Nothing's completely safe. Even using a genuine anonymous remailer can leave you at risk; your email could be intercepted between your computer and the remailer, for instance. As the *Frequently Asked Questions About Anonymous Remailers* document (`http://www.cs.berkeley.edu/~raph/remailer-faq.html`) says, "Hard-core privacy people do not trust individual remailers...[they] write programs that send their messages through several remailers...only the first remailer knows their real address, and the first remailer cannot know the final destination of the email message."

I "Borrowed" a Picture, and Now They're Suing Me!

As you've seen throughout this book, grabbing things from the Internet is as easy as stealing from a baby—but there's none of the guilt. It's so easy and so guilt-free that many Internet users have come to believe in a sort of "finder's keepers" copyright morality. If it's there, and if you can take it, you can use it.

The law says otherwise, though. Here's a quick summary of copyright law: If you created it, it belongs to you (or to your boss if he paid you to create it). You can put it anywhere you want, but unless you sign a contract giving away rights to it, you still own the copyright. You don't have to register copyright, either.

Can I Take It for Personal Use? In most cases, you probably can. When you connect to a Web site, all the things that are transferred to your computer end up in the cache anyway. However, some enthusiastic copyright lawyers claim that the use of a cache is in itself illegal, that even storing images and text on your hard drive goes against copyright law.

Copyright law is quite complicated, however, and this summary misses many essential details. The important thing to understand is that it *doesn't* belong to you if you didn't create it! Unless something has been placed on the Internet with a notice explicitly stating that you can take and use it, you can take it for personal use, but you can't use it publicly. You can't steal pictures to use at your Web site, for instance. (Even if there is a notice stating that the item is in the public domain, it may not be. After all, how do you know that the person giving it away created it?)

Copyright law even extends to newsgroups and mailing lists. You can't just steal someone's poetry, story, ruminations, or whatever from a message and distribute it in any way you want. It doesn't belong to you. Of course, if you are concerned that your work will be taken from a newsgroup or mailing list and distributed, don't put it there!

I Downloaded a File, and Now My Computer's Queasy

Yes, you know what I'm talking about: computer viruses. These nasty little programs get loose in your computer and do things they shouldn't, like wipe your hard drive or destroy the directory information that allows your computer to find files on the drive.

First, my role as contrarian dictates that I inform you that much of the fuss about viruses is greatly exaggerated. When something goes wrong with a computer, a virus usually gets the blame. An example of how the virus threat is exaggerated is the famous Good Times virus. This virus never existed; it was a myth from the start. The story was that an email message containing a virus was being passed around the Internet. The story was obviously wrong because a plain email message without a file attached cannot contain a virus.

Only files that "do things" can contain viruses. That includes program files, as well as document files created by programs that have macro languages. For instance, a variety of Word for Windows and Excel macro viruses just appeared in the past few years (what took them so long?). If a file can do nothing by itself—if it has to have another program to do something to it—it can't carry a virus. A plain text file (including text messages) can't do anything, and .GIF or .JPG image files cannot cause harm. (I'm just waiting for the next big hoax: Someone will start a rumor that there's an image file used at many Web sites that contains a virus and that all you have to do is load the page with the image to infect your computer.)

Yes, viruses do exist. Yes, you should protect yourself. There are many good antivirus programs around, so if you plan to download software from the Web (not just images and documents from applications other than advanced word processors), you should get one. But no, it's not worth losing sleep over.

The Least You Need to Know

- Yes, there's sex on the Internet, but not as much as the press claims. Get a filtering and blocking program if you want to keep the kids away.
- Email can easily be stolen or forwarded. Don't write anything that you could be embarrassed by later.
- People on the Internet sometimes lie (just like in the real world). They may not be who they say they are (or even the sex they claim to be).
- Internet addiction? Snap out of it! (Or go online and get some help.)
- You can search thousands of newsgroups at once, with systems such as DejaNews, to see what people are saying about you.
- Your boss can find out which Web sites you are visiting, so watch out!
- Credit card transactions made on the Internet are safer than those made in the real world.

- Anonymous email accounts can protect your identity in email and newsgroups.
- You don't own what you find on the Internet; it's copyright protected.
- Viruses are relatively few and far between; but it's a good idea to protect yourself with an antivirus program.

Chapter 13

21 Questions: The Complete Internet FAQ

In This Chapter

- Shell accounts, finger, and Winsocks
- Changing your password
- Why some programs won't run in Windows
- Can you sell fish on the Internet?
- Slowdowns and connection problems
- Staying anonymous and much more

In this chapter you will find answers to some questions you may have and a few problems you may run into—everything from the meaning of certain terms to solutions for certain problems.

1. What's a Shell Account?

You may remember me telling you (back in Chapter 1, "The Internet: What's It All About?") that a few years ago most people dialing into a service provider were using dial-in terminal accounts. These are often known as *shell* accounts. If you have a TCP/IP account with a service provider, you probably also have a shell account. Or if you sign up with a Web-hosting company to host your Web site, you'll probably get a shell account, too.

So you have a choice: You can connect to the Internet via the fancy graphical software, or you can connect using the bland command-line interface. Why bother with the command line when you can have the splashy graphics? The answer to the next question will provide an example of why you would want to, and when you look at the finger command later in this chapter, you'll see another example.

Most service providers give you a free shell account when you sign up for a PPP account. Others have the nerve to charge extra for the privilege. You shouldn't have to pay extra for it.

2. How Do I Change My Password If I'm Using a PPP Connection?

The fact that this is even a problem strikes me as a little strange. Many service providers don't provide a convenient way for you to change your password with a dial-in direct connection, yet they'll tell you that you should change your password frequently for security's sake. They *could* provide a Web form, but most don't. Many Web-hosting companies don't provide a password either. So how *do* you change your password?

Not a Good Sign Some major service providers don't let you change your password at all. You have to call and ask them to do it for you, which is a *very* bad way to go about it!

If you are with an online service such as MSN, AOL, or CompuServe, the main program probably has some kind of password menu option. But if you are with a service provider, you may have to connect to their system with a terminal program. You need to get to the menu system used by people who are not fortunate enough to have a dial-in direct account. Find a menu option that says "Account Assistance" or something similar, and then look for one that says something like "Change Password."

But how do you get to the menu you need to change your password? One way is to connect using a simple serial-communications program (such as Windows 3.1's Terminal or Windows 95's HyperTerminal) or any commercial or shareware terminal program. You dial the phone number for your shell account and then log in, but you'll have to ask your service provider for information because the login instructions may be different. If you want more information about this procedure, you should see the first edition of this book; send email to `ciginternet@mcp.com`, type the word **first** in the Subject line, and leave the body of the message blank. You'll get Chapter 6 in an email response message.

The other way is to connect to the Internet in the manner you usually employ and then open a Telnet program. Connect to your service provider through Telnet, log on to your shell account, and then go to the change-password menu option. Call and ask your service provider which Telnet address to use.

3. What's a Winsock?

Winsock is short for "Windows sockets," and it's the program used by Microsoft Windows to act as an interface between TCP/IP programs running on the computer and the Internet itself. Just as a printer needs a printer driver to interface between the programs and the printer, the Internet needs a driver to interface between the programs and the Internet. In the Windows world, that driver is known as a Winsock. If you have a Macintosh, you don't have a Winsock, of course, but you still need TCP/IP software.

If you use Windows 3.1, you have to acquire a Winsock program separately—it doesn't come with the operating system. Most service providers and online services now include Winsock with the software they provide you (you can install it yourself if need be; one of the most commonly used ones is Trumpet Winsock, which you can find at many software archives. In Windows 95, 98, and NT, Winsock is built-in, so you don't need to get a separate program. (However, you may need an advanced degree in networking to figure out how to use it.) The easiest way to handle all this is to get an installation program from a service provider or an online service that installs and configures the Winsock for you.

4. Why Won't Netscape Run in Windows 95?

This problem is not quite as common as it used to be, but it's still around; in fact, it got me just the other day. Suppose you are using Windows 95 and have connected to an Internet service provider that gave you Windows software to install. Then you go to the Netscape Web site to download the latest version of that navigator, or maybe you download the latest version of Internet Explorer. Which version do you pick? Why, the 32-bit version, of course, the one designed for Windows 95, 98, and NT. You install the program, and try it—but it doesn't work. What's going on?

The problem may be that, although you are using Windows 95 (what's known as a 32-bit operating system), the Winsock program you are using is a 16-bit program. Remember, the Winsock is the "driver" that connects your programs to the Internet. The Winsock is installed when you install the software needed to dial into the Internet. To run a 32-bit program (such as the Windows 95 versions of Netscape or Internet Explorer), you must use a 32-bit Winsock!

A year or two ago, many services were still providing 16-bit Winsocks, even though millions of people had Windows 95. Although most online services and service providers are now providing 32-bit Winsocks, some of the more inept services are still working with 16-bit Winsocks. If your service provider is still using an old 16-bit program, your only options are to stick with 16-bit programs (those created for Windows 3.1) or to convince the service provider to help you set up Windows 95's, 98's, or NT's Dial-Up Networking software—or if they won't help, to find another service provider that will.

Anytime you run a 16-bit Winsock, you are stuck with 16-bit Internet programs. If you are trying to install a 32-bit Windows program and can't get it to work, start by checking to see if you have a Winsock designed for Windows 95 or NT.

5. Why Won't My Browser Display This or That or the Other?

When you buy a TV, you expect to be able to use it to watch any program on any channel you have available. You don't expect to see error messages telling you something in a program can't be displayed or messages saying that if you want to see a particular program you'll have to install the *Geraldo* plug-in.

That's not the way it works on the Web. Browsers behave differently. Some browsers won't work with JavaScript or Java (or you may have turned off these things in your program preferences). Old browsers can't display frames and can't work with plug-ins—or if you have a recent browser, maybe you haven't installed the plug-in that a particular site requires.

You can avoid some of these problems, but by no means all, by working with the most up-to-date version of Netscape Navigator. You can get away with using the most recent version of Internet Explorer, too, although it's likely that it won't be quite as up-to-date as Netscape Navigator. But whichever browser you choose, there will *always* be certain features that won't work properly.

6. Can You Sell Fish on the Internet?

This is a real question that someone asked me during a radio show interview. (The question came from a fisherman in Alaska who was looking for new markets.) And I don't have the definitive answer. All I can say is, "maybe." But you'd better have a really good plan!

I don't know how you can go about selling fish, but I do know that you can sell various kinds of stuff—real stuff, not other Internet services. The editors took a poll and told me they'd seen salad dressing, teddy bears, model horses, live horses, legal services, picture-scanning devices, Internet tutoring, and real estate for sale. There are also books, CDs, and videos—as well as hot sauce, pizza, a newsletter for writers of children's stories, and all sorts of other stuff. Of course, all these people are not necessarily making money doing this, but some most certainly are.

CDnow sold 16 million dollars' worth of music CDs in 1997, for instance, and that company was started by 24-year-old twin brothers. More modest successes abound. I know a small publisher selling more than $30,000 worth of books a year through his Web site; a company that sells a remote control "flying saucer" (it's actually a helium balloon) gets a significant portion of their income from the Web; and a fantasy-sports software company finds many new customers on the Internet. My own Web site (`http://www.poorrichard.com/`) is most definitely making a profit, and sales are growing.

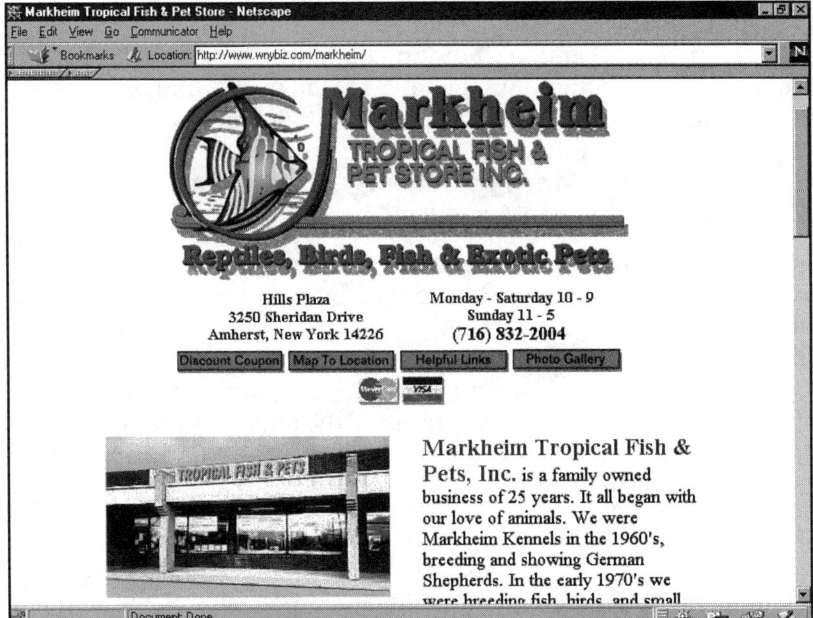

Maybe you can sell fish on the Internet.

7. If I Have a Fast Modem, Why Are Transfers So Slow?

You've just installed a fancy new 56Kbps modem, the very latest in modem technology you've been told, and still some Web sites are about as speedy as molasses on a cool day in Iceland. What's going on here? Your information has to pass through many computer systems, along lots of lines; hey, it may be coming from halfway across the world, after all.

Think of this transfer across the Internet as a relay race. The information you want is passed from person to person, maybe dozens of times, between the Web site and you. The last person in the chain is that speedy 56Kbps modem you bought. But when you look at the others involved in the race, you see that some are as athletic as Roseanne, and others are as fast as your grandmother. Still others may be very fast, but they've got other jobs to do, too. They are involved in hundreds of relay races at the same time! If you are at a very popular Web site, for instance, hundreds of other people just like you are trying to get information at the same time, and that relay runner might be having serious problems keeping up. (In any case, your 56Kbps modem almost certainly isn't operating at 56Kbps—see Appendix A, "Finding Internet Access and the Right Equipment.") I know I've told you that the Internet is a bunch of telephone wires connected to each other, but the truth is that it often operates like millions of bottlenecks strung together on a long piece of string.

If it's any consolation (and it probably isn't), it's not just you having problems; millions of other people are sitting at their computers in Alberta, Arizona, Austria, and other places beginning with different letters, saying, "I just bought this 56Kbps modem. Why did I bother wasting my money?" Why would anyone bother to get a fast modem? Because with a slow one, you'll be even slower. The Internet isn't slow all the time, so the faster your modem, the faster data transfers will be.

Another reason that your traffic might be slow is something called *differentiated service levels* or *preferential packets*. Information sent across the Internet is sent in small packets of data, each packet containing the address that's needed to get it to where it has to go. The packet can also include priority information. There are reports that the companies owning the Internet backbones are now selling priority service to major corporations. (A backbone is a major line on the Internet; you might think of the line from your computer to your service provider as a path, the line from your service provider to the backbone as a road, and the backbone as a major freeway.)

If a backbone company sells preferential treatment, it means that information going to or from the preferred site goes through right away. Any other packets of information have to wait in a queue. Each time a preferred packet arrives, that packet goes to the front of the queue. Mid-afternoon in North America is often a very busy time on the Internet anyway; corporate employees come back from lunch and log onto the Dilbert site or perhaps even do some work. But if those employees are getting preferential treatment, then it's even slower for the rest of us. So if your packet is sitting in a queue on a backbone on the other side of the country, it doesn't matter how fast your modem is—the packet can't get to you!

8. Will the Internet Kill Television?

No. Using the Internet is active; using the television is passive. Remember, television was supposed to kill both movies and radio, but both seem healthy enough today. For that matter, movies were supposed to kill theater, and theater (if I remember right) was supposed to kill rock paintings. Anyway, do you really want to watch *Titanic* on your computer?

9. Why Isn't Anyone Reading My Web Page?

I guess you heard the nonsense that "A Web page is a billboard that can be seen by millions," and you believed it. Let me put it this way: There are 250 million people in the United States, but if you put up a *real* billboard in the United States, will 250 million people see it? I won't bother answering that.

The Web is not a highway, and your page is not a billboard. If you want people to come to your Web page, you have to promote it. Don't believe all that "If you want people to come to your Web site, it has to be compelling" nonsense either. A Web page has to serve a purpose; if it serves its purpose well and is well-promoted, it can do well (even if it doesn't use Java to display some pointless animation).

10. How Can I Remain Anonymous on the Internet?

Many people are concerned with keeping their privacy and anonymity on the Internet. In particular, women who like to spend time in chat rooms often feel the need to put up a protective wall between themselves and other members. If a relationship develops with someone online, they want to be in control of how much information about themselves they allow others to discover.

There are some basic strategies you can use to maintain your anonymity on the Internet:

- Get an account with an online service or service provider and obtain an account name that is nothing like your own name. If your name is Jane Doe, use an account name such as *HipChick* or *SusanSmith.*
- Many online services enable you to enter information about yourself, also known as a profile, that others can view (in chat rooms, for instance). If you are with an online service, make sure your profile is empty.
- If you are with a service provider, ask your provider to disable finger for your account. (Finger is a service that other Internet users can employ to find information about you—see the next section.)
- Once you are on the Internet, be careful not to leave identifying information when you're leaving messages in newsgroups, working with mailing lists, and so on.

Although these strategies won't ensure full anonymity, they work pretty well in most cases. To find out who HipChick or SusanSmith is, someone would have to persuade your service provider to divulge information. That's not impossible, but in most cases, it's unlikely (unless you're doing something to incite the interest of the police or the FBI).

You can also get a free email account from Juno, Yahoo!, Hotmail, or many other companies. When you fill in the form identifying yourself, dissemble (the word used to be lie, I believe, but politicians thought that word too coarse). See Chapter 12, "Staying Safe on the Internet," for more information on staying safe and anonymous.

11. What's Finger?

With the finger UNIX command, you can retrieve information about other people on the Internet if you have just a little bit of information. You can use this command in either of two ways:

- Log on to your shell account and get to the command line (you should find a menu option somewhere that will take you there; ask your service provider if you can't find it). At the command line, type **finger** and press **Enter** to run the command.
- Install a finger client, a program that allows you to run finger from within your graphical user interface—from Windows or the Macintosh, for instance.

Some You Win, Some You Lose Many service providers completely disable finger requests. Others disable certain types of requests. For instance, if you were to try a command like **`finger smith@big.net`**, some service providers would send a list of all the account holders called Smith, but some providers simply wouldn't respond.

Suppose you've seen the `HipChick@big.net` email address and want to find out about HipChick. You use the finger command **`finger HipChick@big.net`** and press **Enter**. A request for information is sent to big.net. You *may* get such information as the account holder's real name, which is why I told you to make sure finger is disabled if you want to remain anonymous!

12. Can Someone Forge My Email?

A year or two ago I saw a message in a mailing list from someone complaining that an email message to the list was forged. Someone else had sent a message using this person's email address. Another member of the list wrote a message telling her that she should be more careful. He said (a little bluntly) that if she left her computer unattended she should expect trouble. Thinking I'd play a little game, I sent a forged message to the list in *his* name. (No, I didn't know him, and I definitely didn't have access to his computer.) "That'll teach him," I thought, "He should be more careful."

It's very easy to forge email messages—so easy, in fact, that I'm surprised it doesn't happen more often. (It probably happens more often to people who spend a lot of time in newsgroups, mailing lists, and chat rooms—where it's easy to get into fights—than to people who use other services.) A person can forge a message simply by entering incorrect configuration information into a mail program or, better still, the mail program of a public Web browser. However, before you run out and play tricks on people, I should warn you that this mail can still be traced to some degree. (It might be difficult, though, for anyone other than a police officer with a warrant to get the service providers to do the tracing for him.)

How can you avoid this problem? There's not much you can do except keep your head down and stay out of "flame wars" (which I'll discuss next). You *could* digitally sign all your messages, although that may be overkill.

13. What's a Flame?

I've heard it said that the Internet will lead to world peace. As people use the Net to communicate with others around the world, a new era of understanding will come to pass...blah, blah, blah. The same was said about the telegraph and the television, but so far, there hasn't been much of a peace spin-off from those technologies! But what makes me sure that the Internet will not lead to world peace (and may lead to world war) is the prevalence of flame wars in mailing lists and newsgroups.

A *flame* is a message that is intended as an assault on another person, an ad hominem attack. Such messages are common and lead to flame wars, as the victim responds and others get in on the act. In some discussion groups, flame wars are almost the purpose of the group. You'll find that the Internet is no haven of peace and goodwill—and I haven't even mentioned the obnoxious behavior of many in chat rooms.

14. I'm Leaving My Service Provider. How Can I Keep My Email Address?

I currently have three Internet accounts. Over the past few years, I've had dozens of accounts, and that means I've had dozens of email addresses. Although this is unusual, it's certainly not unusual for people to have a handful of accounts as they search for the best one. Unfortunately, keeping your friends and colleagues up-to-date on your email address is a real hassle. If only there were a way to keep the same address, even when you changed providers...

There just might be. You can register your own *domain name*. You do this through InterNIC, and you can find instructions for doing so at `http://rs.internic.net/` or at `http://www.worldnic.com/` (the second site will cost $10 more, but is much easier to use). It costs $70 for the first two years and $35 a year after that to keep the domain name. Many service providers will register a domain for you, but they may charge you an additional fee to do so.

Once you have your own domain name, you can set up a mail service (search for **email service** at a search site such as Yahoo!) and assign the domain name to that service. Then all your email addressed to that domain will be sent to the service, which will store it in your POP (Post Office Protocol) account. You'll use a mail program to download your mail from there. (When you register a domain name, you have to already have chosen a service, because the email service provider has to set up its computers to recognize the name.) If you plan to set up a Web site with a Web-hosting company, then you can register the domain to that company's servers, and you'll get your email there.

Once you are using an email service or getting email through a Web-hosting company, it doesn't matter which service provider or online service you use to get onto the Internet. You can change from one company to another as many times as you like, and you'll still be able to get to your mail through the email provider or hosting company. And if you ever decide to move your domain name to a different email provider or hosting company? Then find the new company and transfer your domain to it. Whether you change email providers, hosting companies, or Internet service providers, you can always keep your email address. Email services start at around $5 a month, and even Web-hosting accounts are available for less than $10 a month.

Another way to keep your email address is to sign up with a free or low-cost email service. A number of these are around now (search at `http://www.yahoo.com/` for **free email service**). These services are usually free because they sell advertising that is shown when you get your mail. If you don't mind that, though, this is a good way to get and keep an email address, regardless of how many times you change your service provider. One of these companies (MailBank: `http://mailbank.com/`) has bought up thousands of domain names based on people's last names, so for $5 a year you can have an address that uses your last name as the domain name: john@kent.org, fred@smithmail.com, and so on.

15. Why Can't I Get Through to That Site?

You'll often find that you cannot connect to sites that you've used before or that you've seen or heard mentioned somewhere. You might find Web pages that you can't connect to, FTP sites that don't seem to work, and Telnet sites that seem to be out of commission. Why?

The first thing you should check is your spelling and case; if you type one wrong character or type something uppercase when it should be lowercase (or vice versa), you won't connect. (The following figure shows the dialog box Netscape Navigator displays when you've typed the name incorrectly.) Another possibility is that the service you are trying to connect to might just be very busy, with hundreds of other people trying to connect. Depending on the software you are using, you might see a message to that effect. Or it could be that the service is temporarily disconnected; the computer that holds the service might have broken or might have been disconnected for service. Finally, the service might not be there anymore.

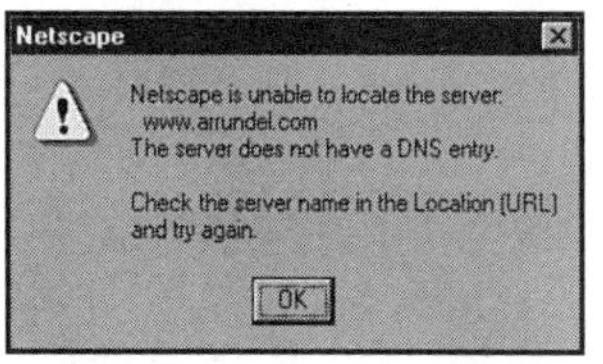

Oops! I mistyped the URL, and my browser can't find the host.

Trying again a few times often helps; you'll be surprised just how often you can get through to an apparently dead site just by trying again a few moments later. Also note that some software is a little buggy. For instance, some browsers seem to hang up and appear unable to transfer data from a site at times; but canceling the transfer and starting again often jump-starts the process.

Don't Place the Blame Too Quickly

Often it's your service provider, not the site you are trying to connect to, that's having problems. Try connecting to a variety of sites, and if you can't get through to any, it's probably a problem with your connection to the service provider or with the provider's system. Try disconnecting and logging back on.

16. Why Won't This URL Work?

URLs are a special case because even if they don't seem to work, you may be able to modify them and get them to work. First, make sure you are using the correct case. If a word in the URL was shown as uppercase, don't type lowercase (if the URL doesn't work with some words uppercase, though, you might try lowercase).

Second, make sure you are using the correct file extension if there is one. If the URL ends in .HTM, make sure you are not typing .HTML, for instance. If the URL still doesn't work, start removing portions of the URL. Suppose you have this URL:

```
http://www.big.net/public/software/
macintosh/internet/listing.html
```

Check This Out...

Remove the Period When you type a URL, don't type a period at the end. You may find URLs in books and magazines that appear to end with a period because they are used at the ends of sentences. But real URLs don't end with periods, so make sure you don't include the periods when typing.

You've tried using both `listing.html` and `listing.htm` at the end, and neither seems to work. Drop `listing.html` and try again. You may get a document with links to something you can use. If you still don't get anything, remove the `internet/` part (in other words, you are now typing just **`http://www.big.net/public/software/macintosh/`**). If that doesn't work, remove the next part, macintosh/. Continue in this manner, removing piece after piece, and in most cases, you'll eventually find something useful.

17. Why Do So Many People Hate AOL?

It's an unfortunate truth that America Online members have a bad reputation on the Internet. You may run across rude messages in which people insult AOL members or treat them as if they are the scum of the earth. Here's what happened. AOL, like all the online services, decided that it had better get Internet access in a hurry. So it started adding Internet services, and it added newsgroup access quite early. All of a sudden, about a gazillion AOL members flooded onto the Internet in a rush that would have had the bulls at Pamplona running in the opposite direction. Millions of AOL members overwhelmed these discussion groups with questions such as "How do you download files from this group?" and "Where are the pornographic pictures?" Of all the online services' members, AOL's members were probably the least computer-literate. (AOL had targeted the "family" market, while CompuServe, for instance, had been a geek service for years.)

The Internet had been, until just a few months before, a secret kept from most of the world. All of a sudden, it was as busy as a shopping mall on a Saturday afternoon, and every bit as cultured. And there was an obvious scapegoat: all those people with @aol.com email addresses! Unfortunately, you might still run across anti-AOL bias on the Internet.

18. My Download Crashed, So I Have to Start Again. Why?

Most online services use file-transfer systems that can "recover" if the transfer is interrupted. For instance, if you are halfway through downloading a file from CompuServe when your three-year-old kid decides he wants to see what happens when he presses the big red button on the front of your computer, all is not lost. After you reboot the computer and reconnect to CompuServe, you can begin the file transfer again. But you don't have to transfer the whole thing; instead the transfer begins in the middle.

However, that won't work on the World Wide Web, for the moment at least (Web browsers will eventually be able to resume interrupted downloads, but they can't yet). It *can* work on *some* FTP sites, with *some* FTP programs though, which is one reason that FTP can be so useful. If you prefer to use your Web browser for transferring files, though, you'll have to keep your kid away from the computer (or try covering the button with a piece of card).

19. Where Do I Find...?

You're in the wrong chapter; see Chapter 11, "Finding Stuff."

20. Should I Start My Own Service Provider Company?

No.

21. Why Not?

One of the most common questions Internet writers get asked is, "How can I set up a business as an Internet service provider?" The easy answer is, "If you don't know, you shouldn't be trying." It's a very complicated—and currently very competitive—business. If you don't know what it takes, you probably don't know how little you know, and you shouldn't be trying. After all, over the next few years, thousands of Internet service providers will bite the dust as the big telecommunications companies get in on the act. Why add your blood, sweat, and tears to the pile? You can run many other businesses with a better chance of success. Or, if you really want to bankrupt a business, pick one with lower initial costs.

Just One More Question...

You're going to come away from this book with lots of questions because the Internet is big, there are many different ways to connect to it, and there's a huge amount of strange stuff out there. I hope this book has helped you start, but I know you'll have many more questions.

Once you are on your own, what do you do? Try these suggestions:

- *Get the FAQs.* FAQ means "frequently asked questions," and it refers to a document with questions and answers about a particular subject. Many newsgroups and mailing lists have FAQs explaining how to use them, for example, and Web sites often have FAQ pages. Look for these FAQs and read them!
- *Continue your reading.* I've written about a dozen Internet books and need to sell them, so continue buying (and reading) them. Well, okay, there are other writers putting out Internet books, too (you may have noticed a few). To become a real cybergeek, you'll need to learn much more. So check out a few of these books.
- *Read the documentation.* There are literally thousands of Internet programs, and each is a little different. Make sure you read all the documentation that comes with your programs so you know how to get the most out of them.
- *Ask your service provider!* I've said it before, and I'll say it again: If your service provider won't help you, get another service provider! The Internet is too complicated to travel around without help. Now and again you'll have to ask your service provider's staff for information. Don't be scared to ask—and don't be scared to find another provider if the first one won't or can't answer your questions.

The Least You Need to Know

- A shell account is a dial-in terminal account. You may have a free shell account, and you may need to use your shell account to change your password.
- Getting rich on the Internet is a lot harder than it's been made out to be.
- You may have a fast modem, but if the Internet is busy, things will still move slowly.
- Use an email service if you want to be able to switch between service providers without changing your email address each time.
- You can be anonymous on the Internet if you are careful.
- If your service provider won't answer your questions, you need another service provider!

Chapter 14

Ideas

In This Chapter

- What use is the Internet?
- Using the Internet for business and pleasure
- Finding information online
- Music and culture
- What else do you want to do?

Throughout this book, I've explained many of the services the Internet can provide. But you might now be wondering "What good are these things?" Unfortunately, until you get onto the Internet, get hooked, and forget that you have responsibilities out in the "real" world, it's difficult to understand what the Internet can do for you. (Imagine, for a moment, the Neanderthal thawed out of the ice and introduced to modern technology: "Okay, so I can use this soap stuff to remove the smell from my armpits, right? What for?") This chapter gives you a quick rundown on just a few of the ways in which ordinary (and some not-so-ordinary) folks are incorporating cyberspace into their daily lives.

Keeping in Touch

The world has shrunk over the past few years—at least for those of us in cyberspace. I hadn't spoken with my sister in a decade or two, but now that she's online I hear from her every week or two (every day or two if her computer's acting up). My brother lives a continent away, but I hear from him frequently via email. An old school friend and I planned a trip to Iceland, using email to swap lists of things we'll need. Just recently I've received email from several people I'd worked with a decade ago in another life. Email is a wonderful system—sort of like the U.S. mail on amphetamines.

Meeting Your Peers

Many people use the Internet as a way to keep in touch with their peers. They can find out about job opportunities, new techniques and tools used in their business, or problems they've run into that they think *surely* someone else has experienced. The mailing lists and discussion groups provide a fantastic way to meet other people in your business field.

Business Communications

As I write this book, every now and then I have a question for the editor. I simply write the message and click a button, and off it flies. Later, when I finish this chapter, I'll send the document file via email, too. Then later still, after the chapter's been edited, the editor can send it back via email. I'll change the edits back to what I originally wrote and then send it back yet again. (Editor's note: Yeah, that's what *he* thinks!)

Many businesses have discovered that the Internet provides a rapid communications tool. Why type a letter, memo, or report into a word processor, print it out, put it in an envelope, take it to a mailbox (or call FedEx), and wait a day or five for it to arrive when you can send the same word processing document and have it arrive a minute or two—even a few seconds—later?

Product Information

We live in an instant gratification society, the entire purpose of which is to get toys into your hands faster and faster. Do you need information about that new car you want to buy, for instance? If so, go to `http://www.edmunds.com/` to check it out (you learned about Web addresses like this in Chapter 3, "The World of the World Wide Web"). As you can see in the following figure, the page contains the car's specifications as well as a picture of it. You can drool over it—and even find out just how much the dealer paid for it.

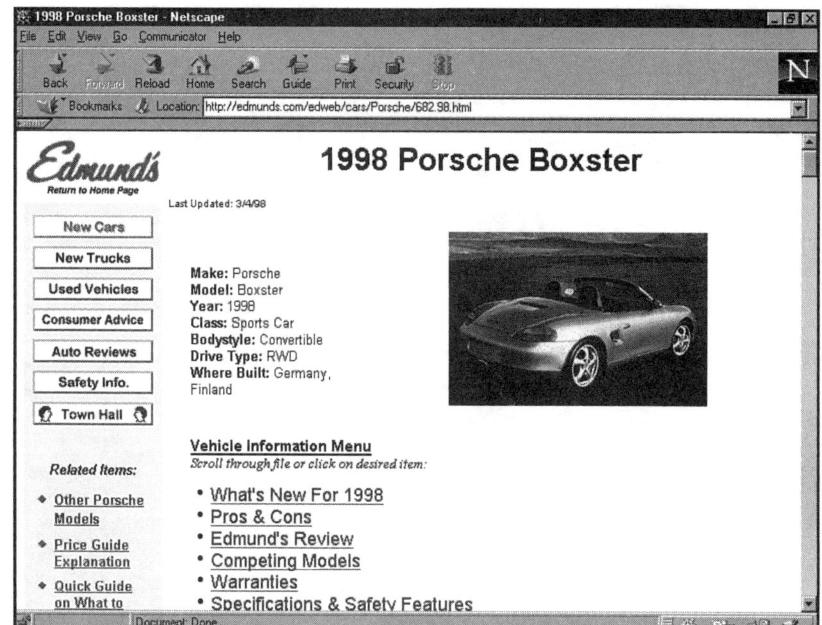

With what you'll save on this baby, you'll be able to buy Internet access for the rest of your life!

Product Support

There's a downside to the Internet of course: It's run by computers, which, as we all know, are the work of Satan. Still, the next time your computer does something weird or you need a new print driver, go online and find the fix or software you need. Many computer and software companies, perhaps most, now have an online technical support site. Although it would be nice if all these sites were well-designed, some of them are as easy to use as running shoes on a frozen lake.

Getting Software

We're back to instant gratification. You know that program you just saw advertised in *Internet Windows Computing World* magazine? Want to try it out? Go online and download a demo right now! There's no more waiting. Pretty soon everybody will be buying software and transferring it straight to his computer.

You can use one of the Internet's great shareware libraries, too. The following figure shows the TUCOWS site. TUCOWS, The Ultimate Collection of Winsock Software, is a library of shareware Internet programs for Microsoft Windows 3.x, 95, 98, and NT; they have Macintosh and OS/2 software, too. You can find it on the Web at `http://www.tucows.com/`.

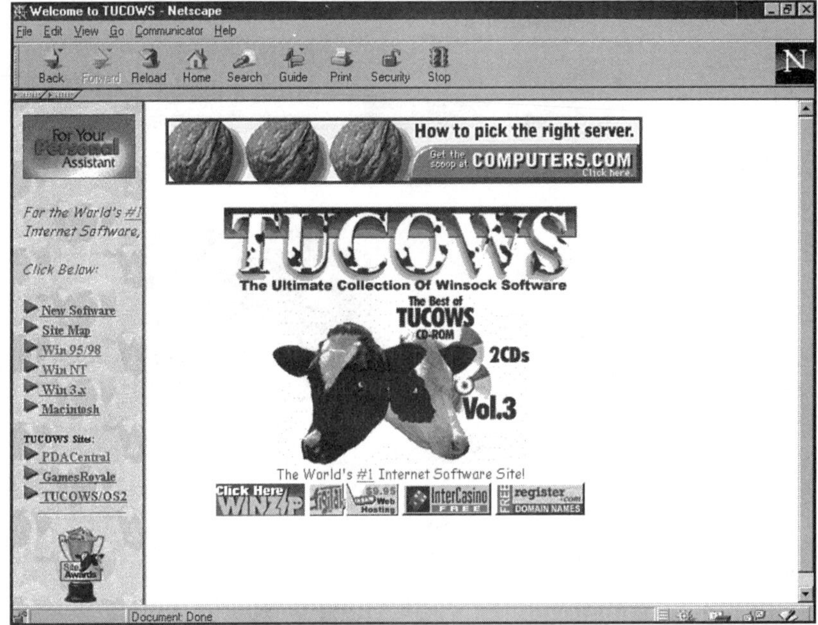

TUCOWS: The Ultimate Collection of Winsock Software (they have Macintosh and OS2 stuff now, too).

Research

If you are writing a school paper, researching a book, or planning a vacation, the Internet contains a cornucopia of illuminating tidbits. It's *not* a library (contrary to the nonsense of those in the Internet community who got a little carried away with their predictions), and it will be a long time before it can replace one. Still, it does give you access to huge amounts of useful information that's just waiting to be used.

Suppose you are planning to visit, oh, I don't know, how about Iceland? Get onto the World Wide Web and search for Iceland (you learned how to search for stuff in Chapter 11, "Finding Stuff"). What do you find? A hundred or more sites with information about Icelandic travel, sports, culture, media, real estate (there's no way *I'm* moving there), news, and more.

Visiting Museums

I suppose you can't afford to visit the Louvre *and* the Smithsonian this year. What a shame. Still, you can get online and see what you are missing (see the following figure). The potential here is greater than the reality. Maybe someday most of the masterpieces in the world's great museums will be online; but right now, many museums just provide one or two pictures and information about which subway to take to get there.

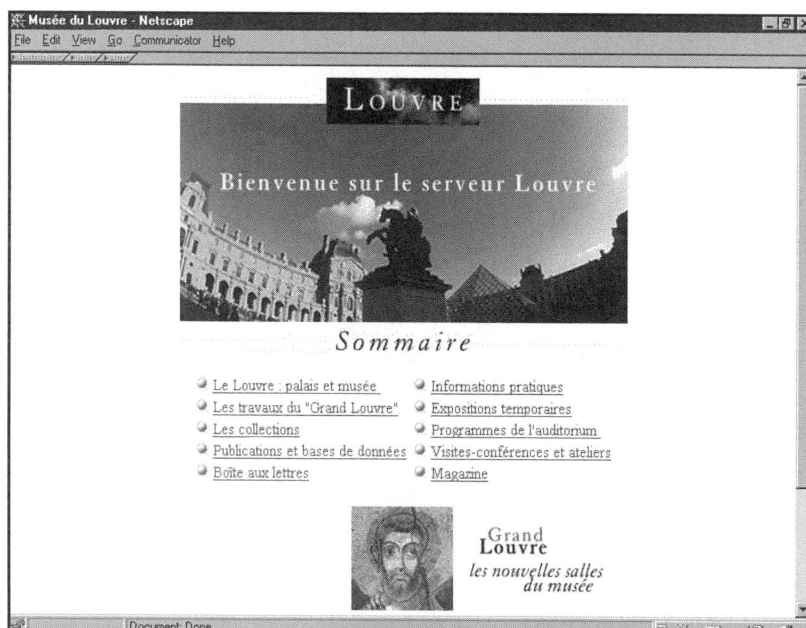

Visit the Louvre this summer from the comfort of your own home (`http://www.louvre.fr/`*).*

Finding Financial Information

Want stock quotes? How about information about competitors or about online banking services? You'll find it on the Internet. You can find links to great financial services at the search sites discussed in Chapter 11. Or try Yahoo! Finance (`http://quote.yahoo.com/`) or InvestorGuide (`http://www.investorguide.com/`).

Music

If music is your passion, you'll be happy to know that you can hear some of the latest from the music world when you find it on the Internet. Try IUMA, the Internet Underground Music Archive (`http://www.iuma.com/`). Would you prefer bagpipe music or film scores? Maybe you want to buy some CDs (see `http://cdnow.com/`). Whatever you're looking for, you can find it on the Internet.

Magazines and 'Zines

You'll find thousands of magazines and 'zines online. (For the not-quite-so-hip among you, a *'zine* is a small magazine, usually published on a shoestring by someone with three or more pierced body parts.) You'll find underground books and comics, as well as newsletters on almost anything you can imagine (and probably a few things you can't imagine). A good place to start is the E-Zines Database at `http://www.dominis.com/Zines/` or the E-Zine List at `http://www.meer.net/~johnl/e-zine-list/`.

Hiding from the Real World

There's a wonderful cartoon that is legendary in the computer world. It shows a dog in front of a computer terminal, and it has the caption "Nobody knows you're a dog on the Internet." It's unfortunate that the need exists, but quite frankly, there are people who use the Internet to hide from the real world. For one reason or another, they have trouble with face-to-face relationships, yet on the Internet they can feel safe and part of a community.

If You *Can't* Get Out

Some people would love to have more face-to-face relationships but for some reason can't get out to meet people. Perhaps they are elderly or disabled or have been posted to the Antarctic. Or maybe they're not leaving their apartment for fear of being served a Kenneth Starr subpoena. Regardless of the reason, the Internet provides a link to the rest of the world for those times when you can't physically get somewhere.

Shakespeare on the Net

A little while ago I met a fellow computer book writer who stages Shakespeare plays in IRC (Internet Relay Chat). This chap (he's English) takes a play, modifies it slightly to his taste (he recently staged an updated version of *Macbeth*), and breaks it down into its individual character parts. He sends each "actor" his lines only, no more. Each line has a cue number, so the person playing the character will know when to type the lines. Then they start, each person typing his or her lines at the appropriate cue position. It's an act of discovery for all the "actors" because they don't know what the other characters will say until they say it. Strange, but strangely fascinating.

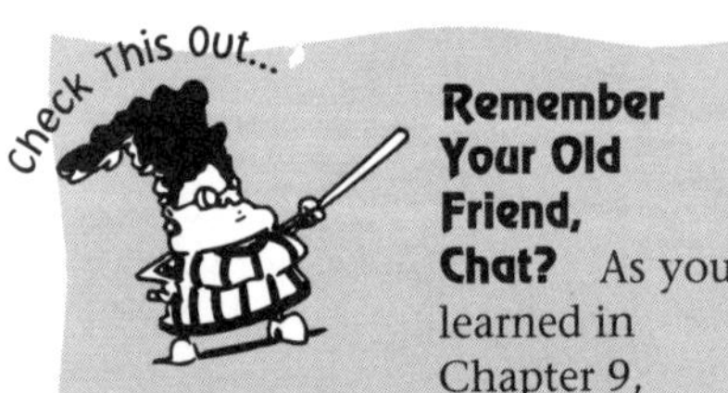

Remember Your Old Friend, Chat? As you learned in Chapter 9, "Yak, Yak, Yak: Chatting in Cyberspace," IRC is a chat system. You type a message, and it's immediately transmitted to all the other people involved in the chat session. They respond, and you immediately see what they have typed.

Joining a Community of People with Common Interests

Suppose you have some, er, let's say unusual interests. You believe the U.S. government has been chopping up aliens for years—or maybe that it's in cahoots with aliens. Or suppose that, by chance, you are consumed with a hatred of purple dinosaurs (one in particular, anyway) or that you feel compelled to tell others of your latest, um, erotic experience in the air.

Now suppose that, in your neighborhood, there are few people who share your interests. Who do you share your thoughts with? Where can you find a sense of community? On the Internet, of course, in the newsgroups and mailing lists (see Chapters 7–8). (And yes, the examples suggested above are real examples.) You may be surprised at the sort of people you find online. It's not all techno-chat. I have a friend who's a member of a discussion group on the subject of renovating antique tractors, for instance!

You Don't Trust Your Doctor

I must admit I don't have a lot of faith in doctors. Grandma was right: Stay away from hospitals—they're dangerous! Many people go to the Internet in search of the answers their doctors can't provide. Whether you have a repetitive-stress injury, cancer, or AIDS, you'll find information about it on the Internet. Want to try homeopathy, acupuncture, or just figure out what leeches can do for you? Try the Internet. Be careful, though. Although you'll find a lot of useful information, you'll also run into some pretty strange ideas, many of which have as much relation to reality as Charles Manson does.

Shopping

Much of the press seems to think that the raison d'être for the Internet is for K-Mart and Sears to find another way to sell merchandise. Internet shopping has been grotesquely overrated for several years—but recently it's taken off. It's not living up to its potential yet, but nonetheless, millions of people are making purchases on the Internet. In particular, they're buying books, CDs, and software. But they're also buying telescope lenses, clothing, and even groceries.

Cybersex

The Internet provides a wonderful form of communication for those who seem to have trouble finding others with similar sexual proclivities. This is by no means a minor part of cyberspace; some commentators even claim that the sexual use of online services played a major part in their growth. (That's probably not so far-fetched an idea to anyone familiar with America Online's tremendously popular chat rooms.) You can get online and talk about things that your parents or spouse might consider *very* weird, with people who consider them quite normal.

Political Activism

As they say, political activism infects every form of human communication—or was that pornography? Anyway, the Internet is the latest frontier for political activities, providing militia groups a means of keeping in touch and providing Democrans and Republicats a place to seek votes.

Subversion

The Internet provides a great way to subvert the political system in which you live. That's right, you too can publish information that your government doesn't want published, whether it's information about how Nutrasweet was created as part of a plot to take over our minds or what was going on during the latest coup. Perhaps the most quoted such event was the last coup in Moscow, during which much information was exported through the Internet. Closer to home, the Internet has become a thorn in the side of the U.S. government as it makes the distribution of encryption software so easy.

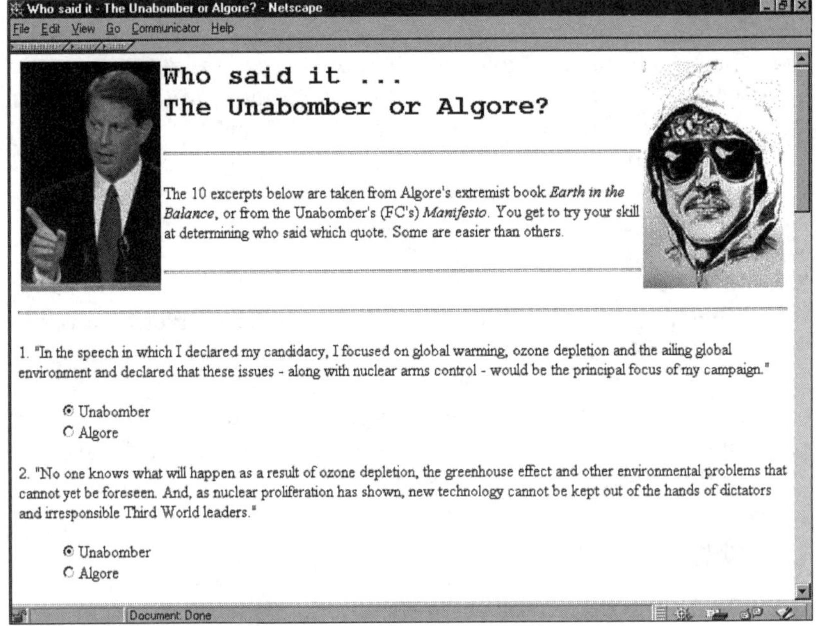

Here's a snap of the Political Activism section—or the Subversion section, perhaps.

Looking for Work (and Help)

Thousands of people are looking for work on the Internet, and thousands more are offering both full-time and contract positions. Many professional associations have special mailing lists used for transmitting job leads. Do a little research, and you could have dozens of leads arriving at your home every day. Check out this site for starters: `http://www.4work.com/`

Clubs and Professional-Association Information Sources

Are you running a large club or professional association? Why not set up a Web site? Your members can then check the Web site to find out when the next meeting is being held, search a database of fellow members, find out about the association's services, and more. Potential members can find out how to join, too.

Mating and Dating

Do people *really* meet online and get involved in romantic relationships of various kinds? Yes, they really do. I'd be inclined to make a joke about it, except that I have a friend who met a man online who eventually became her husband and the father of her child.

Long-distance Computing

Being a computer geek comes with a real disadvantage: You always seem to be working. If you find yourself wishing you could get to the programs on your desktop computer while you are on vacation or are visiting relatives or clients, for example, you may have considered buying one of those remote control programs. You install the program on your laptop and then dial into your desktop machine. The program enables you to copy files between the computers and even run programs across the connection.

As you might guess, however, the long-distance phone calls can get very expensive, but now there's a new way to do it. Some of these programs let you make the connection across the Internet. So if you use a national service provider that has phone numbers throughout the United States, (or even an international provider or an online service that has numbers throughout the world), you can dial into a local number and connect to your computer across the Internet and pay only a fraction of the long-distance charge. Even if you don't want to go to quite these lengths, you can still log in and pick up your email wherever you happen to be.

Books

You can write books about the Internet. According to modern polls, there are now 5,357,131 people writing books about cyberspace, the Internet, and how we won't have to blow our noses ourselves 10 years from now because the Internet will do it for us. (Seriously, though, a recent survey found that more money is spent on books and magazines about the Internet than is spent buying things on the Internet! So much for the computer revolution killing off paper publications!)

What Did I Miss?

In addition to the ideas I've listed in this chapter, you could probably find a few thousand other uses or more. The Internet is huge, and it's diverse; it's whatever you make of it.

The beauty of the Internet is that although people begin as observers, they end up being participants. They become active in discussion groups and perhaps even start their own groups. They often create their own Web sites.

Take a look at the Internet to see what's out there and how other people are using it. Who knows? You might soon find that it becomes part of your life. (Don't say I didn't warn you!)

Part 4
Resources

You'll find reference information in this part of the book. There's a glossary of Internet terms and a quick look at the new Internet tools built into Windows 98. I'll tell you where to find the software you need: programs to help you on your travels around the Internet, games, print drivers, and unlimited other things. I'll also give you some background information about picking a service provider, in case you don't have Internet access yet or you want to find a new provider.

You'll also find out how to use the email responder, a system some readers may want to use to retrieve chapters that explain how the Internet used to work (and still does for the unfortunate users stuck with old technology).

Appendix A

Finding Internet Access and the Right Equipment

If you are reading this, either you don't have an Internet service provider (ISP) or you are considering changing the one you have. Let's deal with the first major question: Which is the best Internet service provider?

I Want the Best! Where Do I Get It?

Ah, so you want the best Internet account you can get. If that's the case, be prepared to empty your bank account. You're going to need a special high-speed line from the phone company, a fast computer with special hardware to connect it to that line, a system administrator to set it up and maintain it, and on and on.

But for the rest of us, the ordinary Joe or Jane who wants to get hooked up to the Internet, what's the best way to do it? There's no easy answer to that, unfortunately. It's rather like asking, "What makes the best spouse?" Everyone has a different answer. A service that you think is good might prove to be a lousy choice for someone else.

Basically, what you need to do is pick a service provider that is cheap, helpful, and has a reliable and fast connection to the Internet and easy-to-install software. Of course, that's very difficult to find. I've had Internet accounts with a couple of dozen providers, and I haven't found one yet that I would rave about. They've ranged from pretty good to absolutely awful.

What's a Reasonable Cost?

Over the past few years Internet-account charges have gradually moved away from a per-hour basis and toward a flat fee. You pay for unlimited access, so whether you use the service for one hour a month or a hundred, you pay the same price. For instance, you can get a CompuServe account that allows you to log on for as long as you want for $24.95 a month; America Online (AOL) will charge you $21.95. Special offers can sweeten the deal; AOL, for instance, will give you a 50-hour free trial and, when you sign up, will give you your first month free.

For a while, $19.95 seemed to be the normal flat fee charged, but the rates seem to have crept up a little—and then down a little. But it's still possible to find much cheaper rates. I've seen $17.95 a month, Yahoo! has recently started advertising $14.95 for its new service, and I recently saw one ISP charging $12.00. If you rarely use the Internet, you can probably find a company that will charge by the hour; CompuServe charges $9.95 for five hours and $2.95 for additional hours, for instance.

Unlimited Access What does unlimited access *really* mean? It means that you can use the service for as many hours as you can connect and remain connected. Which may be many hours less than the number of hours in a month! Busy signals may often thwart your attempts, and even if you can connect, you may find that your connection is dropped frequently.

Note, however, that some Internet service providers—as opposed to online services such as CompuServe and AOL—may charge a sign-up fee, perhaps as much as $25 to $50. And they generally don't offer a free trial period (although some of the larger companies do give the first month free).

Free Internet access may be on the way. Industry analysts say that a number of large companies are planning to provide their customers with free Internet account—open a bank account, get a free Internet account—as a way of creating customer loyalty. So the pressure on access rates seems to be downward, perhaps all the way down to zero.

Tips for Picking a Provider

Consider the following guidelines when you're trying to find an Internet service provider:

- The major online services often make it very easy to connect to the Internet: You just run the setup program and away you go.
- On the other hand, the major online services tend to be a bit more expensive (although their prices have dropped greatly, and the difference is no longer so significant). Some of them also have a reputation for having very slow and unreliable connections to the Internet. But then, so do many Internet service providers!
- There are a lot of low-priced Internet service providers (in Colorado, for example, there are about 70), and the competition is stiff!

- Unfortunately, many low-priced services have customer service that matches their prices—they are often not very helpful. To work on those services, you need more than a little of the geek gene inside you.
- On the other hand, some of these services *are* very good and will help you hook up to the Internet at a very good price.
- Make sure the service has a toll-free or local support telephone number—you'll almost certainly need it!
- A number of large national Internet service providers, such as WorldNet (owned by AT&T), EarthLink, and PSINet, often have very good prices ($20–25 a month for unlimited usage, for instance). In addition, in some areas, they might even have good service.
- There are no hard and fast rules! A service that is very good in one area may be lousy in another. And a service that your friend says is really good may be very good right now and absolutely awful next month.

Finding a Service Provider

If you don't have an Internet account yet, but you want to find one, I can help. Here are a few ideas for tracking down service providers:

- If you're using Windows 98, try the Internet Connection Wizard. This program has a referral service that may help you find a service provider in your area.
- Look in your local paper's computer section; local service providers often advertise there.
- Look in your city's local computer publication for ads.
- Check the Yellow Pages' "Internet" category.
- Ask at your local computer store.
- Check for ads in one of the many new Internet-related magazines.
- Look in a general computer magazine (many of which *seem* to have turned into Internet magazines).
- Ask your friends and colleagues which local service providers are good (and which to avoid).
- If you know someone who has access to the World Wide Web, ask him to go to `http://www.yahoo.com/Business_and_Economy/Companies/Internet_Services/Internet_Access_Providers/`. Or, better still, say, "Go to Yahoo! and search for *service provider*." You may not know what that means, but your friend probably will (check out Chapter 11, "Finding Stuff," for more information). You'll find

information about many service providers and even some price comparisons. (You might also try using the Web at your local library; most libraries have Internet access these days.)

- Another good Web site to try is The List (`http://thelist.internet.com/`), a directory of more than 4,000 service providers. Also, you can try ISP Finder (2,700 service providers) at `http://ispfinder.com/`.

Find a Free-Net

You might also want to look for a *Free-Net*. Free-Nets are community computing systems. They might be based at a local library or college, and you can dial into the system from your home computer. As the name implies, they don't cost anything. (Well, some may have a small registration fee of around $10, but if it's not actually free, it's pretty close to it.)

Free-Nets offer a variety of local services, as well as access to the Internet. You may be able to find information about jobs in the area or about local events and recreation. You may be able to search the local library's database, find course schedules for local colleges, or ask someone questions about social security and Medicare.

Free-Nets usually have a menu of options based on a simulated town. There may be a Community Center, Teen Center, and Senior Center, for example. In addition, there might be an Administration Building (where you can go to register your account on the Free-Net), a Social Services and Organizations Center (where you can find support groups and local chapters of national organizations such as the Red Cross), and a Home and Garden Center (where you can find out about pest control). There might even be a Special Interests Center, where you can chat about UFOs, movies, religion, travel, or anything else. Free-Nets also have a system that lets you send messages to other users.

Free-Net or Freenet?

You'll see the terms Free-Net, freenet, and FreeNet, and maybe even some other variations. All of these terms were service marks of NPTN (National Public Telecommuting Network), which preferred to use the term Free-Net. Note, however, that NPTN is bankrupt and out of business, so feel free to use whatever spelling you want.

Even without Internet access, Free-Nets are a great community resource, especially for home-bound people such as the elderly and handicapped. However, they have serious limitations. Not all Free-Nets will provide full access to the Internet. For security reasons, some may limit certain services. For instance, they may not want you to use FTP to bring possibly virus-laden files into their systems. Free-Nets are often very busy and difficult to connect to. Most importantly, they are generally dial-in terminal connections or shell accounts. You probably won't be able to use the fancy graphical software that makes the Internet so easy to use.

If you still want to find a Free-Net or other form of free access in your area, contact the Organization for Community Networks. It has a Web site (`http://ofcn.org/`), where you can find a listing of Free-Nets and other community networks. (Again, take a trip to your library to use its Internet access, or find a friend with access.) You can also contact this organization at the following address:

Organization for Community Networks

PO Box 32175

Euclid, Ohio 44132

Phone: 216-731-9801

This organization does not have a full list of all the free Internet access systems available, though. Check your local computer paper, and ask at local computer stores (not the big chains, but the mom-and-pop type computer stores staffed by people who actually know what they are selling).

Equipment You Will Need

You're going to need the following items to connect to the Internet:

- A computer
- A modem
- A phone line
- Software

Which computer? You know the story, the faster the better; the more RAM (Random Access Memory), the better. Ideally, you need a computer that will run the nice graphical software that's available for Windows and the Macintosh. If you don't have a computer that will run this sort of software, you can still access the Internet, but you'll have to use a dial-in terminal (shell) account.

For instance, you'll probably want at least a 486, or better, if working in the PC world. You may be able to scrape by with a 386. But most software won't run well on a 286, if at all. (For a shell account, just about any machine is okay.)

A modem takes the digital signals from your computer and converts them to the analog signals that your phone line uses. You plug the phone line into the modem, and, if it's an external modem, you plug the computer into the modem, too. (If it's an internal modem, you install it in a slot inside your computer, and the phone line connects to a socket on the edge of the card.)

When buying a modem, remember the rule of "the faster, the better." Most service providers have 33,600bps connections these days, with many currently switching to 56Kbps. You can buy a good 33,600bps modem for $50 to $100. The 56Kbps modems are more expensive, but see the following discussion of these modems.

You Can Only Be So Tight

If you think $50(ish) for a 33,600bps modem is too much, you need to think long and hard before getting a slower modem. Even a 28,800bps modem will feel sluggish; anything less will be unbearable. (It's difficult to buy a *new* modem that is slower than 33,600bps, but you might find one secondhand—and you might regret your decision if you buy it.)

By the way, don't buy a modem from the *Acme Modem and Hiking Shoe Company* (or from any of the other hundreds of budget modem makers). Anyone can build and sell a modem; however, building a *good* modem is difficult. Modems are complicated things, and the cheap generic modems often do not connect reliably. Buy a modem from one of the well-known modem companies, such as US Robotics, Hayes, Practical Peripherals, or MegaHertz. (Look in a computer magazine, and you'll soon see which modems are being sold by most of the mail-order companies.) It will cost you a few bucks more, but it may save you hours of hassle. You might also ask your service provider for a recommendation on the kind of modem to buy; they should be able to tell you about the ones that work well, and those that don't.

The 56K Problem

Before you buy a 56K modem, you need to understand a few things. First, there were two rival techniques used for making modems transmit at this speed. A new standard was agreed upon quite recently (the V.90 standard), but that means if you buy a modem, you'd better make sure that either it conforms to the new standard or that it can be upgraded to use the new standard. Also, before getting a modem, make sure that the service provider you want to work with can provide 56K connections (many can't) and that the modem you want to buy will work okay with that service. Even though there's a new standard, some reports indicate that there are still compatibility problems; the standard allows for certain differences in the way that information is processed by the modem. Just because a modem apparently conforms to the standard doesn't mean it will work well with your service provider's modems, so ask what you should use.

Note also that although a modem may be rated at 56K, it can only transfer data at high speed one way. Transfers *from* the Internet will occur at the highest connection speed, but transfers *to* the Internet will go at the slower 33,600bps rate. That's okay for most users, who are viewing information on the Web or downloading files.

Finally, even if you do get a 56K modem, it may not transfer at that speed across some phone lines (if it can't reach top speed, it'll still be able to transmit at a lower speed). Few phone lines can handle full 56K transmissions, and some lines are completely incompatible with 56K transmissions. It is worth getting a 56K modem rather than a 33,600bps modem? Consider these problems:

- Many service providers don't have 56K connections.
- Many service providers who advertise 56K connections don't have many connections, so you may rarely connect full speed.
- Your telephone lines may not be able to handle 56K modem transmissions. Although most do, some don't, so talk with the phone company or the service provider you want to connect to. If the lines won't handle 56K, your expensive modem will simply run at the slower 33,600bps rate.
- Even if your phone lines *can* handle 56K transmissions, that still doesn't mean you'll get full-speed transmissions, because the phone lines probably won't handle them very well. You're more likely to connect at around 40Kbps to 45Kbps.

It's up to you. 56K modem prices currently begin at around $75 and go up to around $175, so they're quite a bit more for only a little extra speed in many cases. If you've already got a 33,600bps modem, perhaps even a 28,800bps modem, it may not be worth upgrading. If you're buying your first modem, or if you have a 14,400bps modem or slower, you should seriously consider getting a 56K modem.

If you'd like more information about 56K modems, including lists of service providers who work with them, ways to test your local phone lines to see whether they'll handle 56K modems, and lots more, check out these sites:

- 3Com, the manufacturer of the US Robotics modems: `http://www.3com.com/56k/`
- The 56K Modem Info Center: `http://www.sirius.com/~rmoss/`
- The No Hype 56K Modem Page: `http://www.mactimes.com/lowend/56k/index.html`
- 56K.com: `http://www.56k.com/`

You Want Something Faster

Yes, there are faster connections—for some of us. The following sections give a quick rundown of other possible types of connection that might be available in your area.

ADSL

This may be our best hope. It's a new telephone technology due to be introduced in some areas late in 1996. Oops, that's what I wrote a couple of editions ago, and here we are in 1998 and we still don't have it. Still, it's promised in some areas by the summer of 1998 and in most of North America by late 1998. And if you believe that it will *really* be widely available by then, try to be a little less gullible. I'm still keeping my fingers crossed for ADSL connections soon, but realistically speaking it can't possibly be widely available for another year or two—the phone companies simply don't have enough people to install all the equipment that's needed. In my area, for instance, I was told that it would be available by June of 1998. And indeed it is...just not for my home, apparently. Although it's available in this area, it's not available for everyone in this area, because many buildings are too far from the phone company's central-office switch. Now I'm told "the second half of 1998." I'm not holding my breath.

Even if you can get an ADSL line, what will you connect to? America Online says it will open up ADSL lines, and other service providers will get ADSL service, too, but how quickly? You may have to sign up for Internet service with your local phone company, and the local phone companies have proven themselves completely incompetent at providing Internet access. (Here's an example: My phone company recently changed their login script without telling their subscribers, so people could no longer connect. I guess they were looking for a way to cut back on system congestion.)

ADSL will provide extremely fast connections. There will be various choices, beginning at around 256Kbps (about five or six times the speed of a fast modem) and going up to 7Mbps (about 125 times faster!). Prices will begin at around $60 a month (including Internet access). There will also be a setup charge, and you'll have to buy a card to go into your computer. A good place to learn about ADSL is the ADSL Forum (`http://www.adsl.com/`) or your local phone company's Web site.

ISDN

ISDN is an old Albanian acronym for "Yesterday's Technology Tomorrow—Perhaps." ISDN phone lines are fast digital phone lines. This technology has been around for years, but the U.S. phone companies, in their infinite wisdom, figured that we really didn't need it. Of course, now they are scrambling to provide it, spurred on by the increasing number of people who use the Internet. Still, in some areas, if you call the local phone company and ask whether you can have an ISDN line, you might hear something like "Sure, move to Germany."

ISDN Modem

An ISDN modem is not really a modem. The word *modem* is a contraction of two words: modulate and demodulate, which are the terms for the processes of converting digital signals to and from analog phone signals. Although the ISDN adapters are called ISDN modems, the signals are digital all the way: there's no modulating and demodulating being done.

Don't bother to get an ISDN line until you find a service provider who also has an ISDN connection; currently most don't. You'll be charged at both ends, by the phone company (who will charge to install and maintain the line) and the service provider (who will charge extra for the privilege of connecting to the Internet with it).

Not surprisingly, prices are all over the place. To use ISDN, you'll need a special *ISDN modem*, as it's known (more correctly, an ISDN *adapter*). That'll cost around $350 to 450, but prices are falling. Then you pay the phone company to install the line (between $0 and $600—don't ask me how they figure out these prices), and you'll pay a monthly fee of $25 to $130. You'll have to pay both the phone company *and* the service provider an extra fee for this special service.

I recently had ISDN installed and discovered a few oddities about this technology. It requires that large holes be dug in your yard, generally by a small group of rotund men who stand around in front of your house staring at the hole. It may take a dozen visits from the phone company—they may even try to install it a couple of times after they've already installed it once. It may also require the destruction of the neighbor's shrubbery. Even then, it may not work well; I eventually gave up and went back to using a normal modem.

Satellite

For the next few years, only one satellite service will be available in North America, the DirecPC from Hughes Network Systems (`http://www.direcpc.com/` or call 800-347-3272). Other companies plan to introduce satellite service, but the earliest such service can begin is around 2002.

Prices of DirecPC have dropped quite a bit over the past year or two. It now costs about $250 to buy the equipment, and $229 to pay someone to install it. (There's also a product called DirecDuo, which combines Internet and TV service.)

DirecPC connections are at 400Kpbs, seven times faster than fast modems (although some service plans only provide 200Kbps). Note, however, that DirecPC only transmits data *to* your computer. You still need a phone line and an Internet service provider to transmit data *out*. When you connect to a Web site, for instance, the instructions to the Web server go along your phone line to the service provider; then the data from the Web site goes up to the satellite and down to you.

Various rates are available; full unlimited 400Kpbs access will cost $170 a month (plus your Internet service provider's fee). The lowest rates are around $20 a month; that rate provides 200Kpbs transmissions for 12 off-peak hours a day.

Cable

The cable companies have been promising Internet access for some time, even running ads implying that they were *already* providing Internet access. And one day they just might. But for the moment, don't hold your breath, or you'll turn blue long before you connect to the Internet via cable. It will be several years before Internet access is widely available through cable (although if you're lucky enough to be in a test area, you may be able to get it right now).

Here's what I suggest, though. Call the cable company and ask. They may be installing Internet access, or about to start, but may be keeping it quiet because they know they won't be able to keep up with demand. My cable company says they're beginning Internet access in my area next week, and will install a connection at my home within the next two weeks. But they're not advertising this new service, even to existing cable customers.

Prices and capabilities vary. Some systems require that you use a phone line at the same time that you use the cable connection because the cable system will only transmit to your computer; there's no data transfer the other way. On the other hand, some systems are bidirectional; you won't need a phone connection. Prices for installation range from around $100–$300, with a monthly fee of $30 and up.

Transmission speeds vary, but can be very, very fast: uploads at 200Kbits/sec to 500Kbits/sec, and downloads of from 1.5mbits/sec to 3 or 4mbits/sec.

T1 Line

This special type of digital phone line is about 10 times faster than ISDN, but it costs a couple of thousand dollars or more for the equipment and then somewhere from a few hundred to a couple of thousand dollars a month to run. Although this solution is okay for small businesses who really need fast access to the Internet (very few really do), it's out of the price range of most individuals.

For now, most of us are stuck with modems. With luck, they're 33,600bps modems or perhaps 56Kbps modems, which are slow but affordable. But don't get too jealous of people using faster connections. The Internet can be very slow at times, and even if you have a very fast connection from your service provider to your computer, you may still find yourself twiddling your fingers. For instance, when you're using the Web or an FTP site, the server you've connected to might be slow. Or the lines from that server across the world to your service provider might be slow. Or your service provider's system might be clogged up with more users than it was designed to handle. So just because you have all the equipment you need for a fast connection doesn't mean you'll get a fast connection.

For instance, as a recent ISDN user I should point out that you might be disappointed if you invest in that technology. It's okay sometimes—and at other times, it's simply not worth the extra cost. A neighbor said to me recently, "Won't it be great when the Internet runs fast, you know, a megabyte a second or whatever?" And I replied, "Sure, but won't it be great when the Internet runs at 28.8!"

Index

Symbols

A

B

C

D

N

O

P

Q

R

S

T

U

V

W

X

Y

Z